TRIUMPHANT WARRIOR

The Legend of the Navy's Most Daring Helicopter Pilot

Peter D. Shay

CASEMATE

Philadelphia & Oxford

Published in the United States of America and Great Britain in 2019 by
CASEMATE PUBLISHERS
1950 Lawrence Road, Havertown, PA 19083, USA
and
The Old Music Hall, 106–108 Cowley Road, Oxford OX4 1JE, UK

Copyright © Peter D. Shay, 2019

Hardback Edition: ISBN 978-1-61200-763-2
Digital Edition: ISBN 978-1-61200-764-9 (ePub)

A CIP record for this book is available from the British Library

Printed and bound in the United States of America

Typeset in India by Versatile PreMedia Services. www.versatilepremedia.com

For a complete list of Casemate titles, please contact:

CASEMATE PUBLISHERS (US)
Telephone (610) 853-9131
Fax (610) 853-9146
Email: casemate@casematepublishers.com
www.casematepublishers.com

CASEMATE PUBLISHERS (UK)
Telephone (01865) 241249
Fax (01865) 794449
Email: casemate-uk@casematepublishers.co.uk
www.casematepublishers.co.uk

Front cover: Weseleskey standing by a UH-1B helicopter. (Courtesy of A. E. Weseleskey)
Back cover: Vinh Long runway. (Courtesy of A. E. Weseleskey)

MANHOOD

A MAN'S USEFULNESS DEPENDS UPON HIS LIVING UP TO HIS IDEALS INSOFAR AS HE CAN.

IT IS HARD TO FAIL BUT IT IS WORSE NEVER TO HAVE TRIED TO SUCCEED.

ONLY THOSE ARE FIT TO LIVE WHO DO NOT FEAR TO DIE AND NONE ARE FIT TO DIE WHO HAVE SHRUNK FROM THE JOY OF LIFE AND THE DUTY OF LIFE.

Theodore Roosevelt

Contents

Preface

When I set out on this journey, I was determined to pen a biography of a naval aviator whose personal pride, naval career, and future life were profoundly impacted by a singular helicopter mission. However, on discovering that he was also an integral part of a unique ground battle that has not received much historical recognition, I decided to explore what happened in the early morning hours of January 31, 1968. I then interviewed as many participants as possible (including Army personnel) who engaged the enemy during the Tet Offensive Battle at the Army Airfield located at the Mekong Delta town of Vinh Long. For many reasons, this battle was historic, but what stood out most were the successful efforts of brave Navy aircrew personnel, who although not trained as infantrymen, helped repel a large ground force of Viet Cong fighters, whose goal was the overthrow of the base.

While the bulk of this book was written more than ten years ago, the story told will always be relevant to those of us who not only appreciate naval aviation and heroism on the field of battle, whether it be on the ground or in the air, but also see an obligation to give credit to those who fought for our country. The culmination of this book represents a historical account that should have been told long ago. I take full responsibility for how much dust it gathered before I had the personal wherewithal to pick it up again. As I view it in retrospect, I could say that due to a variety of circumstances and reasons it was put off; but to be more straightforward with readers and with myself, the actual reasons why it was not published before now are as follows: I was, in fact, serving with the navy unit during the period in which the story takes place, and personally knew many of the individuals whose personal accounts can be found in these pages. I felt that I had a profound duty to honor their thoughts and feelings. At what I thought to be near completion, the emotional toll my sense of duty took upon me began to weigh too heavily. As I read and absorbed each witness's account, I became more and more personally involved; and felt a greater level of responsibility to the importance of each word. Despite all the work I had already put into telling this story, not being certain I was doing it justice made setting it aside the better part of valor.

In that context, I must take a moment to apologize to my fellow veterans, those whom I interviewed and recorded and who were able and willing to piece together and share their deepest memories (and for some their darkest nightmares) of what took place 50 years earlier, in what now has become such a distant place, simply called Vietnam.

Even more regrettable is that more than a few important witnesses are gone now. They will never have the opportunity to read and appreciate their contributions to the completed work. Such warriors and people who gave to their country include: Eugene Rosenthal, Glenn Wilson, Tom Olezeski, James Walker, C. J. Roberson, Jerry Wages, Joe Bouchard, Chuck Fields, Sam Aydelotte, and others, whose names I may have missed but whose contributions are invaluable. These men have been and always will be part of the unique history of Helicopter Attack (Light) Squadron Three—the Navy "Seawolves."

Several minor edits have been made, and nearly all the photographs shared with me have been given credits. I have done my best to refrain from writing with any particular bias, though it is difficult not to form an opinion as to the dynamics of what happened six weeks after the offensive when a unique and daring helicopter rescue mission ensued on March 9, 1968.

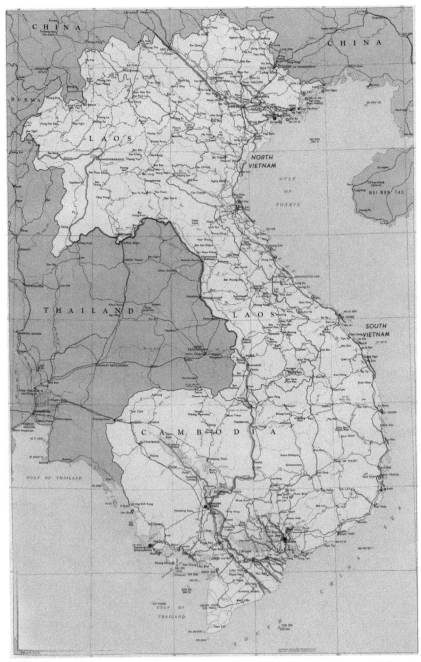

Vietnam. (Indochina Atlas. United States Central Intelligence Agency, Office of Basic Intelligence. Washington, D.C. 1970)

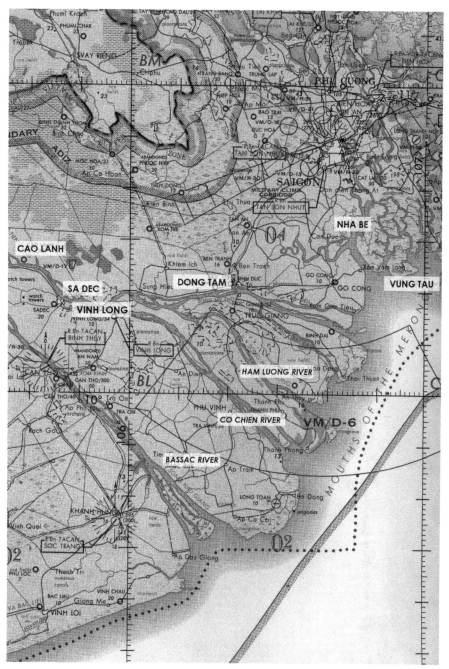

The Mekong Delta and Vinh Long area of navy operations. (Courtesy of U.S. Mapping Agency)

Introduction

Inherent in "A Navy Flyer's Creed" is the power of inspiration: "My country built the best airplane in the world and entrusted it to me. They trained me to fly it. I will use it to the absolute limit of my power. With my fellow pilots, aircrew and deck crews, my plane and I will do anything necessary to carry out our tremendous responsibilities."

"When the going is fast and rough, I will not falter. I will be uncompromising in every blow I strike. I will be humble in victory. I am a United States Navy Flyer."

In Vietnam, barely a month after the start of the Tet Offensive in 1968, one such proud United States Navy flyer applied the fundamental but sometimes forgotten maxims expressed in this creed. And he dared to risk not only his naval career, but the lives of his fellow aircrewmen in rescuing a wounded U.S. Army advisor whose time had nearly run out and whose loss of blood meant that he was only moments away from certain battlefield death.

The pilot, Lieutenant Commander Allen E. "Wes" Weseleskey, had been assigned at the Vinh Long Army Airfield as the Assistant Officer in Charge of Helicopter Attack (Light) Squadron Three, Detachment Three (HA(L)3, Det. 3). His controversial mission took place on March 9, 1968 on the outskirts of Sadec, a small city in Kien Phuong Province in the Mekong Delta region of Vietnam.

To say that there was turmoil and chaos during this period would be a serious understatement. Unknown to the soldiers on the ground at the time, the sailors on the waterways, the pilots in the air, or the grunts in the hills, five months earlier in November 1967, America's most prominent general was ordered to fly to Washington to brief the President on the progress of America's war against the communists in Vietnam.

General William C. Westmoreland had already served nearly four years in Vietnam, having arrived two months after the overthrow and assassination of South Vietnam's President Ngo Dinh Diem. So by the time of his visit to Washington, he, more than others in the military establishment, had the knowledge of the status of the war effort. And since he was known to visit troops all over the country, he had knowledge that was first-hand.

On November 15, during a refueling stop in California, he was greeted by a group of newsmen. He told them, optimistically, "I am very encouraged. I have never been more encouraged in the four years I've been in Vietnam. We are making real progress."[1]

The morning after his arrival in Washington on November 16, Westmoreland briefed a closed session of the House Armed Services Committee. He told the mostly skeptical committee representatives, that with the progress being made on the battlefield, the United States could commence a "phase out of U.S. troops in two years or less."[2] And four days later he spoke at the National Press Club, telling his audiences, "We have reached an important point when the end begins to come into view."[3]

This was not the first time that rosy assessments for the outlook in Vietnam had been expressed. In January 1963, Admiral Felt, commanding the Pacific Fleet predicted, while in Washington, that the counterinsurgency would be defeated "within three years."[4] General Paul D. Harkins, formerly a protégé of General George Patton in World War II, and then serving as the first commander of the U.S. Military Assistance Command, Vietnam (COMUSMACV) proclaimed that "I am an optimist."[5] He considered the date realistic but "believes we can do even better."[6] Even Secretary of Defense Robert S. McNamara and General Maxwell D. Taylor (Chairman of the Joint Chiefs of Staff—JCS) had reported to President Kennedy that it was "their judgment that the major part of the U.S. military task (in the Republic of Vietnam) can be completed by the end of 1965."[7]

Within two and a half months after his return to Vietnam in 1967, Westmoreland and his supporters were shocked by being caught totally off guard by the ferocity of the Communists' Tet Offensive of January 31, 1968, and the ensuing countrywide battle that rocked the convictions of the sages and believers in Washington as well. And by the last week in February, Westmoreland, in concert with Joint Chiefs of Staff Chairman General Earle Wheeler, was requesting reinforcements for the armed forces: an additional 206,000 troops, 108,000 of them earmarked for Vietnam.[8] Westmoreland was suffering his first major defeat in leading the war effort, and his appeal for reinforcements was opposed by McNamara, just two days before the latter's farewell as Defense Secretary.

Westmoreland would never recover from his rosy November assessment, and by the end of March, General Creighton W. Abrams was chosen as his successor. What did not help Westmoreland's reputation for his war management efforts was Abrams's March 29 response to President Johnson's question regarding the necessity of a troop increase. The President was pleased to hear Abrams say, "Oh, no, sir, Mr. President, we've got plenty of troops."[9]

The 1968 Vietnamese Lunar New Year, designated as Tet Mau Ton by the Vietnamese people, began as an annual holiday celebration but instead turned into a countrywide battle that set the stage for beginning of the end of the Vietnam War—seven miserable years later in 1975. During the offensive, thousands of American servicemen died as did tens of thousands of Vietnamese from both sides.

Before the holiday, a single North Vietnamese artillery shell lobbed into the American outpost at Khe Sanh exploded and killed 19 U.S. Marines. During the opening hours of the attack in South Vietnam's capital, Saigon, 27 lightly armed U.S. military policemen were killed by the attacking VC (Viet Cong) fighters. The fact that an even greater number of the attackers lost their lives offered no solace. This battle was a rude awakening for America and her allies, who had already invested so many lives and so much capital trying to defeat the perceived threat of world Communism.

When men are in combat, they become focused on where they are serving, having a "here and now" mentality. They do not have the time or inclination to concern themselves with military engagements being fought in other corps or provinces. Although many *New York Times* reporters were on assignment in Vietnam, recent issues of the newspaper with "All the News That's Fit to Print" were not to be found in-country (except many days later, if brought over on a flight from the United

States). And even then, who would have the time or inclination to peruse the painful details documented in the paper? Nevertheless, after the first few days of Tet, news started to travel fast. In February and March 1968, the degree of devastation and destruction occurring throughout the country became widely known, and it was news of despair. American soldiers, allied forces, the Army of the Republic of Vietnam (ARVN), and countless innocent civilian bystanders were losing their lives, homes, and places of work. Included in the bad news for Americans were the attack on the embassy compound in Saigon, the catastrophe occurring in the historic city of Hue, and the constant pounding of shells into Khe Sanh and Con Thien. And, of course, there were overwhelming attacks in all of the Mekong Delta provinces. The U.S. Army Airfield at Vinh Long was nearly overrun by the VC and nearly abandoned by the American defenders. So, in early 1968 the entire country was in the midst of a cataclysm.

The ensuing chaos and instant unraveling of military strategy had become so threatening and problematic for America's war effort that ordinary caution was thrown to the wind. The threat of enemy forces regrouping to attack Saigon became all too real. On February 13, a flight of three B-52 Stratofortress bombers was given bombing coordinates only 15 miles from the capital. So at midday, hundreds of bombs rained down on the small village of Nhi Binh, in Hoc Mon Province. Since the Viet Cong were everywhere else but not there at the time, 45 civilians, but no combatants, were obliterated in the torrid midday sun. The cause of the mistake would never be told to the American public, other than it was an errant B-52 strike.

Some of the printed issues of the American military publication *Pacific Stars and Stripes* listed casualties as never before: February 12, 1968, listing names of 41 Americans who died;[10] February 13, 1968, listing 168 reported deaths;[11] February 14, listing 58 reported deaths;[12] February 18, listing 56 reported deaths, 57 missing;[13] February 19, listing 61 reported deaths with 38 Army soldiers missing.[14] Closer to the date of Weseleskey's rescue mission at Cao Lanh (described in this book) the March 6 issue of *Pacific Stars and Stripes* listed 68 deaths and 26 soldiers missing in action (MIAs). The headline story of this issue was "REDS OPEN FIRE ON ALLIED BASES." The opening paragraph reads,

"Communist forces sent hundreds of rockets and mortars slamming into allied air bases, command posts and other installations Monday in the heaviest series of coordinated shelling in more than two weeks."[15] The Communist onslaught was unrelenting.

For reasons not easy to comprehend, the March 9 rescue mission almost did not take place. Had it not, that would have been one of this war's many travesties. Military actions are not usually analyzed with hypothetical hindsight. Yet, individually, each battle, especially those costing American lives, even one life, should be open to retrospective thinking. Historically, there have been individual acts of courage and self-sacrifice without which the results can never be known. For certain, the outcome on March 9 would have been more tragic than it was if the U.S. Navy gun-ship helicopter had not touched down in the midst of a fierce battle. It would have barely been a footnote, a statistic—one or two more American deaths in a delta rice paddy—another listing of casualties' names and services in *Pacific Stars and Stripes*. During some weeks of reporting, especially during Tet, the lists of those killed in action (KIAs) took nearly a full column of space in that military journal.

The author was able to reconstruct most of this story through eyewitness interviews with U.S. Army and Navy veterans. Fortunately, most had clear memories of their experiences. And, of course, who might guess how accurate the account was for former Viet Cong General Pham Phi Hung, who recollected being at the battle site, in charge of leading the enemy in their attempts to shoot down the helicopters and cause as many casualties as possible? His 816th VC Battalion was focused on ambushing and destroying the elements of the ARVN's Ninth Infantry Division searching for them that day.[16]

Trying to jar old memories to find out exactly what happened was not a simple or pleasant task. War memories are special, and after 34 years, they become blurred, not simply because of the passage of time but also because they seem surreal, given their very nature. Battlefield events just do not seem to stay connected with logic and therefore remain vague and doubtful in the folds of our memory. They are conveniently blurred or forgotten and bear no relation to most men's present or post-war future lives. Those actual events are unique and, in many ways, bizarre—simply unbelievable, unfathomable.

During a conversation with me over drinks at the bar of New York's Seventh Regiment Armory's Open Mess in May 2003, one of the U.S. Army advisors assigned to the ARVN's Ninth Infantry Division who was rescued on March 9, 1968, Medal of Honor recipient, retired Army Colonel Jack Jacobs, spoke to me about his recollection of the rescue. When I related to him that the Navy officer who made the rescue had become the target of an Article 32 investigation (precursor to court martial), it suddenly cleared his surreal memory of lying in a hospital bed and being visited by a naval officer in an "ice-cream suit" (Navy summer whites uniform) assigned to investigate that pilot who, a week or so before, had flown into the jungle to save his life. Jacobs was reassured to learn that this bizarre memory had indeed been true.

So the memory persists, on its own, for its own sake, during the endless passage of time. Might it be befitting but discomfiting for this memory of Jacobs to be awakened, put into order and clarified? There will always be some doubt about new facts, such as those discovered by Jacobs. However, while these facts might resolve one of the mind's distant memories/mysteries, they may also disturb the mind's equilibrium.

But this author is not here today to focus on the subconscious, since wartime events occur completely outside of the mind (unless you're daydreaming); they are external to normal thought processes and are purely physical and require physical reactions. This is not to say that there isn't a great deal of training about how to defend against and defeat the enemy, but these reactions to outside stimuli are more second nature than cognitive.

What is it that one does to become a military hero? Is it a matter of being in a particular place at a certain point in time and reacting to something extremely dangerous, sometimes in a carefree or perhaps risky manner, to save the lives of people on the verge of becoming countable war casualties? Placed on a scale of deliberate or spontaneous acts, throwing oneself on a live hand grenade and facing almost certain death to save the lives of comrades would seem to be near the extreme end of the spontaneity side of the scale. Such an act actually occurred on Peleliu Island in 1945 when Marine First Lieutenant Carlton R. Rouh dove onto a just-released Japanese grenade in order to protect two of his men (amazingly, he survived the blast). On the cognitive end of the scale, would be crash-landing a fighter aircraft behind enemy lines in North Korea to save a squadron-mate unable to get out of his burning aircraft. It would seem to have been pretty well thought-out by Lieutenant (junior grade) Thomas J. Hudner, Jr. in order to have been effectively executed. Even though the rescue attempt failed and the young Navy lieutenant's own F4-U aircraft was destroyed in the process, after initially being lambasted and considered for a court martial, he was awarded America's highest medal.

Do we value one of these rescues more than the other? Probably not, since both were rewarded with the United States' highest decoration for bravery—the Congressional Medal of Honor. (Not that Hudner did not place his life on the line. However, Hudner did not face certain death, only possible death. He must have thought through the possibilities for himself and factored in the odds of his landing in time to help squadron-mate Jesse Brown extricate himself from his disabled aircraft.)

There is one thing for certain. Cognitive choices are probably the more difficult to make than spontaneous choices, since many servicemen would probably elect not to make a rescue attempt, when the odds are heavily stacked against success. It's easy to rationalize not risking your life—and perhaps the lives of your crew—when the relentless firepower of the enemy forces is apparent and it is realized that if the rescue is attempted, one squadron policy or another would be violated. Sure, fly around the rescue site, try to call for help, suppress fire, call the base for advice. But don't go in and get your butt kicked. Although it's easier and much less risky, it is not necessarily the coward's way out of the dilemma. It is what is expected.

When reading the profiles of more than 100 of America's military heroes in *Medal of Honor* by Collier,[17] it is difficult to avoid comparing one hero to another and asking, "Was this act of courage more heroic than the other?"

Final judgment for issuing the Medal of Honor is made after witness statements are perused and analyzed by the various levels of military bureaucracy. We can only wonder what medals might have been awarded to those men in combat units at sea, in the air, or on the ground, when all hands are lost and there are no witnesses able to come forward.

In America, we do very much care about awarding medals to deserving recipients, living or posthumous (in care of their loved ones), and we even care to honor those Americans who could never be identified. The Tomb of the Unknowns was created by Congress in 1921 to honor all the unidentified soldiers who had perished in World War I. Those American soldiers who rest in this sarcophagus in Arlington National Cemetery facing the Potomac River remind us "that no member of the American armed forces, wherever he or she serves or however he or she falls, is forgotten. The profound association of the Medal of Honor with the tomb is a reminder that all who give their measure for their country are heroes."[18]

CHAPTER ONE

Early Navy Operations in Vietnam

Bob Spencer: "Gentlemen, it's time to build a squadron."

Commander Spencer standing in his office.
(Courtesy of Seawolf family)

It was in 1966 that the United States Navy began to expand its nascent riverine warfare operations in the Mekong Delta using small craft called PBRs (Patrol Boats, River). The watercraft were needed to enable America's naval forces to conduct day and night patrols to keep the commercial traffic flowing throughout the vast network of rivers used in transporting rice from the Mekong Delta rice bowl to the great northern urban population center around Saigon, the capital of the Republic of Vietnam (South Vietnam).

Secretary of Defense, Robert S. McNamara, granted initial authorization for the watercraft in August 1965, and it was a month later that Navy brass met in Saigon and decided to assemble a force of 120 boats to patrol the Mekong Delta and the Rung Sat Special Zone, with the expansion target date of early 1966. Not long afterward, on December 18, the River Patrol Force was created under the code name Operation Game Warden and designated Task Force 116.[1]

Early in the war, the U.S. Army had begun to assert its increasing presence in the southern part of the country designated as IV Corps and had already been tasked to protect the 31-foot boats trying to interdict enemy vessels and tax collectors on the delta's rivers and canals. Attacks on Vietnamese sampans and junks from along the riverbanks were so frequent and severe that many local rice farmers had to resort to transporting their harvest by a much longer route, traveling northwestward to the Cambodian border to successfully complete the trip. Consequently, the primary mission of the newly arrived Navy boats was to keep the rivers open to enable processed rice to move northward via the shortest route.

Aggressive patrolling by the heavily armed and speedy, but fragile fiberglass PBRs resulted in more frequent attacks by the ever-present yet elusive black-pajama-clad Vietnamese Communist fighters. The consequence of these attacks was a sharp increase in the casualties incurred by the American sailors manning the boats. Thus the Army had no choice but to assist the Navy and deploy helicopters to protect the Navy boats from destruction. These operations required much night flying and coordination with the Navy's riverine units, not an area of the Army's expertise. At the same time, the Army's expansion of ground operations increased its own requirements for the helicopters, resulting in a serious competition between the two services for them.

Early in 1966, the policy heads at CINCPACFLT (Commander in Chief, Pacific Fleet), responsible for the administration of all forces in Vietnam, had become acutely aware of the requirement for armed helicopter support for riverine operations and had recommended to the Department of Defense the establishment of an armed Navy helicopter squadron in Vietnam.

The planners specified the need for 44 Bell UH-1B Iroquois operational helicopters, 12 UH-1B pipeline helicopters, and 10 UH-1B training helicopters, for a total of 66. These single-engine helicopters had been used by the Army in Vietnam since 1962 and within four years had established a reputation for reliability and versatility. They were outfitted for close air support with the M-16 weapon system comprised of four external M-60 machine guns and two rocket pods, each housing seven 2.75-inch rockets.

In line with that request, several months later, in October 1966, CINCPACFLT also considered assigning the new AH-1G Cobra helicopters to the Navy but because they would not become operationally available until 1969, it was decided that "44 operational UH-1Bs would be acceptable to provide the earliest capability."[2]

But as sound as the request had seemed, "Those requirements were negated when the Secretary of Defense charged the Army with providing attrition aircraft and Navy aircrew training."[3] A decision had thus been made that would have lasting impact on the establishment and early operations of the Navy's critical air support program.

While awaiting the formal policy approval, the Navy was able to make a deal for some Army UH-1B model helicopters and form its own combat unit. Still, since the Army had priority for the UH-1Cs coming off the assembly line from Bell Helicopter, the Navy was assigned those UH-1Bs that had just been overhauled and were ready for redeployment to Southeast Asia. Those aircraft, inherently ideal for the mission of river patrol, nevertheless had serious shortcomings. The airframes had already been flown in combat and in many cases severely damaged and probably overstressed. In comparison to the newer "C" models being developed, they had less power, had older armament systems, and had a less maneuverable rotor system, the main element for controlling the aircraft. But because they were all the Navy could get, they were accepted.

The Navy Department had not initially planned for this mission and had no squadron designated for it, so aircrew personnel were requested from Helicopter Combat Support Squadron (HC-1), located at Ream Field in San Diego. In March 1966, Defense Secretary McNamara specifically approved the request from Paul Nitze, the Secretary of the Navy for the initial loan of eight UH-1Bs from the Army. It was to be followed by another 14 aircraft, as Navy aviation personnel became available to man them, raising the total to 22. McNamara, at CINCPAC's request had, in fact, approved doubling the number of aircraft to 44. However, in December 1966, Nitze's staff turned down the request for the second group of 22 aircraft, citing a shortage of second-tour helicopter pilots.[4] Surprisingly, only eight months later, in August 1967, there were 100 naval aviators assigned to the Navy's newly formed squadron, Helicopter Attack (Light) Squadron Three (HA(L)3), nicknamed "The Seawolves."

The arrangement for having Navy pilots fly Army helicopters was so accelerated that the Army became tasked with furnishing transition training to Navy pilots and their crews after they had arrived in Vietnam. In addition, all support functions were to be provided by the Army, including aircraft maintenance and provision of ammunition, fuel, spare parts, and support personnel. Barely a month later, the first six aircrews from HC-1 had been selected, had received their new assignments, and were on their way to the Republic of Vietnam.[5]

For the most part, pilots volunteered to become part of this unique squadron unit heading to Vietnam for actual front-line combat duty. An Officer-in-Charge (OINC), Lieutenant Commander Joseph P. Howard was selected from HC-1 at San Diego, and off they went to the Mekong Delta, in support of inland riverine operations.

It was decided that the unit's headquarters would be in Vung Tau, a former French beach resort east of the Delta. It was organized into four detachments (Numbers 29, 27, 25, and 21), each having two aircraft, eight pilots and eight gunners/crewmen. Detachment 29 was assigned to LST 786, *Garrett County*, a former World War II ship, designed to support two helicopters flying off her deck. She was located on the Bassac River, one of the critical tributaries of the Mekong. Detachment 27 was assigned to Nha Be, an important river town at the junction of the Long Tau and Soirap Rivers near Saigon. Detachment 25 would be at Vinh Long Airfield, an Army base adjacent to the Co Chien River. Lastly, Detachment 21 was assigned to LST 821, *Harnett County*, located upstream from Vinh Long and also anchored towards the center of the wide Co Chien.

During the winter of 1966, Commander Robert W. Spencer, a 37-year-old youthful and spirited officer who had begun his career as a naval aviation cadet, was serving on board the USS *Valley Forge*, LPH-8, as its Air Boss. After transporting the entire 326th Marine Amphibious

Battalion, including equipment, to the port city of Danang, the ship returned to the Long Beach Naval Shipyard where Spencer took off for a family medical emergency.

Having performed in a commendable manner for two years, Spencer felt not only prepared, but primed for an assignment to command his own squadron. So one of the first phone calls he made upon his return was to his career detailer at the Bureau of Naval Personnel (BUPERS) asking for a squadron command assignment. The news was disappointing: "I wasn't selected."

Barely a week later, on February 14, while still ashore with his family, he was called by his commanding officer, Commander Charlie Carr, who told him, "You've been selected for squadron command. You've got a squadron."

Spencer replied, "You're pulling my leg. I just spoke to those folks and they said I wasn't selected."

Carr insisted, "You've got a command and I am making you available because I want you to have it."

Spencer asked, "What is it?"

When Carr told Spencer that the squadron was called Helicopter Attack (Light) Squadron Three (HA(L)3), Spencer was flabbergasted. He was excited but also felt somewhat wary, since he hadn't a clue as to the nature of this organization. "What was this helicopter squadron?" Spencer wondered. He had been named HA(L)3's commanding officer before he knew anything about it.

Carr then told Spencer, "I want you to detach immediately, proceed to Fort Benning for six weeks, then from there to Camp Pendleton with the Marines for weapons training. When Spencer finally received his written orders, they already had him set to "report in-country by May 5th."

For Bob Spencer, this would seem to have been an ideal opportunity, considering his qualifications and experience. First, he was interested in commanding a squadron, as it was for him a normal and necessary career sequence assignment. Second, he had combat experience and an excellent record flying attack and close-air support missions in the Navy's formidable single engine AD Skyraiders over Korea in 1952. As a 22-year-old naval aviator just out of flight school, then Ensign Spencer was chosen by VA-65's squadron flight leader to be his wingman as the second aircraft in a flight of 35 that successfully attacked the strategic and heavily defended Suiho hydroelectric plant in North Korea.

Spencer finished his Korean War tour aboard the USS *Yorktown*, flying a total of 42 combat missions alongside much more seasoned former World War II aviators. Of the many lessons learned in Korea, he could apply several to flying armed helicopters over the jungles, rice paddies, and rivers of Vietnam. They included ensuring that pilots remained conscious of but not fixated on their targets. He had learned that pilots should not fly directly over the enemy target and never fly parallel to terrain features so as to avoid being in the enemy's line of fire and thus becoming an easy target. Adding to his credentials, Spencer had extensive experience as an instructor at the home of naval aviation at Pensacola, Florida both in SNJ and T-28 fixed-wing aircraft in 1954 and in HUP and H-13 helicopters from 1962 through 1964.

Prior to reporting to Fort Benning for training in the UH-1 helicopter, Spencer was tasked with putting together his team of officers, including the executive officer (XO) and the department heads. While he was in Long Beach, to his complete surprise, fellow Navy Commander Con Jaburg flew in from San Diego to meet with him and excitedly requested that he be his XO. Sensing that their "personalities just did not join," Spencer was not entirely comfortable, but he nevertheless decided after speaking with BUPERS that he would not create a negative issue. Therefore, he gave his approval. Besides, since Jaburg was so passionate about wanting the position, it might just be a blessing.

In retrospect, under the circumstances, Spencer felt that he didn't have the time to peruse "500 service records trying to determine or hand-choose these people." Did Spencer feel rushed? "I detached in February, had six weeks TAD at Benning" (for UH-1 helicopter indoctrination and 20 hours of flight training). After Fort Benning, "I had to go to Camp Pendleton (for weapons familiarization) and to Survival, Evasion, Resistance, and Escape (SERE) school at Warner Springs, California, and then report to the senior naval officer present in Vung Tau, Republic of Vietnam no later than 5 May." Since there were no other senior naval officers present in Vung Tau, CDR Spencer had essentially been instructed to report to himself.

After his arrival in Vietnam, things did not get any simpler for Spencer. After flying into Saigon and receiving the standard briefing at the Navy's fenced-in and heavily sandbagged Annapolis Hotel, he flew with Jaburg and his "priceless and invaluable" Operations Officer Commander Ron Hipp to Vung Tau to get things going. Since no preparations had been made for their arrival, their first night was spent sleeping on cots in the hallway of an Army-run Vietnamese hotel. To find sleeping quarters, Spencer and his initial cadre of officers had to find berthing at the Cat Lo Coast Guard facility, a 15-mile ride from Vung Tau. Two weeks were spent there until permanent sleeping accommodations could be arranged at Vung Tau.

Spencer eagerly looked forward to at least one exciting event, the official commissioning of the squadron he had been designated by the Navy six weeks earlier to command. But even here, luck of the dice didn't seem to roll for him as he discovered that the official commissioning ceremony of HA(L)3 had already been held in Vung Tau on April 1 by his HC-1 predecessor, LCDR Joe Howard. Undercutting Spencer by handing him the throne without the coronation would not bode well for the subsequent relationship between the Navy's Vietnam command and the new helicopter squadron.

Spencer was utterly dumbfounded at the first briefing he received from the earlier assigned HC-1 personnel. In Howard's absence, it was Lieutenant (junior grade) "Pistol" Boswell who imparted his wisdom to Spencer and his top officers. In a little area of the hotel serving hamburgers, "Pistol" started his briefing with, "Skipper, you're going to love it here. All you have to do is fly and shoot." Spencer recollects thinking hard, then getting up and walking to the men's room, putting on his "sheriff's badge" (commanding officer's pin) and returning to the table. He then looked at his XO, looked at his Ops Officer, looked at Pistol and said "Gentlemen, it's time to build a squadron."[6] And so, after an incredibly disorganized and rocky start (and Spencer knowing it and not liking it), he assumed his assignment as Commanding Officer (CO), Helicopter Attack (Light) Squadron Three; it was the first armed helicopter squadron ever commissioned in the United States Navy.

In the next few weeks, additional aircrew personnel started arriving in Vietnam. Many of them were flown directly to the detachments to which they had been assigned. Most of the time, the new arrivals were picked up at Tan Son Nhut Airport in Saigon by the smiling HC-1 crews, who had been anticipating their replacements. They were very much welcomed by their HC-1 predecessors, who for the most part were ready to return to HC-1 in the United States after serving one-year tours in Vietnam. However, there were also HC-1 personnel who had not yet completed their tours and were assimilated into the newly minted HA(L)3.

Assignment of personnel to the four detachments was decided upon by Spencer and his department heads at their headquarters in Vung Tau. They spent a great deal of time selecting the officers in charge (OINCs) since these were the most critical assignments and it would be their leadership that the squadron would be relying upon for successful detachment operations. The squadron's leadership had hoped for strong, organized, calm lieutenant commanders. For the most part, the transition from HC-1 to HA(L)3 was smooth. However, in one of the detachments, flying off the *Harnett County* (LST-821), there existed a band of individualists, nicknamed Rowell's Rats, who had apparently not been very closely managed by the leadership of HC-1 or for that matter by any senior officer in Vietnam. This might have been expected since the parent squadron was thousands of miles away across the Pacific and had, in fact, loaned its personnel to another area of operations. Even then, it was apparent that they were probably not supervised very closely by the senior command of Task Force 116, the Navy's operating task force in the Mekong Delta. Rowell's Rats had a reputation that fit their detachment's namesake. It was reported that they were disobeying orders, flying regularly in violation of sound tactics and bent on wantonly destroying many targets of their own choosing. Ultimately, the OINC had to be relieved and returned to Vung Tau to complete his tour writing a tactical doctrine.

The first group of second-tour aviators to arrive in Vietnam was a motley group, with each pilot hoping to enhance his career with a one-year tour of duty in a combat zone. It is doubtful that any of these pilots had been schooled in or had much knowledge of fighting Communist guerrillas following the tactics and strategy outlined in Mao Tse Tung's treatise on protracted guerrilla warfare. Nor had they read Bernard Fall's *Street Without Joy*, describing his experience as a journalist documenting the French fighting and getting mauled by Viet Minh forces, thereby serving as a clear warning to the United States military as to what it might expect on the ground.

Perhaps naively, these volunteers placed career opportunities ahead of common sense and history, but since America was expanding the war effort and had all the necessary manpower and equipment, it seemed like an interesting and not too dangerous place to be. Why not fly for a year, experiencing the southern farming culture and the scenic view of farmers working their rice paddies while wearing funny-looking conical hats? While in Vietnam, get some experience shooting at a lightly armed enemy wearing black pajamas, get a few R&Rs in Asia, and go back to the States with points for a promotion and a bunch of medals to emblazon their Navy blue uniforms. Except for the slight risk of becoming a casualty, why not?

Some of the officers came from the HC (helicopter combat support) community, while others transferred from the HS (anti-submarine warfare) community, with many of the junior officers transferring over before their first sea duty tour was completed and many others arriving directly from the training command, as Spencer had done similarly, 15 years earlier, in Korea.

Return from SERE school, May 1967. Standing, *left to right:* R. Stanger, H. Guinn, C. Biller, C. Myers, J. Bolton. Kneeling: J. Gilliam, P. Shay (author), J. Luscher. (Author's photo)

CHAPTER TWO

Wes Weseleskey's Early Life

Sally Weseleskey: "He what? He volunteered?"

High school prom with Wes and Sally. (Courtesy of A. E. Weseleskey)

One of the officers selected to be OINC of an HA(L)3 helicopter detachment was Lieutenant Commander Allen E. Weseleskey, son of a Russian immigrant coal miner. Raised in western Pennsylvania, Weseleskey's first learned language was Russian, which he speaks fluently to this day. Born on June 19, 1935, young Weseleskey seemed to be destined to live out his life in the way of the Eastern European family system: each generation of males was to live with, be raised by, and ultimately support their parents. When Weseleskey reached the age of 14 and was informed by his father that he would be going to "Pitt" he was flabbergasted, thinking for a moment of his future as a student at the University of Pittsburgh. "Could my father have perceived that I wanted to get a college education?" he thought.[1]

This early illusion was short lived, because his father meant the coal mine "pit." And before he knew it, his father changed the date on his birth certificate and sent him out for a job. Because he had no intention of going into the "Hole" as his family predecessors had, Weseleskey "fooled the old boy" and got a higher-paying job in the Open Hearth department at Allegheny Steel Mills in Breckenridge, Pennsylvania.[2] Weseleskey chose this position not simply because it was cleaner and he wouldn't have to live with being coated with the black, slimy, smelly coal dust when he returned home every night, but because working at the huge Number Two hearth gas furnace offered more rapid pay increases and the possibility of promotion. He had had enough of coal and seeing his father coming home every day with his hair, hands, fingernails, and ears coated with black grease. He was ready to leave the horrible conditions that existed in the Bairdford coal mining camp 60 miles northeast of Pittsburgh.

But by age 16, Weseleskey had had enough of this manual labor. There were other opportunities in the world. After seeing the brighter side of life as a result of being mentored by a former USAAF World War II B-24 pilot, Dr. Dwayne Wareham, his high school band director, he got himself ejected from his house by expressing his opposition to the way he was being treated and became a "street person." After spending some time working odd jobs, sleeping at friends' and relatives' homes, and receiving encouragement from his mentor, Weseleskey was able to audition successfully for the band and music department at the elite Valley Forge Military Academy outside of Philadelphia. After making the cut at Valley Forge as a tuba player, he was able to break with tradition and launch his own career, starting with a quality education. The academy was an all-boys boarding school serving for some (including wealthy families, such as the Mellon banking family) as a transition before entering college. His 1953 graduating class comprised 150 students.[3]

Just prior to being accepted at VFMA in 1951, young Weseleskey met shy and petite Sally Bilbie, born in 1935 a few months earlier than he, at a Saturday night dance party at his grade school's gymnasium. They each entered by purchasing an admission ticket for 25 cents. After being introduced by a friend and after a brief exchange of teenage pleasantries, Wes asked this cute blond nicely shaped in a light sweater and wearing a poodle skirt, if she would dance with him. According to Weseleskey's lucid memory, after the first dance there was mutual swooning over each other, and after the second dance, he proposed to the adorable damsel. He recalls, "I knew right then and there, I had just met the future wife of my lifetime."

Thus, the relationship with Sally began when she was 16, and he, born a few months after her, a mere 15 years of age. After several night rendezvous, he built up enough courage to ask Sally on a date. Without a car, he had to take a Pittsburgh bus from his home in Springdale and then hitchhike or walk the last two miles to her home in New Kensington. Her parents were very friendly and he felt welcomed there. Since her mother Mae played the piano and father Ed, the banjo, one evening Wes brought his tuba and they all joined in a jam session. Wes appreciated for the first time feeling what he had been missing at his home, being part of an "all American family."[4]

Fortunately for Wes, VFMA also had a junior college program, which he qualified for with a financial scholarship. In 1955, after having completed the junior college and having run out of scholarships, he enlisted in the Navy with his mother's permission. Having been motivated by seeing the movie *The Bridges at Toko-Ri*, which told the Korean War story of an attempted but doomed rescue of a downed fighter pilot by a heroic helicopter crew, featuring compelling acting performances by William Holden and Mickey Rooney, Weseleskey decided to enlist at the Naval Air Station in Willow Grove, Pennsylvania, where he was able to take and pass the NAVCAD (Naval Aviation Cadet) battery of tests. His good fortune prevailed and before he knew it he was on his way to becoming a naval aviator. He entered flight school at Pensacola as a member of Class 22–55 in July 1955.

During his rigorous high-pressure training period at Pensacola, Weseleskey had no desire to attend the ACRAC dances arranged in cooperation with the local townsfolk, many of whom sought after future pilot husbands for their nubile, mostly Southern Baptist daughters. The supervised dances were a welcome respite for many of those flight students thousands of miles from home to enjoy. It was a great relief from the pressure of academic classes, strenuous physical training and constant discipline from Marine Gunnery Sergeants.

Instead, Weseleskey kept to his studies and pined for his fiancée. So after considerable thought and consideration and with a huge amount of risk, he and Sally took the plunge, entering into wedlock on July 27, 1956, which in effect violated his training contract which forbade NAVCADS (naval cadets) marrying prior to receiving their wings and being commissioned as naval officers.[5]

After 18 months of training, Wes received his coveted "wings of gold" on March 1, 1957. During the same ceremony he was commissioned as a naval officer: an ensign reservist. He was given orders to VAAW 35, an all-weather attack squadron flying Douglas Aircraft's Skyraider ADs out of North Island, California. There he received training in night attack tactics and gunnery, which included firing 20mm cannon and 2.75-inch rockets, mostly from low altitude. Wes accumulated more than 1,200 flying hours in Skyraiders aircraft type and 400 hours of gunnery/weapons exercises. He recalls the precise method of attack on a ground target: commence attack at 160 knots and 2,000 feet and break off at 800 feet, but not less than 500 feet and a half mile from the target. No doubt, this training experience would highly qualify him for his assignment flying attack helicopters in Vietnam less than ten years later. It also seemed that at the outset, HA(L)3's newly designated commissioning and commanding officer, Commander Robert W. Spencer, and Weseleskey were of the very few who had any degree of combat/weapons type of flying.

Weseleskey, realizing the importance of being augmented into the regular Navy (which would guarantee him a full career as a naval officer), kept on applying for augmentation over the years but would be denied five different times. Being that the regular navy had more stringent educational requirements as compared to the naval reserves the main problem for him was that he did not have a college degree, a prerequisite for augmentation. The other half of the problem was that he was prevented from getting into college because he was not in the regular Navy. This would not be the only paradox that Weseleskey would face in the future.

In 1958, Weseleskey deployed with his squadron aboard the aircraft carrier *Hancock*, CVA-19. Being assigned to this huge squadron manned by 122 pilots, Weseleskey started to realize that his hope of joining the regular Navy might never come to fruition, simply because he might not be needed. So during one of his squadron's exercises aboard the ship, he decided to take a few hops in the odd-looking tandem rotor HUP with HU-1, the Fleet Angels helicopter squadron serving as plane guard for the fixed-wing squadrons. In the 20 hours he flew with them, he enjoyed hovering the helicopter and being challenged by the complexity of flying this type of aircraft.

Thrilled by his experience, he decided to make the transition into helicopters, which served two goals. The first was that since he had already received his commercial license in flying fixed-wing aircraft, qualifying in rotary-wing aircraft would give him greater commercial value should he not receive his desired augmentation and be forced out of the Navy. The other goal was that, since helicopter aviation was still a fledgling part of the Navy (helicopters made their initial appearance in the Navy during the Korean War in the early 1950s), he might become of greater value to the Navy. So it was back to Pensacola for transition flight training to helicopters. Soon after becoming fully qualified, he was off to the small Pacific island of Guam (initially without his wife Sally, as she was about to deliver their second child) for an assignment in search and rescue.

During check-in at Guam, Weseleskey met the departing Lieutenant Commander Sam Aydelotte, the station ordnance officer. Aydelotte recalled meeting the young "JG" and selling him his beat-up '52 Plymouth convertible, his station clunker, affectionately named "Blue Beetle" that he had recently fitted with a $30 Sears top for $150.00.[6] Ten years later, Weseleskey would again meet Aydelotte, but it would be for a month while on a detachment in Vietnam and, just as before, it was prior to Aydelotte's transfer.

After completing his two-year Guam assignment, Weseleskey still had not received an augmentation approval letter. Even his accomplishments in flying 24 successful rescue missions did not seem to help him. With a wife and two small children, he needed financial security. So he decided that although he loved the Navy and wished to remain in it, he would change services and apply to the Army to become a warrant officer, where there was an implied guarantee of a career. The Department of Defense had authorized inter-service transfers since it did not wish to lose experienced aviators from its other services while many positions were available with the Army. On the same day that he completed his application to fly with the Army, he finally received his augmentation and could once and for all settle down to having a Navy career. The year was 1961.

His first set of orders as a regular Navy lieutenant was to Ground-Controlled Approach (GCA) Unit 52, a heretofore non-existent unit. He was sent to air traffic control school in Olathe, Kansas to receive training as a final controller and air traffic control officer. After completing four months of this intensive schooling, where he was one of only two men out of 65 who passed the five-hour FAA final exam, Wes was ordered to Washington, DC, to serve as assistant officer in charge of the GCA unit at the presidential heliport, located at NAS Anacostia, which was a three-minute flight from the White House. He was also assigned to be the division officer of the base's emergency crash crew and boat rescue crew. While on assignment there he was able to continue accumulating flight time by flying with the Marine presidential helicopter squadron (HMX-1) at Quantico, where he was permitted to sign for a helicopter. NAS Anacostia closed soon afterward, becoming part of Naval Station, Washington, DC. Its aviation activities were transferred to and then reopened as NAS Andrews at the eastern part of Andrews Air Force Base.

Finally, in 1963, after completing this assignment, Weseleskey was ordered to college at The Naval Post Graduate School at Monterey, California. Because of his love of history and geography, Weseleskey chose to enroll in the political science curriculum. One of the other components of the school at Monterey was a safety officer program, in which Weseleskey was thrilled to enroll. In 1965 he graduated with a baccalaureate degree, whereupon he received orders to a mainstream Navy helicopter squadron in Norfolk, Virginia, tasked with antisubmarine warfare. While at Helicopter Anti-Submarine Squadron Three (HS-3), he served both as Quality Assurance Officer and Safety Officer and cruised on board both the *Randolph* and the *Essex* aircraft carriers.

Sometime in late 1966, the squadron received a classified dispatch requesting volunteer pilots for a helicopter attack unit soon to be established in Vietnam. This dispatch was sent to all Navy helicopter units, including those at the Naval Air Training Command (the author was able to volunteer for this same unit directly after his graduation from Helicopter Training Squadron 8—HT-8.) "Having an attack background, I volunteered,"[7] Weseleskey bluntly spoke. Of the 50-member squadron, only three pilots volunteered to fly with this new, yet to be named squadron, and be stationed in a war zone: Lieutenant Jimmy Glover, Lieutenant (junior grade) Jim Sprowls, and Lieutenant Commander Allen E. Weseleskey. By the time of his decision, Weseleskey had accumulated more than 1,000 hours of flight time in the twin-engine Sikorsky SH-3 all-weather helicopter, affording him the confidence of a seasoned aviator.

To explain the small number of volunteers, it had to be understood that the members of the Navy helicopter establishment such as HS-3 seemed comfortable with the known security of belonging to a stateside squadron and deploying aboard ship for a few months at a time. Not that the perils of night flying off an aircraft carrier, looking for phantom Russian submarines trying to shadow our great fleets, was less of a worthy career choice than actually confronting a real enemy as was to be anticipated in Vietnam, it was simply what was known at the time—the battle of the Cold War. And adding to the pilots' comfort in serving with HS-3 in Norfolk was the fact that their wives would get to know each other and become part of a large squadron family, which was very typical for a stateside squadron. It was also encouraging that people from very different backgrounds could come together to serve with such a unified purpose.

Another reason for the low turnout of volunteers to fight a war with rounds of bullets flying at you from different directions was not nearly as obvious. What would an officer say to his wife and young children? "I am volunteering to go to Vietnam and get shot at." Or, "I need to get away from you for a year and live in Asia." In some cases, perhaps an officer did want to escape from a failing marriage. Or, an officer trying to have a successful career but plagued with poor fitness reports and thus not having a great opportunity for advancement might fit into another category of volunteers. But this situation would have to occur at Weseleskey's rank or above, as more junior officers were rarely passed over and therefore did not have this problem. And since Weseleskey had things starting to go his way, even receiving his augmentation, he was not in great need of combat credentials for his future career.

Then what did lead Weseleskey to volunteer for combat service in Vietnam? According to Weseleskey, he, Glover, and Sprowls all felt very strongly about the national interest in preserving the sovereignty of the Republic of South Vietnam. But for a man such as Weseleskey, this simply did not sound like the whole story, considering his persistence as a poor youth who sought out a higher education and as a helicopter pilot wanting to stake his position as a career officer in the regular Navy. Perhaps there was also an element of truth to the scuttlebutt heard in Vietnam that Weseleskey felt that a successful combat tour would enable him to rise to flag officer, thus becoming Valley Forge Military Academy's first alumnus to achieve that high rank.[8]

Hardly anyone who had previously signed up with the Navy to fly helicopters expected to fly in real combat, as opposed to theoretical Cold War games with the Russians. The exceptions were the HC/combat support helicopter detachments of pilots flying off aircraft carriers in the western Pacific, who might be called upon to make rescues in North Vietnam territory (even though this was usually left to the Air Force launching helicopters from northern air bases in South Vietnam).

It would seem at the time that any flight officer volunteering for duty in Vietnam would be placing his marriage at risk. For this reason, some volunteers (not just Weseleskey at HS–3) did not tell their wives the truth. But could it really be hidden from one wife in a squadron with dozens of the wives knowing each other?

Initially, Wes had informed his wife Sally of receiving orders to a newly formed squadron being assigned to operate in Vietnam. The orders were sent to HS–3 via a BUPERS naval message dated February 21, 1967 directing Weseleskey to report initially to the 10th Aviation Group at Fort Benning for UH–1 training.[9] The orders stipulated that after completing the transition to the UH–1, Weseleskey was to report to COMPHIBTRAPAC for three weeks of survival/counterinsurgency training. After these training cycles, the orders directed Weseleskey to report to OIC, HC–1 Detachment Vung Tau, Republic of Vietnam.[10]

When she first heard the news, Sally was shocked with disbelief. Because of the dangers inherent in combat, she was frightened to hear this, but she understood that it was what her husband had been trained for. She was also highly supportive both of America's efforts in Southeast Asia and her husband's service career. But she was also very concerned by this news because she was now raising four children—the oldest nine and the youngest seven months of age. She thought about the demanding task of raising her children alone, and for close to fourteen months. (Typical squadron cruises were never more than a few months duration.) Nevertheless, she was able to reconcile with the idea and accept it without showing her emotions.[11]

At the squadron's going away party for the three pilots soon to be departing, a few of the wives (unaware of what Wes might have told his wife) approached Sally and jokingly asked her that since her husband had "volunteered" for duty in Vietnam, was she having marital problems. Her response was, "He what? He volunteered?" This surprise detail about her husband's career move almost cost Weseleskey his marriage.

According to Sally, when she did hear this news, "it was simply crushing to me.... We had gone to a farewell party, and after having a few drinks the Navy wives started chattering about those pilots who had volunteered to fly combat in Vietnam. And some of them proudly boasted that since their own husbands did not volunteer, they knew which wives had the bad marriages," implying that Sally was one of them. Sally was devastated by this news, at first for discovering it related to her in such a blunt manner and then by realizing its depressing reality.

For several days, as the truth sank in, she had a very hard time emotionally and really suffered. But how could she divorce a man, the father of their children, the man she fell for when she was in high school? Sally recalls being more disappointed by not having been informed in advance about Wes' volunteering, than in the actual details, presented a few days earlier. But because of their deep relationship, Wes and Sally were able to talk over the issue and resolve any misunderstanding and disappointment. Sally was able to forgive her husband.

The wives, showing typical respect for Navy tradition, offered to let Sally remain in the officers' wives' club for the duration of her husband's absence, even though he would no longer be in his former squadron. But by this time, she was thinking to herself, "Are you kidding me?" And feeling that the wives had treated her so callously, she decided not to accept their offer, given their lack of good judgment and hostile manner. She decided to readjust her social plans for the next year by planning to spend time with friend and neighbor Marge Roberson, wife of Weseleskey's new HA(L)3 squadron-mate, Master Chief C. J. Roberson. Besides, with their young boys being in the same Cub Scout troop, they would most likely have a lot more in common. Sally felt relieved by this new relationship and soon discovered it to be her "saving grace."[12]

Sally and Wes, over the following few weeks, were able to patch up the issue so that when he departed, there were no hard feelings, only love, understanding, and Sally's appreciation for Wes's patriotism. Sally knew that she would be able to immerse herself in her favorite activity—being a mother—after he departed. She would also be able to look forward to seeing him at some point, in Hawaii during an "R and R" break from his tour in Vietnam. And Sally would never hear again from the HS-3 wives, with the exception of scuttlebutt about some broken marriages.

The three HS-3 pilots—Glover, Sprowls, and Weseleskey—left HS-3 during the latter part of February 1967 and were together throughout the entire cycle of training until their arrival in Vietnam two months later. The training started with two weeks of UH-1 familiarization at Lawson Field on the Fort Benning Army base, near Columbus, Georgia, after which the new squadron members headed to Warner Springs, California for the excitement of SERE training. Finally, it was off to the Marine facility at Camp Pendleton for weapons familiarization, including handling and firing light and heavy machine guns, and the M-14 rifle and throwing hand grenades (flight school had included only hand-gun training). But it was the nine training flights at Fort Benning that seemed to generate the most excitement for the new combat pilots, who were making Navy history and flying U.S. Army helicopters in the process.

The two weeks of classroom and flight training commencing on March 7 climaxed with an extraordinary event on the last day of school. It was graduation day and would be clearly remembered by all of the Navy pilots having the experience of participating in the weapons firing at the aerial gunnery range.

Weseleskey recalls the picnic and party atmosphere, with Army officials and others wandering into the reviewing stands to observe the spectacle. It seemed to have the drama of the kickoff of an Army-Navy football game.

Since this was the finale of the first UH-1 training class of HA(L)3, in attendance was HA(L)3 Commanding Officer Spencer, his top lieutenants, Commanders Jaburg and Hipp, and a slew of other experienced pilots, including Lieutenant Marius Gache, LCDR George Crowell, and, of course, LCDR Weseleskey. In addition, also in attendance were those youthful pilots who had just completed flight school: Ensigns Robert Britts, Jim Burke, and Morris Steen. Although none was aware of it yet, they were all destined to become part of naval aviation history.

According to Spencer, the gunnery exercise almost did not take place. The Army had only reluctantly opened the range because "the Air Force had been there previously and had fired a rocket into downtown Columbus."[13] But apparently, the Army was comfortable with the experience level and professionalism of the Navy pilots, who were badly needed in Vietnam to relieve the Army of one of its most challenging assignments. Since the Army UH-1 instructor pilots were combat veterans, having flown countless hours in Vietnam, they were able to get their students trained to a high level of proficiency.

Spencer was perturbed when he discovered that there was a shortage of ammunition that would result in the allocation of only a half hour of gunnery to each of the HA(L)3 pilots. For Spencer this was inadequate. So he called one of his Washington contacts and had the Navy dispatch an R-5D aircraft loaded with Navy ordnance to enable his pilots to receive what he considered to be a bare minimum of experience. "That was Navy ordnance we were loading down there," according to Spencer.

The UH-1Cs were each loaded with their maximum of 14 rockets and two sets of fully armed externally mounted dual machine guns (with a total of 5,000 rounds of 7.62mm ammunition). Four copters at a time flew in a daisy chain in the direction of a couple of old tanks and other stationary targets set before a large rambling hill on one of the Fort Benning ranges. Between the two pilots in each helicopter sat an Army instructor. For Weseleskey as well as for Spencer this was the young and daring Captain

Robin Miller, who would be soon returning to Vietnam for another tour. (The highly decorated captain would complete three tours in Vietnam, earning the Army's highest medal, the Distinguished Service Medal, before being put out of action by an enemy round that struck his hand.)

Spencer was flying the lead aircraft in the daisy chain of helicopters, which were about to open up their relentless firepower onto the metal detritus, including an old Sherman tank, onto which they had fixed in their gun sights. Spencer recalled one young instructor telling him "not to worry about hitting any of these things because they've been out here for years and nobody's hit any of them yet." So he said to him (with obvious pride in his fledgling unit), "you've never had the Seawolves here," to which the officer replied, "I don't know what you're talking about."

"During the first firing run the grandstands were empty. By the time we landed and rearmed, every senior officer and his wife and children were out there in the grandstands like it was a Blue Angels' show. They gave us a standing ovation when we were rearming. They stood up and applauded and saluted and everything else. There wasn't one target out there that had escaped a hit. And they thought that was absolutely phenomenal," Spencer stated. So after initially having concerns for his assignment commanding the new squadron, he was thrilled that his pilots were such high performers. He probably started to dream about future successes when his operating fire-teams would have to square off against living, moving enemy targets as focused on killing his crews as they were intent on killing them.

Weseleskey was delighted that he was able to hone his gunnery skills on the Army range. And he was pleased to have been instructed by the experienced Captain Miller, whom he was destined to meet again six months later, when they both would be stationed at the Vinh Long Army Airfield in Vietnam. Weseleskey also felt proud of his new squadron's first moment of glory.

After completion of their training, although having fewer than 20 UH-1 hours, Spencer issued Weseleskey and the other seasoned pilots their designations as aircraft commanders and fire-team leaders. He declared them ready and able to assume their roles when they would reach their assigned detachments.[14] And within six weeks this group of 20 naval aviators would be in Vietnam for their one year of combat duty serving their country in its fight against the Vietnamese Communists and against the specter of Communist world domination.

Weseleskey as musician at Valley Forge Military Academy. (Courtesy of A. E. Weseleskey)

Wedding as a U.S. Naval Cadet. (Courtesy of A. E. Weseleskey)

Weseleskey and Sally's four sons: Edward, Scott, Bruce, Jon. (Courtesy of A. E. Weseleskey)

Weseleskey's fixed wing squadron assignment after flight school. (Courtesy of A. E. Weseleskey)

CHAPTER THREE

Assignment at Detachment One

Marius (Matte) Gache: "We started getting better equipment...
the whole squadron benefited."

Weseleskey standing by UH-1B helicopter. (Courtesy of A. E. Weseleskey)

In early May, Weseleskey arrived in Vietnam with his squadron-mates. After a short stay in Saigon for in-country indoctrination, he caught a bumpy ride in a twin-engine C-7 STOL Caribou cargo plane to HA(L)3 headquarters in Vung Tau. There he would spend another two weeks before he was off again to Binh Thuy Air Base on the Bassac River a few miles north of the provincial capital Can Tho.

On May 17, 1967, Weseleskey received his written official designation as the new Officer-in-Charge of Detachment One, signed by HA(L)3 Commanding Officer Robert W. Spencer. It read:

> As detachment Officer-in-Charge you shall:
> Be responsible for the safety, well-being and efficiency of those personnel under your command.
>
> Exert every effort to maintain your detachment in a state of maximum effectiveness for combat service consistent with the degree of readiness prescribed by higher authority.
>
> Report any deficiency which appreciably lessens the effectiveness of your detachment.[1]

Weseleskey was initially given his OINC assignment by the squadron's leadership, who needed someone of his caliber and experience to help bring the nascent squadron into the fold of integrated operations with the other Navy Game Warden units patrolling the rivers.

Spencer recalled that when he first met Weseleskey at the Army's UH-1 training unit at Fort Benning, "Al was full of energy." Spencer thought that he was going to be "my ace in the hole. He was a mover." He considered it a friendship that had blossomed. "For three months he was my right-hand man. I would have died for the dude."[2]

In the second Seawolf Gram sent to the detachments in June 1967, Spencer could not have had more pride in Weseleskey's other fascinating hallmark: poetic expression. Before leaving for Vietnam, Weseleskey looked at his four sons, studying their concern about his upcoming combat assignment. One night he put together his thoughts and wrote the following poem, the thrust of which was the expression of his eldest son, Eddie:

A Nine Year Old Man by Allen E. Weseleskey

"What are you doing Dad?" My boy fondly asked.
"I'm packing my things Son; I have a great task."
"But you've just returned From the ship this day;
My brothers and I thought Here at home you'd stay."
"That was my wish Son To be with you here,

But my orders say hurry My son is a big boy But I paused as I saw it	Leave ones I love dear." And big boys don't cry, That tear in his eye.
He knew I was going He tried to be brave, "I know you must go Dad, The pride that I feel	To the war in Vietnam. A Nine Year Old Man. You make me quite proud Can be said out loud:

It's the Pledge of Allegiance
My Country 'Tis of Thee
The Star Spangled Banner
The Home of the Free."

"Be careful each day Dad We want you home safely I cherish his words For me they have Meaning	But do your job well, I'm sure you can tell." They ring clear and true. Do they—for YOU?

Feeling it worthwhile to share his feelings with the Commander-in-Chief, he sent it to the President of the United States. Weseleskey's wife Sally forwarded to him the following reply:

Dear Mr. Weseleskey,

Thank you for sharing with me the pride and happiness you find in your son.

To answer your question, the words of your Nine-Year-Old Man have real and deep meaning for me. I think millions of Americans would react with equal admiration to this testimony of family patriotism.

We are grateful for your courage and dedication to the cause of freedom. May God accompany you to Vietnam, comfort you in the hours of family separation, and reward you with the blessings of that peace we are determined to achieve.

Sincerely,
Lyndon B. Johnson

A UH-1B helicopter arrived to pick up Weseleskey to transport him from Binh Thuy to LST 838, the *Hunterdon County*, a 300-foot World War II vessel taken from mothballs, restored, and fitted as a floating mobile PBR (Patrol Boat River) base. With a platform able to accommodate two Seawolf helicopters, the ship had been anchored at the mouth of the

Bassac River. Piloting the aircraft was Detachment One OINC Lieutenant Commander George Rockwell, who had earned the reputation as one of the finest officers in HC-1. His detachment, nicknamed the Flying Squirrels, had earned a reputation for reliability and agility in providing support for the LST's PBR boats. Weseleskey was not surprised to see him looking delighted. He had an air of satisfaction resulting from knowing that Weseleskey was assigned to relieve him of the job he had nearly completed. The date was May 13, 1967 (a few days prior to his official designation date).[3]

Weseleskey felt comfortable in his new environment, knowing he had assigned to him two outstanding second-tour pilots, Lieutenants Marius (Matt) Gache, having reported in from Toms River, New Jersey and Jim Glover, whose home was a small town in Arkansas. Staying on with the new detachment was Lieutenant (junior grade) Web Wright, a U.S. Naval Academy graduate and a pilot from HC-1 with six months of duty remaining in Vietnam. Weseleskey considered these officers outstanding aviators, very capable of performing combat missions in the UH-1B, and was confident that they would become the anchors of his combat detachment.

After two weeks and a series of orientation flights with Rockwell, Weseleskey, on May 29, flew his first flight as aircraft commander. He and his new detachment were then transferred to the newly arriving LST 786, *Garrett County*, while Rockwell sailed with *Hunterdon County* to Vung Tau, where he would finish checking out of HA(L)3 in preparation for his return to CONUS. So, with his nine flights and 14 hours of UH-1C time at Fort Benning and the 26 UH-1B flight hours he accumulated in Vietnam flying off the LST, Weseleskey "felt like I could handle the job" as leader of the detachment.[4]

The *Garrett County* was a World War II, 342-feet-long tank landing ship built in 1944 with a flat hull that was originally manned by the Coast Guard and assigned to the Asia Pacific region. After being decommissioned and placed into mothballs after the war, it was upgraded and prepared for flight operations and re-commissioned in 1966 for use in Vietnam. Since it was not designed for deep sea operations, it was a perfect fit to be anchored in the middle of any of the branches of the relatively shallow Mekong River.

The first 20 Seawolf pilots assigned to man the helicopters, who had just arrived, spent their first two weeks having their service records evaluated and being positioned by Spencer for assignments either to detachments or at the headquarters in Vung Tau. This southern coastal city also served as a beach resort for servicemen given in-country R&R. Named Cap Saint Jacques by the French during their rule of the country, it catered to Saigon's rich and famous elite. Officers not sent directly to detachments would have to wait until Spencer and his staff decided that it was their time to be assigned.

At the time of Spencer's arrival, there were only eight helicopters in support of the four Seawolf detachments. But more aircraft were arriving each week, and they were being put into service as quickly as possible. Some came from as far away as the Army re-work facility in Corpus Christi, Texas, while others came right from the Army in Vietnam.

The influx of personnel to man these aircraft continued at a rapid pace as did the expansion of detachments and new responsibilities for the squadron. By the first of August, there would be over a hundred officers assigned to HA(L)3. Since everything was happening so quickly and personnel were being shifted about seemingly haphazardly, many of the newly arrived pilots, especially the junior officers arriving right out of flight school, were a little impatient and eager to get into the air and to participate in the squadron's challenging assignments. While there were many second-tour officers coming to Vietnam for career enhancement, there were also many junior pilots coming for their once-in-a-lifetime adventure.

In early June, the squadron headquarters was still getting settled, and it would not be until the beginning of July that operations personnel would be located in the new office spaces in the hangar area. Most of the former HC-1 personnel who were completing their one-year tours had already returned to CONUS. Also, by early June, Spencer had finished making his selections for the detachments. However, there was a constant stream of aviators and enlisted personnel and aircraft being fed to the squadron.

The maintenance department was gradually being built up to service the helicopters, but Spencer found that the aircraft being issued to the squadron were not in particularly good condition, making the department's work difficult. He recalled that when he first arrived in country there were serious aircraft maintenance problems and "there were only three aircraft flying out of the eight that they had."[5] Nevertheless, Spencer had to be practical and make do with the aircraft he was getting and hope that, over time, things would improve.

At the fixed bases located in Vinh Long (Det. 3), Nha Be (Det. 2), and Dong Tam (Det. 7), it was easy for the pilots to get their flight time flying the newer model UH-1C gunships or UH-1D Slicks with the overworked Army. Usually, the OINCs did not object to having their younger pilots get flight time and combat experience. Many of the Army pilots were seasoned, on their second tour of duty in Vietnam and with experience as instructors. The fact that many of them had not received the same intensity of instrument training that the Navy pilots had did not seem to matter, especially in Vietnam where nearly all helicopter flying was done according to visual flight rules, both during the day and at night. And the fact that many of the Army pilots were warrant officers, not commissioned officers, did not matter either. The Army pilots were highly admired for their experience, their courage, and for their acceptance of the newly arrived, inexperienced Navy counterparts. While letting the Navy pilots fly with them, the Army pilots demonstrated patience and understanding, being aware that very few of the Navy people had ever flown helicopters in combat.

Weseleskey was barely broken into his new detachment as OINC when he began to demonstrate the aggression, decisiveness, and courage that would characterize his entire tour in Vietnam.

In command of a helicopter fire-team on June 10, 1967, Weseleskey came to the rescue of a U.S. Army Special Forces unit on patrol in the enemy-controlled Long Toan Secret Zone, engaging in a fierce firefight with a force of local Vietnamese Communist guerillas. Weseleskey had his fire-team take the fight directly to the attackers, who redirected their firepower in the fire-team's direction. This distracted the enemy from their primary target, enabling the Army patrol to secure a more advantageous position from which to direct fire more accurately toward the enemy fighters.

After his copters had expended their ammunition, Weseleskey had them return to the *Garrett County* to rearm and refuel, enabling them to come back to the battle scene as quickly as possible. Again, Weseleskey's fire-team was met with a barrage of enemy gunfire. Relentlessly, Weseleskey and his wingman returned fire, disrupting the enemy attack and causing them to break off the engagement. For this action, Weseleskey and his crews were awarded medals, with Weseleskey in particular earning the Distinguished Flying Cross.[6]

Less than two weeks later Weseleskey, acting as the fire-team leader of the detachment's two heavily armed UH-1B gunship helicopters, along with his wingman, Lieutenant Tom Glover, was on standby alert the night of June 20, 1967. The weather was typical of the spring monsoons in the country's southern part. The skies were overcast, with a ceiling below 600 feet, making the flying conditions extremely demanding on the crews. But at least there weren't any squalls with heavy blinding downpours predicted.

To further tax the pilots' flying skills and complicate their missions, the old UH-1B helicopters were constantly plagued with mechanical problems, some of which were serious and unpredictable. The HA(L)3 aircraft lacked radar altimeters, rendering accurate altitude assessment nearly impossible. And, of course, when the aircraft might return to the LST over an hour after having been called on a mission, if there was a barometric altitude change, the approach to the ship and the descent onto the deck had to be made completely visual to avoid making a landing with incorrect altitude. This would not be easy for a naval aviator trained to fly at night by relying on accurate instruments.

So when the ship's CIC notified them at approximately 2030 that they were to be scrambled to support a small Special Forces Green Beret reconnaissance unit under heavy enemy fire that had sustained serious casualties, the Weseleskey fire-team sprang into action. After a short briefing on the location of the friendly troops requesting both firepower and evacuation in the Long Toan Secret Zone, the two helicopters lifted off into the dark night and headed toward the action.

It took them more than 20 minutes to arrive on the scene. With the help of a "Spooky" C-47 aircraft flying above the clouds and dropping high-intensity parachute flares to illuminate the area, the fire-team was able to direct its machine-gun and rocket fire to within 50 meters of the encircled men. When the flares' illumination started to flicker, Weseleskey and Glover had to make the transition to flying on instruments while still keeping one eye on the ground. During this phase, the door gunners raked the perimeter of the location, suppressing most of the enemy fire. During the firing passes, the copilots contributed to the effort with accurate machine-gun fire from their sight-adjustable side-mounted M-60 machine guns.

But the emboldened enemy persisted in their fire, and when the timing was in their favor, the Communist gunners resumed their heaviest fire, which now included trying to silence the guns of the two helicopters. The battle between the enemy gunners, hiding in tree lines and behind the walls of dikes and invisible, except for their tracer fire, and the heavier firepower of gunship rockets and machine guns, resumed during repeated passes at the enemy locations. The opposing sides traded rounds as if it were a boxing match. Who would win the aerial standoff?

Finally, during a lull, a U.S. Army "Dust-Off" helicopter arrived in the area and started to make an approach to evacuate a seriously wounded Special Forces officer who had lost an arm to an exploding enemy hand grenade. During the approach, the Army pilot became badly disoriented in the night haze and broke off his approach.

Weseleskey had to decide whether to land his own aircraft, putting his crew at great risk, in order to make the evacuation and save the young officer's life. He decided against this, electing instead to encourage the Army pilot and accompany the Dust-Off back into the landing zone while having his wingman stand off and cover them both. The door gunners had to focus on firing at the perimeter of the landing zone, not so much for the sake of killing the enemy, but rather with the goal of forcing them to keep their heads down. To accomplish this, they had to spray the area with M-60 rounds, with the main concern of not firing on friendly troops. To avoid firing on friendly troops was of course an absolute requirement.

Weseleskey had to use his experience, intellect, training, and intuition to make his decision, and it had to be the right one. There were many factors to digest and integrate into his thoughts without the luxury of having time to deliberate. But most importantly, he had to weigh the odds of success and consider the lives of his crews. For Weseleskey and his team flying a helicopter at 80 knots during a firefight, fear would inspire them to take action, to get the job done. For the courageous, fear acts as a catalyst producing adrenalin to go forward, not retreat.

Perhaps there would be time later to devise a tactic to return to reengage and destroy the enemy. But at this moment, survival was paramount. So Weseleskey's decision proved correct, and the Dust-Off made the pickup of the Army officer and evacuated him to the nearest field hospital for treatment.

After the mission was completed, the aircraft fuel indicators of both of the aircraft displayed a low fuel state, requiring an immediate and direct return to the *Garrett County*. Since Weseleskey's wingman, Lieutenant Glover, had his fuel indicator nearly on the empty line, he was given priority on landing. As in many rescues, the range of the number of different problems faced always presented a challenge to the fliers, as they did on this night.

This successful mission earned Weseleskey and his aircrew Distinguished Flying Crosses. It was performed with the crews of both gunships working in concert to accomplish the rescue. Actions like this one would add to the laurels of HA(L)3 and allow it to earn its reputation as the squadron that never turned down a mission.[7]

A variety of problems started to manifest themselves both at the land-based detachments and on board the LSTs. At Vinh Long, the new OINC, Lieutenant Commander Chuck Myers, wanted a tactical radio available in the officers' quarters' office. He was able to acquire a few radios, UHF and FM. While he and Lieutenant (junior grade) Mike Louy were trying to install an antenna on the roof of the corrugated metal Quonset hut it inadvertently came into contact with overhead electric wires, giving both of them a powerful shock and causing them to roll off the rounded structure. A few days later, Weseleskey visited them at a hospital in Saigon. He was able to see the burn injuries on their hands and on the bottoms of their feet. Myers had a two-inch diameter blackened gouge in the sole of one of them. It was not a pretty sight. Louy's more serious injuries resulted from his fall off the structure. They spent more than ten days being treated at the Saigon facility. Louy was then transferred to the U.S.

Naval Hospital in Yokosuka, where he would be spending many more weeks of treatment and rehabilitation.[8] Myers ultimately returned to Detachment Six in Dong Tam, where he completed his tour. Louy made it back to Vietnam from Japan, finishing his one-year tour in Detachment Four on the *Garrett County* and being promoted to lieutenant prior to being rotated back to CONUS.

Weseleskey had received his earlier Detachment One OINC assignment on May 17. He observed that the aircraft in his detachment seemed to have been nursed along and were not in the best condition, but they were flyable. One of the problems he immediately recognized was the lack of accounting data for any Navy supply chain for the UH-1B aircraft. This resulted in the squadron being dependent on the Army for its supplies, not something traditional Navy squadron officers had ever thought they would have to deal with. In addition, the trip to Vung Tau from the lower Bassac River took too long to make every time a part was needed. It was much more convenient to fly into the Army airfield at Vinh Long, which also happened to be the location of HA(L)3 Detachment Three. Since the Vinh Long Army facility had to service four platoons of its own UH-1 Charlie and Delta model aircraft, it also served as an intermediate maintenance depot for them. As a generous favor the Army facility unflinchingly provided support for the HA(L)3 aircraft. One additional benefit for Weseleskey's detachment was that documentation was not required for them to receive supplies for their helos, saving them time filling out paperwork.

But this maintenance solution had one distinct logical disadvantage. The Army naturally gave priority to the readiness of its own aircraft, sometimes extending the time required for Navy helicopters to get needed parts and service thereby reducing their availability. And since the Navy Seawolves were on standby for combat support of PBR units and Navy SEALs and had a 24-hour-a-day readiness requirement as a quick reaction force, the riverboat crews could be in jeopardy.

In June 1967 Spencer and his staff were becoming aware of the seriousness of the deficiencies of the old UH-1B aircraft the squadron was receiving from the Army, helicopters that were essential for getting the operating detachments to function and provide support for the Navy's river patrol units. Spencer recalled not only that "the Army had stripped every aircraft of anything worthwhile before they delivered them and lost several pilots just flying some of that junk to us," but that "had we not accepted them, we would have been out of business and back home in disgrace within 60 days."[9] With regard to one aircraft received by the squadron, after a cursory examination, the squadron's personnel "removed 350 pounds of paint and found six cracks in the tail pylon."[10] Nevertheless, Spencer had strong faith in crews' ability to adapt to and overcome the aircraft deficiencies.

For Weseleskey, the lack of readiness was beginning to gnaw at him; he expected more support from the squadron folks, who now seemed to him like outsiders concerned with other issues. He had been OINC for less than a month when he started to feel that "as we got into an increasing number of firefights with the ubiquitous enemy, it became apparent that we couldn't maintain the guns because the gun barrels and other parts were being worn out from heavy use. We had difficulty getting replacement parts. We had already used up the PBRs' spares and any spares the ship had, so we requested parts support from our parent squadron in Vung Tau. We were told to call Saigon and to order parts that way."[11] He felt that they were "totally irresponsive with no reason given." He remembers being told "you have to get your own parts. Call Saigon and get your parts." Weseleskey recalled that "I didn't have a telephone, so I sent a message laying out the lack of parts support and therefore the lack of ability to support the PBRs and SEALs."

Understandably, some friction started to develop between Weseleskey and the CO and XO. He did feel though that Commander Ronald Hipp, the operations officer, was somewhat understanding. Hipp told him, "We're doing the best we can; we're still trying to get established here."

Then, "when the squadron sent us a couple of replacement aircraft that were actually 'downed' aircraft, it was the straw that broke the camel's back. One aircraft had 10 'downing' discrepancies, while the second one had 4 'downing' discrepancies." Two of his aircraft commanders, Lieutenants Gache and Greenlee returned from a mission saying that the helos were "totally unsafe to fly."[12] (Gache had an even better recollection of the condition of the aircraft in a May 20, 2004, phone interview with the author.) According to Gache, when they first arrived on board the *Garrett County*, the aircraft seemed to be "cast offs, in poor shape, with maintenance being marginal, at best. We didn't have any support. We were told to get weapons and parts off the ship's allowance, but they were not set with allowances to support our aggressive actions. We soon ran the ship out of parts to support even themselves and the assigned PBRs."[13] One officer even described the helicopters as being held together with wire.

Since the significance of these problems was that the detachment would not be able to support PBR operations on the rivers, thereby endangering the lives of the sailors, Weseleskey, protective of his crews and acutely aware of the predicament facing him, "had Jimmy Glover, the detachment maintenance officer, and Greenlee take the aircraft up to Vinh Long, where we got a copy of the 'yellow sheets' noting the 14 total 'downing' discrepancies between the two aircraft."[14]

At Vinh Long the aircraft had been turned over to the Army's 611th Transportation Company for a thorough inspection. This unit had had years of experience maintaining the UH-1 aircraft. The unit's maintenance supervisors reported on their DA Form 2404 (Equipment Inspection and Maintenance Worksheet) ten serious gripes on one aircraft (BUNO 64–14003) and four on the other. Of the ten listed gripes marked with a large "X" there were remarks such as "Right Igniter Intermittent," "A/C Engine Hangs Up On Start," "Starter Generator Leaking," "Bolt Loose Swash Plate Gimbel Pins," "Tail Rotor Cracked Leading Edge," "Tail Boom Cracked."[15]

Although these problems were remediable, they would take some time to repair. Weseleskey recalled that, "Glover sent me a message stating that it would be five days getting one of the aircraft repaired. So we had to tell the PBR units that there would be no air support," effectively causing them to cancel their operations. (This, of course, reflected badly on Weseleskey's reputation as OINC.) "I waited until they got back and looked over all the paperwork and that night put together a message to send to the home squadron relating to their lack of quality assurance (of maintenance work performed) and support for the fighting guys and that it would have to be a 'blood priority.' I felt that someone would have to get killed before we could get their attention."

Weseleskey's detachment had flown on many successful missions, but his aircraft were still in need of parts, especially M-60 barrels. So finally, after he reviewed the "yellow sheets" describing the discrepancies for the two helos that had just returned from Vinh Long, his frustration got the better of him. Even though Weseleskey understood and empathized with the CO's conundrum: how to conduct the supporting flight missions without downing aircraft that were declared unsafe to fly, felt obligated to take action and decided on June 28 to fire off a message to HA(L)3 headquarters (with the help of both Glover and Gache) warning the squadron of the consequences "of possible investigation by higher authority."[16] And, with the support of his pilots and crews, Weseleskey decided to draft and fire off a separate message to both COMNAVSUPPACT SAIGON and HA(L)3, with an information copy to COMNAVFORV (Commander Naval Forces Vietnam). The message was simple and direct. Under the heading of "M60 MACHINE GUN SUPPORT" and with the date-time group showing as "280450Z JUN 67," it read as follows:

> LIAISON WITH PARENT SQUADRON TO OBTAIN REPLACEMENT PARTS FOR M60 MACHINE GUNS HAS MET WITH NEGATIVE RESULTS.
> HA(L)3 STATES LST 786 SHOULD FURNISH EQUIPMENT SUPPORT. HA(L)3 REFERENCES CONVERSATION WITH COMNAVFORV....
> SHIP HAS NO ALLOWANCE FOR SUPPORT OF UH-1B WEAPONS SYSTEM, M60 OR XM-16.
> THIS DETACHMENT IS DOWN FOR PARTS ON 3 M60 WEAPONS.
> URGENTLY REQUEST RESOLUTION OF PROBLEM AND IMMEDIATE SUPPORT TO CARRY ON SQUADRON PRIMARY MISSION UNDER GAME WARDEN.[17]

A day later he received a response to his message from COMNAVSUPPACT SAIGON calling for action from the *Garrett County* and HA(L)3 and making other forceful recommendations. This response was sent within one day, in light of the wording of Weseleskey's original message: "Urgently request resolution of problem and immediate support to carry on squadron primary mission under Game Warden."[18]

Although both the squadron's leadership and Weseleskey were trying to resolve the same issue, it was Weseleskey's direct, audacious approach after repeated failures to obtain the support to carry out his assignment that led to his professional demise. Weseleskey received the following message:

As of 2 July 67 LCDR A. WESELESKEY WILL BE RELIEVED BY LCDR R. J. JONES AS OINC 116.1.1.4. (Weseleskey's numerical designator) LCDR JONES WILL REPORT ON BOARD 1 JULY 67.[19]

So that was it for Weseleskey. Although he had energetically and faithfully performed the duties prescribed by his designation letter (set forth at the beginning of this chapter), he was in hot water because he had not adhered to the strict rules on chain of command. He was ordered back to Vung Tau in ignominy, and his naval career was placed in jeopardy. And Weseleskey would never receive credit for the positive results of his insubordinate messages. But according to Gache, "We started getting better equipment as a result of this message. The whole squadron benefited."[20]

The extreme reaction to Weseleskey's direct communication being sent over the heads of the squadron's leadership in Vung Tau, thus bypassing the chain of command, may have been intended to set an example for the other detachment OINCs. It might also have been a venting of frustration on the part of the HA(L)3 staff, who were still trying to survive their first months of existence. It was unlikely to have been based on emotion—Spencer recalled that, "Throughout my 30-plus years of naval service, neither personality nor emotions ever influenced one of my decisions."[21]

Considering that the Navy rarely relieves commanders of their duties (barring of course, incidents such as a ship running aground), one would think that a personal visit by the commanding officer or by one of his deputies and a stern rebuke would have sufficed to make the point.

Could this harsh measure taken against Weseleskey also have been a warning to the other five OINCs to maintain silence and live with whatever aircraft availability they could achieve with their meager resources and capabilities? One of the results was a rise in trading and dealing in parts appropriated from other bases and flown to the detachments in exchange for rides in helicopters, a perk usually reserved for friends and visitors from Saigon.

Since the Army had a much better organized pipeline for parts, there were plenty of opportunities to "steal" parts. (No one felt any guilt stealing from another service since the parts technically belonged to Uncle Sam anyway.) Of course, the river units being supported did not care how the helo squadrons kept their helicopters flying, as they wanted the Seawolf fire-teams to be available on a moment's notice to suppress the evil emanating from enemy gun barrels and mortar tubes.

Reining in Weseleskey after this incident might have given the headquarters a new sense of importance and confidence in its ability to control the squadron's destiny. However, during this period the squadron was juggling other personnel as well, especially the OINCs. Could this switching of leaders at the combat unit level have had a detrimental effect on the morale of the junior and younger second-tour pilots and eighteen-year-old enlisted men? And what would the consequences be of a policy assigning OINCs to serve from 4 to 6 months on detachment while most of the other aviators and enlisted crewmen would be serving there for 12 months?

Commander Spencer could hardly be held responsible for the brevity of the OINC tours; the policy was common throughout Vietnam. Although many considered the practice detrimental to military effectiveness, Marine and Army officers were being rotated to the rear after they had served six months in command of a combat unit. This procedure was official policy resulting from concern "that the strain of command was such that most men were likely to become tired and less effective after prolonged operations in the field."[22]

The other rationale for short command tours was "the desire of the services to give as many officers as possible a chance to gain command experience and advance their careers." Most officers serving at the company level agreed "that the six-month tour was 'disastrous' for unit effectiveness," with many of them believing "that they had just begun to be fully proficient at their jobs only a month or two before their six months expired." One former artillery battalion commander concluded: "men do not like a change of leadership." He also thought that it "had a deleterious effect on morale as anything (in Vietnam) simply because the new leader is unknown."[23]

It seems that Commander Spencer and his staff paid little or no consideration to the possible consequences of their decision to relieve Weseleskey of his leadership position at Detachment One on board the *Garrett County*.

Cdr. Spencer and Weseleskey at Tuecon Village, left to right: J. Glover, R. Spencer, Weseleskey. (Courtesy A. E. Weseleskey)

Arming the helo on LST 821 *Harnett County*. (Official Navy photo COMNAVFORV)

Launching off LST 821 *Harnett County*. (Official Navy photo COMNAVFORV)

Detachment One pilots aboard LST *Hunterdon Cty*: Standing, *left to right:* R. Hoffstetter, W. Wright, T. Greenlee, E. Moninger. Kneeling: J. Glover, M. Gache, Wes, M. Jaccard. (Courtesy of A. E. Weseleskey)

CHAPTER FOUR

Accidents Plague the Seawolves

Joseph Calamia: "I looked into the pitch-black night.... I could only see the searchlights and hear the humming of the motors of the PBRs."

Joseph Calamia holding the nose cover of a helicopter lost off LST 786. (Courtesy of Joseph Calamia)

During the year of HC-1 detachment operations in Vietnam that began in May 1966, there was only one aircraft accident fatality: door-gunner Aviation Ordnance Airman (AOAN) Roger Childers died in a crash on September 13. There were also two serious helicopter accidents in November 1966, resulting in the loss of both aircraft. Considering that the aircrews had minimal experience flying the UH-1 gunship helicopters and had never before flown combat missions in waterlogged Mekong Delta type terrain, these losses do not seem extraordinarily high.

Unfortunately, along with the rapid expansion of the new HA(L)3 squadron, the momentum of human casualties and aircraft losses increased dramatically. Spencer felt remorse for each loss of life. He saw each of his charges, whether he was a senior officer or an enlisted airman, as a squadron-mate and viewed each loss as both a personal and squadron tragedy. Adding to his woes were the mounting pressures of keeping the aircraft flying in order to fulfill the squadron's operational commitments. Spencer was unable to sleep at night. He did, however, find some time to nap during the day. He knew of the poor condition of the helicopters and was forced to accept it. He fired Weseleskey on June 30 for being too outspoken about the condition of the aircraft and the deficiencies of the system providing them with parts and maintenance.

About two weeks after LCDR Jones had arrived to replace Weseleskey as the OINC of the *Garrett County* (LST-838*)*, he was shuffled off to another assignment and replaced by a self-confident aviator, LCDR Jim Savage. Within a couple of weeks of his arrival at the detachment on July 21, he led his fire-team on a low-level attack on an enemy position located on VC-infested Dung Island while accompanied by a CBS film crew. On the third and last firing pass at the target, while Savage and his wingman, Lieutenant Glover, were flying the same predictable pattern over the terrain and enabling the enemy gunners to predict their path, Glover's helicopter received an enemy round to its main transmission, causing it to go out of control and crash into the shallow water of a rice paddy. Aviation Jet Mechanic Second Class (ADJ2) Donald Fee, the gunner sitting in the cabin with the film crew survived the crash but was trapped beneath the helicopter after it rolled over onto him and despite the frantic efforts by his crewmates, could not be extricated. He drowned while one of his squadron-mates held his hand.[1]

On August 1, young and handsome Ensign James Francis Burke Jr. from Yonkers, New York, and three Army aircrewmen were killed when their helicopter crashed violently into the ground during a fierce nighttime rain squall. Although he had been assigned to Detachment Three in Vinh Long, he had been flying with the Army, and like other Seawolf pilots, had been trying to accumulate some extra flight hours to advance his skills.

On August 17, Aviation Jet Engine Mechanic Airman (ADJAN) Gill Lester Carter from Alexandria, Louisiana, died during an aircraft ditching at sea near Vung Tau after the engine failed. It was reported that he had died after he was struck by a still-moving rotor blade during his attempt to exit the aircraft.

On August 22, Lieutenant (junior grade) Thomas Edward Gilliam, from Rocky River, Ohio, flying as copilot, was killed during a firefight. The bullet that struck him in the side of his chest would have hit his armored chest protector had it not been for the fact that the aircraft was flying parallel to a tree line, a violation of squadron operational procedures.

Then on August 27, the quiet and very likeable Aviation Jet Engine Mechanic Second Class (ADJ2) George Henry Rush Jr. from Detroit, Michigan, serving with Detachment Two in Nha Be, died from injuries suffered during a helo crash resulting from severe aircraft vibrations while his fire-team was conducting a strike on an enemy target in a mangrove swamp in the Rung Sat Special Zone of operations.

A few weeks after Savage's arrival, Lieutenant Commander Robert Johnson arrived on board the same ship to relieve the experienced and talented Lieutenant Matte Gache as Assistant OINC. Gache, a former HU-4 pilot from Lakehurst, New Jersey, who had served many tours aboard small ships (including icebreakers), earning respect as an expert on helicopter small-ship operations, and was a graduate of safety officer school, recalls losing his Asst. OINC title solely in order to enable Johnson, a junior lieutenant commander, to have his chance at command.[2]

At the squadron's headquarters in Vung Tau, LCDR Johnson, reporting onboard from San Diego, had been assigned as the assistant operations officer and the squadron's safety officer. In his capacity as safety officer, he contributed his inputs to the "Wolfpack," the first squadron communiqué to the detachments. In his first blurb on safety, Johnson paraphrased the May 1967 *Army Aviation Digest* article regarding ditching procedures. "It is now a RECOMMENDED procedure to slow the helo to zero airspeed, with a moderate flare. While descending, jettison right-hand door, lock left-hand door open (don't jettison, due to the possibility of striking the tail rotor), keep level and allow the helo to roll whichever way it might go. As it rolls, assist it with a positive application of corresponding cyclic to stop rotor blades. When rotors are stopped, exit to either side as determined by direction of roll."[3] Absent from the safety input was the Navy's mandatory and elementary requirement to use seatbelts and wear life preservers when taking off from ships or conducting operations over bodies of water.

Johnson had been on just a few training missions during his first few days with the detachment. He flew with Gache in preparation for taking over as fire-team leader. During the day, they flew together, and according to one crewman, Johnson was intent on practicing his skills by flying below treetop level around the countryside, occasionally chasing farmers' water buffalos. This risky flying immediately caused concern amongst the crews about his "enthusiastic" personality. During one of his orientation flights on August 3, they landed at a Vietnamese Army outpost in order to purchase some souvenir scarves.

Johnson's blond-haired crew chief, 20-year-old Aviation Electrician Third Class (AE3) Doug Leaf, had been in Vietnam since April after arriving there right out of "A School." Since he had absolutely no helicopter experience, Leaf had to learn everything he needed to know about helicopters and gunnery while in-country. Leaf was somewhat worried about the newly assigned pilot, whom he characterized as a risk-taking "cowboy." Leaf had initially been trained as a door-gunner by very experienced 114th Aviation Company Army aircrews at Vinh Long during the first two weeks of April. He then decided to volunteer to fly off the LSTs, at first the *Hunterdon County*, where he felt he would receive the benefits of good Navy food and a daily clean shower, and later the *Garrett County*. He had flown with and had become accustomed to flying with the Detachment One professionals: pilots Tom Glover, Matt Gache, and the detachment's latest OINC, Lieutenant Commander Jim Savage. Leaf considered them very level-headed and was comfortable riding as a door-gunner in the cabins of their aircraft.[4]

On the night of August 31, aircraft commanders Johnson and Gache, with Leaf as Johnson's crew chief, flew as a fire-team the dusk-to-dark patrol; it was a short flight without incident. They returned to the ship and parked their helicopters at either edge of the 50-by-50-foot flight deck. (With the diameter of the rotor head being 44 feet, only one helicopter at a time could have its rotors turning during landing or takeoff). Gache recalled feeling that Johnson was in need of more flight time and tactics training and experience before launching in his own aircraft. But Johnson was quite gung-ho about taking up his own aircraft at night off the small LST deck. If there was to be a scramble that night, Johnson insisted on launching as commander of his own aircraft and as the fire-team leader. Since LCDR Savage was spending the night in Dong Tam and Johnson was the senior detachment officer present, he was empowered to decide how to conduct the flights.[5]

It was late and Gache suggested to Johnson that he stay awake and be alert, rather than sleep and then possibly awaken and stumble around on the unfamiliar ship in order to locate and man his aircraft. The rain had been pouring earlier, but it had eased to just a mild drizzle. The night was darker than usual because of the low cloud cover. And without the usual starlight it was a black, black night. At their location at the mouth of the Bassac River, the residents' hooches along the riverbanks had their kerosene lamps extinguished. The current moved swiftly. And out on the river, although the winds weren't always constant, according to Leaf, on this night they were strong and blowing from the helicopter's aft as it was parked on the flight deck perpendicular to the length of the ship.[6]

At about one in the morning, there was a scramble with the usual "General Quarters, General Quarters, Scramble the Helicopters" blasting over the ship's intercom. Gache and his crew were ready. They got to their aircraft, flipped on the switches, and got ready to turn up their engine to spool the rotor head in preparation for take-off. However, for the other crewmen, there was confusion. When Leaf got topside, running from his small berthing compartment near the ship's bow, his helmet was nicked by the tail rotor. Noting that he was the only gunner in sight, Johnson told him to go and get crew chief Ott. When Leaf reached Aviation Jet Engine Mechanic First Class (ADJ1) Edwin Ott in the first-class berthing area, he had to awaken him, since he was unaware of his assignment and was still fast asleep. They ran topside and boarded the aircraft.[7]

According to Gache, "we were waiting to get a 'Green Deck' when the lead helo (with Johnson and his crew of Lieutenant Al Bacanscas (copilot), Leaf, and Ott) started lifting off. The ship was still swinging around to give us winds."[8] The bridge personnel advised that it was a RED DECK with the traffic light on the superstructure still red. Following normal procedures, the ship pivoted around on its anchor to enable the helos to be facing into the wind so they could take off and obtain maximum lift.[9]

Leaf recalled that, "earlier in the day I told Ott I had a terrible feeling and that we'd better put on our Mae Wests. That was the first night I had ever worn one, but Ott did not even have a Mae West to wear."

Leaf recalled that the pilot took off barely after the crewmen had gotten into their seats in the rear of the cabin. Leaf was tethered to the aircraft wearing a five-foot-long gunner's belt (also called a monkey belt). He noticed that the wind was blowing from the tail of the helicopter. Because of the confusion, he ended up on the starboard side of the cabin, sitting behind the aircraft commander (he usually sat on the port side, while Ott had customarily manned the starboard side). Things started happening so fast he was not able to coordinate with Ott. Leaf remembers hearing the bridge personnel screaming "Red Deck" and seeing the red signal light glaring brightly in their direction.[10]

Gache, seated in the right seat in the other helo recalled that, "I lost sight of them as they disappeared into the darkness. Gunner Tom Olezeski was standing on my side of the aircraft ready to lock the gun barrels into the M-60s on the flex mounts when he came to my window screaming that they had gone into the river."[11]

Johnson's aircraft crashed immediately upon lift-off. Since the rotor blades had just barely attained their required rotation speed to enable the helicopter to become airborne, and with the severe wind was blowing from behind, the helicopter was unable to attain adequate lift in order to gain altitude. As soon as the rotor blades contacted the surface of the river, the helicopter fuselage pounded the water below and shook from side to side, with its parts disintegrating. Leaf was suddenly pitched forward inside the cabin, striking his face on the back of the pilot's seat, badly breaking his nose and damaging his left eye, severely gashing his left arm, and at the same moment, Leaf recalled, "that is when my lights went out."[12] His protective helmet took such a great hit that it smashed in half and disappeared. (Things were happening so fast that Leaf did not have time to wonder why Johnson took off so suddenly and whether he had panicked on his first night scramble.)

The gunner's belt afforded no protection during a crash; it would only guarantee to keep the wearer from being thrown out of the aircraft. According to Leaf, the detachment had neither a strict policy of the gunners strapping into the aircraft with the seat belts in the rear of the cabin, nor of even wearing Mae West life preservers. Most of the life preservers belonging to the detachments were purportedly unreliable and were not subjected to the normal rigorous standards enforced by a parachute rigger, which the squadron was sorely lacking. Other gunners recalled wearing their Mae Wests only on occasion, and very few used the gunner's belt, if their aircraft even had one. They would use the seat belt, which when extended afforded ample room to enable them to turn in their seats to face outside the helo; when it was fully extended they could put a foot out on the rocket pod and shoot their M-60s 180 degrees under the aircraft pylon.[13]

It was that night, though, that Leaf had had an ominous feeling and put on his Mae West. And it ended up saving him. Leaf did not recall seeing Ott wearing any life preserver as he boarded the helicopter, nor did he see him put on his helmet. (The author's detachment's crews at Nha Be (Det. 2), usually launching their aircraft off the PSP runway and out over the Long Tau River, as a matter of policy always wore Mae Wests over which were worn the armored chest protectors, and were securely strapped in the aircraft, with all hands having their seatbelts fastened.)

When Leaf regained consciousness, he felt the river's mushy bottom and was able to pull one of the two toggles on his life preserver, gaining some buoyancy, slowly bringing him to the surface and enabling him to regurgitate some of the dirty water he had swallowed and to breathe some air into his lungs. In severe shock, he looked around and saw nothing except the lonely darkness as he felt the strong current pulling him away from the ship, toward the river's mouth. He reached for his .38-caliber survival revolver, thinking he could fire a round and bring some attention to himself, perhaps saving him from being lost in the chaos. But as soon as he grabbed it, the gun fell from the grip of the hand of his badly torn-up arm and was gone. He was unable to do much else, also suffering badly from his head and facial injuries. He started to worry about the stiff current pulling him out to sea.[14] Finally, after some hollering to attract some attention, and some overhead lighting being shone by a flare dropped from a circling Douglas AC-47-Spooky aircraft, which fortunately had been airborne in their vicinity, he was grabbed onto and held by Johnson's copilot, Bacanscas, who appeared out of the darkness like an angel. Neither Ott nor Johnson was observed to have surfaced.

Bacanscas had exited the helicopter after it had gone under water. When he surfaced, he heard Leaf, who was now visible, swam over to him, and grabbed him. Luckily, Bacanscas was able to locate the experimental strobe light given to him by Seawolf pilot Bill Martin (who was assigned as OINC of a different detachment) with whom he had trained while back in the States.[15] He depressed its rubber nipple and it lit, its pulsating flashes of bright white light clearly visible in the misty night.

In short order, he and Leaf were located by one of the alert PBR crews, which had just launched from its boom tethered alongside the ship, in search for survivors. The boat crew lifted Leaf (followed by Bacanscas) aboard the small boat. Seeing that seriously injured Leaf required immediate medical attention, the sailors sped back to the *Garrett County*, which now had dozens of personnel peering over the sides of its deck observing the tragedy. A group of organized sailors then cast a line over the side, hooked it onto a life preserver provided by the PBR, and lifted him up to the ship's main deck.

Gache, meanwhile, after having rid his aircraft of its excess weight, including ammunition boxes and unnecessary gear, took off in pursuit of the survivors of the downed helicopter. But Johnson's aircraft had immediately sunk into the murky depths of the Bassac, which even in bright sunlight would be colored a chocolate brown as dark as that of America's Rio Grande. After having searched fruitlessly for ten minutes, he was radioed that one badly injured crewman had been rescued and brought back on board the LST. Gache was then called back to the ship in order to medevac Leaf for treatment. Upon touching down, Gache was "surprised to see Al (Bacanscas) standing next to my window soaking wet since he was not on duty that night." Later that night Bacanscas related to him that "Bob's assigned copilot Lieutenant (junior grade) Tom Anzalone told Al he felt sick, so Al grabbed his gear and ran out to take his place."[16] Gache had the seriously injured Leaf loaded onto his aircraft, and then he took off for the Soc Trang Airfield medical facility.

Joseph Calamia, coming from a Navy family living in El Paso, Texas, whose father served during World War II and whose grand-uncle served on the armored cruiser USS *New York* in 1898, received A-School training as a ship fitter and was all of twenty when he reported on board the *Garrett County* as a fireman striker in 1967.[17] He had been carrying out his 1200–0400 watch duty assignment when he heard all the commotion and climbed up to the flight deck to see what was happening. "When I realized that one of the helicopters had crashed, I looked into the pitch-black night in the light drizzle. I could only see the searchlights and hear the humming of the motors of the PBRs searching for survivors." When he later heard that one of the two missing aircrewmen was Ott, he felt especially sorrowful as it was the more mature Ott who was the one sailor who had befriended him when he reported on board the ship.[18]

For the rest of the night, PBRs searched the area, including the riverbanks, for Johnson and Ott, neither of whom had yet surfaced. Air Force aircraft overhead dropped flares to help in this effort. The LST turned on its spotlights with the hope that the two crewmen would be able to locate their ship, if they had become disoriented and floated downstream. Calamia recalled that a few days later Navy UDT divers searched the crash area for the wrecked helicopter and its victims.

Gache returned from Soc Trang, refueled, and, maintaining his professional calm after the ordeal with which he had just dealt, returned to the formidable darkness of the night sky to resume his search for Johnson and Ott. Nevertheless, after many more hours of searching in concert with the PBR boats, it seemed more and more likely that they would not find the two crewmen. Seawolf helicopters, flying in from other detachments, continued their search for several more days. Even the efforts of the navy divers were unsuccessful at discovering anything more than the helicopter's broken nose cover, which had separated from the aircraft frame on impact with the water.

The violence of the crash did not necessarily mean that Johnson was lost—he was known to be a strong swimmer. But for Ott, there was extra concern. Leaf had known that "Ott could not swim. He never passed Navy swim qualifications."[19] Nevertheless, neither Ott nor Johnson would ever be seen again, and they were declared missing in action.

Leaf recalled his arrival at the Soc Trang hospital, with the emergency medical team calling for the base's doctor, who was socializing at the Officers' Club. The doctor's arrival did not exactly elate Leaf's spirits.

Leaf recalled his being both arrogant and bothered by his freshly injured casualty, the young and torn-up Leaf. The distracted physician sutured the gash on his left arm and put cast material over his nose, so it would set. Jokingly, he threatened Leaf with a court-martial after he vomited on the gurney. Leaf, feeling despair, was hardly amused by this casual, off-handed treatment.

After a few agonizing hours, Leaf was airlifted to the more suitable field hospital at Dong Tam, which although located under a rubberized roof, had a highly professional staff. But things were hectic there as well, with lights occasionally flickering during a mortar attack.

Meanwhile, as more than two days had passed and no one at the detachment knew where Leaf had gone, a concerned Detachment One pilot, Lieutenant Web Wright, one of the few Seawolf pilots graduating from the U.S. Naval Academy (who was later transferred to Detachment Three at Vinh Long), insisted on going to look for him. He ultimately found Leaf at the Dong Tam medical facility. Seeing Wright gave Leaf his first feeling of comfort, the face of a friendly man watching out for his welfare. Leaf was not surprised that it was Wright, since he was the one officer both closest to and showing the most empathy for the enlisted aircrews. Leaf now felt encouraged and, before long, was transferred to the larger medical facility in Vung Tau.

One night, while at the Vung Tau military hospital, Leaf advised one of the attentive nurses that his arm below his elbow just wasn't feeling right. Upon examination, it was discovered that his sutured arm was so severely infected that it was in danger of becoming gangrenous. So the stitches were removed, and the arm was drained of fluids for several days before being re-stitched.

About a week later, the cast and packing were removed from his face. Adding to his misery, it was discovered that his nose was still in very bad shape—it was one inch off center. So he received another operation to restore his appearance. Apparently, the unprofessional and neglectful treatment he had received at Soc Trang only delayed his recovery. Leaf remained in the hospital for between 6 and 8 weeks, where he would mend until he was well enough to return to his squadron.

Given Leaf's severe injuries and only gradual recovery, the squadron leadership decided to assign him to the maintenance department. This is where he would spend the rest of his Vietnam tour, working with the recently reassigned (from Det. One) Lieutenant Jim Glover and trying to help the squadron provide the detachments with better functioning aircraft. He felt that they applied their best efforts to repair the aged and worn UH-1B helicopters, which were regularly brought in for maintenance. Leaf recalled that shortly after his arrival at the squadron headquarters and while he was still recovering, he was summoned to the CO's office, where the accident report he had submitted was being reviewed. Understandably, he told the truth as he saw it and was not too happy recollecting his ordeal and providing his description of the accident that had resulted in the loss of two of his squadron-mates. He recalled balking at the request to modify his statement to reflect less negatively on the accident and the pilot who had commanded and flown the aircraft into the river.[20]

Unfortunately for Leaf, long after having being released from active duty in 1969, it was only in 1980 that, having long suffered from migraine headaches, he was able to receive treatment at a VA hospital that repaired his earlier facial injury while at the same time removing a tumor from under his left eye.

The last in this series of aircraft losses occurred on September 11, when a helicopter had to make an emergency landing because of losing a tail rotor. No serious injuries were reported.

Although the earlier accidents and losses of life began to affect everyone's morale, it was without any doubt, the September 1 crash that really got the attention of everyone in the squadron. Spencer considered Johnson's death "a "major loss to me."[21] Spencer recalled that he had "designated Johnson as safety officer and set him up in a trailer in a hangar." Spencer had been reluctant to send Johnson on detachment, "but I got to the point that I was forced to because he had seen his contemporaries going out to be OINC and he hadn't been going. I got to the point where I couldn't take it anymore. I had to let him go. It lasted less than a week" before Johnson flew into the Bassac. Spencer felt that "he was a very good pilot. But he was flaky and just a little too eager, too soon."[22]

There was no doubt that in early September, Bob Spencer, the commanding officer of HA(L)3 was facing a major crisis in his squadron.

Petty Officer George Rush. (Author's photo)

Helicopter recovered from the crash site. (Courtesy of A. E. Weseleskey)

CHAPTER FIVE

In Transition to Next Assignment

Sam Aydelotte: "His standards were a little higher than everybody else's."

Pilots at Vung Tau Officers' Club. E. Rosenthal (front left), R. Smith (back), S. Aydelotte (front), R. Hofstetter (center sunglasses), J. Savage (front with white shirt), C. Jaburg (right front). (Courtesy of Seawolf family)

Weseleskey spent two months at HA(L)3 headquarters in Vung Tau, in purgatory, for his lack of tact in chain-of-command communications while he was running the detachment on board the *Garrett County*. Wes served in the Administration Department as assistant to the Administrative Officer, Lieutenant Commander Eugene Rosenthal (one of the oldest squadron members, leaving five children at home in Pensacola and its most senior lieutenant commander), giving him time to reflect and to ponder his future. He had just squandered the opportunity for which he had been selected—to lead a unique combat unit created within the historical framework of riverine operations in Vietnam.

Wes often thought to himself, "Was it worth it?" And although he felt sincere remorse for preempting the commanding officer's authority, he also felt convinced that his messages did manage to benefit the squadron. It wasn't easy for him to face his detractors every day, so he kept busy with his administrative tasks, trying to make the best of the situation. Still, his being relieved of his post at Detachment One could well be career-ending.

Weseleskey got along very well with Rosenthal, who certainly knew of his misdeed but was not the type of officer to disparage his assistant. It was probably a good idea for Spencer to assign Weseleskey to the Administrative Department as doing so would likely keep him out of trouble.

Rosenthal was an easy-going, amiable officer, trying to do his best and get promoted to commander. A soft-spoken gentleman, he came to HA(L)3 from an assignment at a naval air station. Weseleskey recalled hearing that Rosenthal's helicopter background was with an HC squadron. Upon his check-in to HA(L)3 Rosenthal was immediately assigned as the Administrative Officer. And since he was the first officer to serve the newly formed squadron in this capacity, he was tasked with keeping the paperwork flowing, especially with regard to the checking-in of newly arrived officers and enlisted personnel.

The administrative work that had to be accomplished at the Vung Tau headquarters was critical, especially in enabling the smooth flow of incoming personnel and their prompt reassignment to the squadron's operational detachments. He worked diligently in organizing the influx of the many newly arrived officers and enlisted men. At the same time, he was tasked with dispatching men who had just completed their tours back to CONUS. This work kept him from receiving an earlier OINC assignment to a detachment. Rosenthal certainly had his hands full.

While in Vung Tau, Weseleskey, like everyone else, dressed in comfortable Army green fatigues. He lived a rather easy life, performing an occasional test flight, and making mail runs to the detachments, but mostly doing paperwork. One day at the end of July, he was tasked to fly to the Saigon mortuary to identify the remains of gunner ADJ2 Donald Fee, who had lost his life in the July 21 helicopter crash off the *Garrett County*.

Since he also had Rosenthal as his roommate, Weseleskey got to know him pretty well. Together, they even went to the hot baths on the weekends. Rosenthal treated Weseleskey well, and they started to form a good relationship. Jointly, they even attended church services, with Rosenthal complimenting his harmonious voice. Weseleskey recalls Rosenthal telling him, "I do not care why you are here" then listing his professional expectations of him. "You keep your nose clean, and we'll get along fine," Rosenthal said.[1]

It was the last week of August, after a couple of boring months in Vung Tau that Weseleskey finally was released from the doghouse and transferred back out to a detachment: Detachment Three at Vinh Long Army Airfield. There he was assigned to serve under OINC Lieutenant Commander Sam Aydelotte, one of the most senior lieutenant commanders in the squadron, if not the Navy.

LCDR Aydelotte, in November 1966, had commanded the primary recovery HS-11 helicopter for the Gemini 12 spacecraft as reported in Naval Aviation News.[2] He had served at Vinh Long since shortly after his arrival in Vietnam. He was sent to relieve the former HC-1, Detachment 25 OINC, Lieutenant Commander Rocky Rowell, who had aptly named his detachment "Rowell's Rats." Since there was no Naval Support Activity (NSA), everything had to be stolen from the Army ("cumshawed" in Navy parlance). It seemed that everyone on the Army base hated Rowell for his tactics in acquiring parts and supplies, and usually they went on high alert when anyone wearing a Navy uniform was nearby. Aydelotte recalled being there barely a week before Rowell was transferred out. Coming from one of the Navy's traditional squadrons—HS-11, Aydelotte experienced a rude awakening in running a detachment at an Army facility.

Aydelotte was pleased to have Weseleskey assigned to him and immediately tasked him as the fire-team leader of the second helicopter fire-team. This was the first time that he had seen or heard from Weseleskey since he had met him years before, when he was completing his tour on Guam in 1957.[3] Aydelotte really liked having Weseleskey as his "Number Two." He recalls that, "he was a great Assistant OINC. I told him to do something, and he did it right away. He did exactly what he was supposed to do. But you have to remember that Al marches to a different drumbeat; everyone is out of step but him." Nevertheless, "he was normally right. His standards were a little higher than everybody else's … a lot of guys did not like him for that."[4]

Aydelotte, in his fourth month at Vinh Long's Detachment Three, felt that he had put in his time with the detachment, and, being prepared to rotate back to the headquarters in Vung Tau, was disappointed in the squadron's leadership for not having had him relieved, since LCDR Rosenthal had been sent to relieve him shortly before. But after flying in two firefights, Rosenthal felt he wasn't ready for the job and returned to his desk in Vung Tau.

When Spencer, the commanding officer, gave Weseleskey his new assignment, he reminded him of the problems he had caused the leadership while on board the LST. Weseleskey was summoned into the CO's office and advised "you will never again be an OINC," to which Weseleskey merely nodded and took in stride since he was determined to make the best of it.

At Vinh Long, though, Weseleskey quickly adapted to the new environment, and as a gunship fire-team leader, he immediately started to lead and train the other members of his team. He flew whenever he could, on his off days even flying with the Army. He thought it beneficial to the squadron to learn some of the Army's advanced tactics, including flying with the "bug ship" team of helicopters, working with high-intensity spotlights illuminating the ground at night, looking for infiltrators and the movement of supplies.[5] Whether day or night, Weseleskey never hesitated to participate in a combat mission.

Weseleskey had been very much aware of and concerned about the recent accident record, even having accompanied Spencer to the site of the crash near Nha Be that took the life of Petty Officer Second Class

George Rush on August 27. So when he was informed of his new collateral duty as safety officer, he felt both awe and delight. It was on September 12, 1967 that he received this unclassified message:

IN ADDITION TO HIS PRESENT DUTIES, LCDR WESELESKEY WILL ASSUME THE DUTIES OF SQUADRON SAFETY OFFICER. THIS ENTAILS THE NORMAL SAFETY OFFICER RESPONSIBILITIES PLUS INSURANCE THAT ALL DETS ARE COMPLTING [*sic* COMPLYING WITH] SQUADRON POLICY, WRITTEN AND ORAL.[6]

Just a day before the message, one of the HA(L)3 helicopters had had to make an emergency landing due to the sudden loss of its tail rotor. There were no casualties. The decision to designate Weseleskey to this assignment, even though he was now serving with a detachment, had probably been made before the latest incident, but more likely in response to the crash off the *Garrett County*, as LCDR Johnson had been the safety officer. Despite the high level of animosity the squadron leaders felt towards him for his earlier transgressions while as OINC of the *Garrett*, it was apparent that in their collective judgment, they still decided that Weseleskey was the officer best suited to the position. They desperately needed someone to help stem the rising tide of accidents and to see the squadron through the crisis in order for them to start meeting their operational commitments and to eliminate or at least reduce the aircraft losses and the loss of irreplaceable lives. The leadership would have to rally behind Weseleskey and instill in the squadron the gravity of the situation and firmly underline that careless flying was unacceptable. There could be no repeats of accidents like the one that occurred on September 1 off the *Garrett County* LST.

Weseleskey recalls being out on a routine mission ten days later, on September 20 and hearing over the radio on the guard channel "This is Delta Control. Seawolf 35 (Weseleskey's call sign), come up on guard frequency for instructions." Wes was ordered to "detach immediately from present position and report to Vung Tau."[7]

So Weseleskey returned to Vinh Long, landed, refueled, and flew to Vung Tau with Lieutenant (junior grade) Hal Guinn as his copilot. The CO's call to Weseleskey for him to fly to Vung Tau must have been extremely urgent, since having Weseleskey depart from Vinh Long would necessitate interrupting his mission and would put on hold the detachment's operational readiness.

After landing in Vung Tau, he reported to the CO and the XO, who had already informed him of his first important assignment as the squadron's Safety Officer. Without much fanfare, Weseleskey was ordered to develop a briefing to put up in the "tank" at MACV headquarters.

Weseleskey had been a safety officer (and a graduate of safety school) at his previous command at HS-3. So barely a few weeks after sending him off to the war zone in Vinh Long in a somewhat disparaging manner, the squadron's leaders now needed him to develop a comprehensive, skin-saving, safety briefing to be presented to General Westmoreland in Saigon. They wanted Weseleskey to prepare the briefing for Commander Spencer to deliver, which would, of course, be according to protocol. And considering the series of unfortunate, but preventable aircraft and personnel losses, the squadron had to be able to convince the general of its innocence. Could Weseleskey pull this off? Would Weseleskey pull off this feat for his superiors?

Weseleskey was given 72 hours to prepare the briefing for the top commander in Vietnam. The pre-briefing was given to the CO, the XO, and to Operations Officer Commander Ron Hipp. It was decided that Spencer and Weseleskey would bring an operational map illustrating the locations of the squadron's detachments. They would have to describe clearly and convincingly the diversity of missions conducted by the squadron, the difficult deployment factors, and the night scrambles, frequently under marginal flight conditions. Spencer would have to convince General Westmoreland and his staff that HA(L)3 operated under conditions more dangerous than did other helicopter units serving in Vietnam. Hopefully, he could spin the vital value of HA(L)3's unflinching support of both Navy and Army units to try to offset its poor safety record.

It was obvious that Westmoreland had discovered that the Army was running out of helicopters to reinforce HA(L)3 since the unit's loss rate was exceeding the replenishment availability rate. Westmoreland himself had to account to SECDEF for the operational readiness of HA(L)3. And since the squadron had been created with an allocation of 22 aircraft for their seven operational detachments, in order for it to continue to function as an operating unit Westmoreland would have to believe that the helicopters he would be allocating to them were going to have maximum utilization, but also be conserved while in HA(L)3's custodianship.

Weseleskey felt that "we developed a very good presentation, and I briefed Spencer on how to effectively present the case."[8] The night before the briefing, the four officers went to the Officers' Club for dinner and drinks, with Weseleskey abstaining. Spencer was appropriately concerned about the briefing he would have to present to the commanding four-star general. This was going to be the moment of his career for him to advance his position—or possibly to be relieved of his command.

"So by the time morning rolled around and we prepared ourselves for the flight to Saigon, it was obvious that Spencer had not slept. And here we were flying north to meet General Westmoreland, the top commander of the Vietnam War, for our safety presentation and Spencer becomes ill. Spencer is trying to save his ass and flies in sick to his stomach. On that day, since the Operations Officer had come along, I sat in the cabin, as Spencer and Hipp flew the aircraft. For comfort and practicality, we all wore freshly laundered fatigues."

The aircraft landed at the Tan Son Nhut heliport designated as Hotel. "As we drive the short distance from the helicopter pad at Tan Son Nhut, it becomes very apparent that Spencer is quite ill. He barfs out the window of the car. As we approach the "tank" at MACV's newly constructed headquarters, again we stop so Spencer leans over into a garbage can. So Spencer tells me 'there is no way that I can stand up and give this briefing.' So, I say to him that I will give the briefing to Westmoreland," which Spencer unhesitatingly accepts.

"After we arrive and I am recognized by the general and his staff while standing in the briefing pit of the theater-like setting, I immediately get down to business and display my maps and charts. I think to myself that I am very well prepared for this event. Although I feel a little anxiety, I am aware that I have a chance to demonstrate my superior knowledge. Although I am not the only officer on the program, it still feels somewhat uncomfortable to me that there are 25 to 35 others in the briefing room. The room is set up like a classroom, with me on a small stage, looking up to Westmoreland and his staff of ten, including communication and intelligence people, sitting in neat rows. There appears to be one naval officer representing CTF116. Westmoreland sits in the center of the front row with his senior deputies, all of them looking at me expressionless. It seems that I am only one of four different officers to make a presentation this day."

"After five minutes of me delivering effective spin, the questions start, mostly from Westmoreland and his operations chief, a major general. I tell them of the uniqueness of HA(L)3's deployment and our 24/7 operational readiness requirement. I say that we provide support for field and riverine forces conducting operations in two dimensions, with HA(L)3 providing the third dimension, by being able to see behind tree-lines and recognize other terrain features where the enemy forces try to conceal themselves. I describe our tactics, which were taught to us at Fort Benning, and our use of the Army Tactics Manual. Many of the questions and answers are between General Westmoreland and me. He is very well prepared, but so am I, in defense of my squadron and my skipper."

"Being addressed as 'Commander,' I have a half-dozen questions politely asked of me. Still, I feel that only Spencer and I have been called onto the carpet, standing in what I feel is a witness box ready to testify and receive judgment. I look Westmoreland right in the eye, with all the confidence I can muster, while Spencer is trying to mask his queasiness with a calm face. During the session, he is given a couple of glancing questions, to which he respectfully responds, 'That's correct, sir.' I see Spencer as looking pale because I know that he normally has a red-toned visage. No one else can discern his condition as he sits up straight and keeps a low profile. Thank God, I think to myself, he's recovered."

"To the question of 'Why are you pilots not able to maintain airworthiness?' I answer honestly about the normal anxiety felt during aircraft launch conditions, maybe having to be made during heavy rains, during unpredictable fog. They are well aware of the downpours occurring during the seasonal monsoons. I tell them, trying to show a sense of urgency: 'When the PBRs call, we know that we have to be out there.' I try to elicit their understanding—and maybe even—a little sympathy."

"He seems to understand our situation, but I am not sure that Westmoreland is buying my story, or whether it is my illusion that he is becoming overwhelmed by my passionate explanations. Or maybe he is laughing to himself. But he keeps his general's expressionless face and poise. I know he is very serious—I can tell just by the image he creates with his highly starched, perfectly ironed shirt that he wears. I started to feel relieved that he never asked 'why are you losing so many aircraft?' To which I would have had to review each and every lousy accident. I immediately conjured up the four accidents during which we lost personnel plus another ditching and the two other minor accidents. I do believe that Westmoreland let us off the hook. After all, Westmoreland knew in his heart that we were operating with old equipment and to our disadvantage, were not being provided with the newer aircraft models, which the Army was receiving. Westmoreland, by having us there and not disparaging us with legitimate criticism, demonstrated his superb leadership."

"After leaving the building I felt very much relieved, and I believe that Spencer felt the same. He thanked me with 'great job.' I believe that he sensed the success of the presentation and was grateful that he still had the command of a squadron. Flying back to Vung Tau, Spencer seemed to feel better, as his color returned and he felt comfortable flying the aircraft."

"After our return to Vung Tau, we discussed the briefing and how we could work together to prevent further mishaps and casualties. Spencer and I agreed to bring the detachments up to standard and to schedule visits and conduct safety briefs. We agreed that I would be the contact for this work. When I advised him of the need for an aircraft for this purpose, he offered his own helicopter, which, although not configured with an armament package, suited the purpose and, if needed, could be rigged with a .50-cal machine gun."

"It was gratifying to me that Spencer and I agreed to seriously address the safety issue, and I hoped that after our experience together at MACV, to be able to make a significant contribution to our squadron. As much as I was interested in accomplishing the HA(L)3 missions, I was also very much interested in preventing the unnecessary loss of the lives of our shipmates."[9] Shortly after being assigned the aircraft, Weseleskey took it upon himself to fly to Detachment Seven in Dong Tam and to Detachment Two in Nha Be in order to conduct the squadron's first safety briefings.

About three weeks later, in the beginning of October, and after flying his new helicopter fire-team in a few firefights and providing aerial cover for SEAL insertions in the area of operations, to Weseleskey's surprise, Aydelotte himself got his transfer notice to report back to Vung Tau, to serve the remainder of his tour as the Administrative Officer. This had Weseleskey scratching his head. What about Rosenthal? Perhaps, the CO had changed his mind about the promise he had made to Weseleskey and decided to elevate his assignment to be the OINC.

Weseleskey often recalled his misinterpretation, years earlier, of his father's intention to send him into the "pit." And before any illusions could be dreamt, there he was, greeting Aydelotte's replacement, Gene Rosenthal. The bosses in Vung Tau must have thought that since they had interacted so well together in Vung Tau, having Rosenthal and Weseleskey paired up again in Vinh Long would solve "the Weseleskey problem."[10]

Seawolf hangar at Vung Tau. (Courtesy of Charles Biller)

Seawolf Operations, 1967. (Courtesy of Web Wright)

Seawolf Operations, 1968 with new logo. (National Archives ref 428-K-58197)

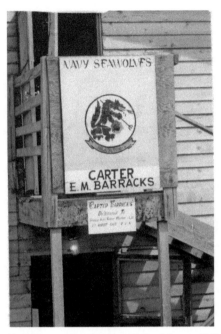

Vung Tau enlisted barracks. (National Archives ref 428-K-58228)

Rebranding an Army helo. (Courtesy of Gordon Daniels)

CHAPTER SIX

Change of Leadership at Vinh Long

A. E. Weseleskey: "I was also very much interested in preventing the unnecessary loss of lives of our shipmates."

Det Three operations area. (Courtesy of A. E. Weseleskey)

Lieutenant Commander Eugene Rosenthal arrived in Vinh Long in October 1967, as the replacement for Lieutenant Commander Sam Aydelotte. It was a relief for Aydelotte, who was now set to return to Vung Tau as Rosenthal's replacement as Administrative Officer, thereby switching assignments with him. Aydelotte had already served as the Detachment Three OINC a bit longer than he had anticipated.[1] Rosenthal had been sent to relieve him once before, more than a month earlier, but after a few combat hops, Rosenthal had decided that he wasn't yet ready for the assignment.

This time, however, Rosenthal was committed to relieving Aydelotte, and there would be no turning back. Even though this squadron policy of rotating officers resulted in the loss of experienced leaders, it was designed to provide each of the many career officers assigned to the squadron the opportunity, regardless of qualification, to lead in combat and to serve as a detachment OINC. Perhaps the squadron did not have much of a choice in the matter since such a disproportionate number of lieutenant commanders were being sent to the squadron by BUPERS in Washington. It was Aydelotte's opinion, that even though many of these volunteers were inspired to serve in Vietnam by a wish to benefit their careers, most of them were sincerely motivated to serve a combat tour with a detachment.

After Rosenthal took over the management of the detachment from Aydelotte, he wanted to strive to improve its performance and to avoid repetition of fatalities such as that of Ensign Burke, back in August, killed while he was flying with the Army. So Rosenthal did what he did best and what he believed would help the squadron, hoping to prove his worth both as a leader and administrator. He was the most senior lieutenant commander in the squadron, and he yearned for promotion to Navy commander, which had eluded him on prior squadron assignments.

Rather than trying to inspire his charges to launch into every mission without considering risk factors, Rosenthal was mindful of his men and wanted to ensure "everyone going back home." He did not think it necessary to fly missions in order to acquire medals. To accomplish his goal, he also wanted everyone to follow the squadron's "SOP" or standard operating procedures. He also thought it prudent to follow the guidance provided in the recently minted HA(L)3 "Detachment Operations Manual" promulgated on July 2, 1967. And to make sure everything would fall into place, he "tried to keep things on an even keel."[2]

After Aydelotte's departure, Weseleskey took the initiative to take Rosenthal on a few flights to familiarize him with the operating area around Vinh Long, as Aydelotte had done for him upon his arrival. He also landed at all the allied outposts so Rosenthal would have the opportunity to meet some of the people for whom he might one day have to provide helicopter support. After a few days, the new OINC took charge of Aydelotte's former fire-team.

Rosenthal had a lot in common with his assistant OINC. He and Weseleskey had worked closely together in Vung Tau doing administrative work. They were both career naval officers: lieutenant commanders with several tours of sea duty under their belts. They were both helicopter pilots qualified in many different aircraft, and both had volunteered for Vietnam service with HA(L)3. Rosenthal and Weseleskey each had proud Navy families including four children. But it was their quite contrasting combat personalities that would ultimately polarize their relationship and inevitably result in confrontations.

Many of the junior pilots had gotten to know Weseleskey, a confident aviator who was not averse to risk-taking and who believed in training copilots and gunners alike to manifest precision in their airmanship, for the sake of their survival and future advancement. It was critical for the aircrews to be trained to function as a team since their lives depended on teamwork. When Weseleskey felt comfortable, he would give the right-hand seat to the junior pilots, the position that had control of the rocket system and from which the aircraft was usually commanded, so they would one day be capable of making the leap into gaining the aircraft commander designation. After enabling them to achieve this experience, he wanted the pilots to qualify for the most responsible flight position—fire-team leader. This flight and combat training also enabled the aircrews to improve their confidence, the most important ingredient for future success. Pretty soon, after witnessing the opportunities being afforded to Weseleskey's crews, some of Rosenthal's pilots wanted to fly with Weseleskey so they could get experience in the other seat.

Rosenthal seemed cognizant of the ongoing safety issues and strove to ensure the survival of his charges. He flew according to the book, exhorting his fire-teams to comply with the squadron's tactics, which were based on the Tactics Manual of the 197th Armed Helicopter Company. Certain cardinal rules he stood by, understandably so, such as making a high reconnaissance pass and avoiding the "dead-man zone" from the ground up to 1,000 feet (many pilots revised that to from zero to 500 feet). Nevertheless, jokingly, some of the gunners grumbled amongst themselves when they were assigned to fly with "nosebleed." Several also thought that his hearing wasn't sharp, as when he failed to hear the pops of incoming enemy rounds just missing the aircraft. And some aircrews even questioned his lack of knowledge of coordinating tactics (even though they were not so well qualified themselves). Nevertheless, many of the gunners liked Rosenthal's fatherly tone and caring manner (he had four children aged 4, 11, 13, and 20)[3] and respected him as a person.[4] One of the more experienced pilots felt a sense of duty to fly with him.[5]

One of the problems Rosenthal faced was that most of the junior officers would fly with the Army, which had two aviation companies stationed at Vinh Long: the 114th Aviation Company (nicknamed the Cobras) and the 275th Aviation Company (nicknamed the Mavericks). These units had been flying out of Vinh Long since the early sixties, and some of their pilots were on their second or third tours. As such, they knew the terrain intimately and what to look for in their search for the elusive enemy, and they often flew aggressively at tree-top level, trying to surprise and sometimes even draw fire from the hidden enemy. Their tactics were uniformly aggressive, therefore running counter to HA(L)3's official policy. This not-so-subtle difference in tactics training would soon become an obstacle hindering Rosenthal's attempt to implement the squadron policy.

However, for the many Detachment 3 pilots and door gunners such as Airman Jack Williamson, they felt it was imperative for them to gain greater experience, which would enable them to more quickly qualify as plane commanders or gunners with HA(L)3. This process gave them the ability both to contribute to the squadron's operational readiness and to receive greater admiration from their peers.

Within a few weeks of Rosenthal's arrival, friction began to develop between Weseleskey and the OINC to whom he now reported. Rosenthal seemed interested in maintaining the status quo and did not feel that he had to push the envelope to achieve the detachment's mission. But, according to Weseleskey, they took into account the attitudes of the junior officers, and the two of them reconciled with Rosenthal agreeing to try to enhance morale.[6]

According to Weseleskey, the situation did not improve that much, and some of the officers would not take meals with the OINC. In addition, some of the detachment's pilots were still flying with the Army, trying to get more experience and flight time. This greatly displeased the new OINC, and rightfully so, since, after the loss of Ensign Burke in August, CDR Spencer had attempted to put the brakes on flying with the Army. Prior to leaving the Vinh Long detachment, LCDR Aydelotte had even advised the 114th Aviation Company's platoon leader, Captain Robin Miller, not to allow Navy pilots to fly with the Army, as it was a helicopter assigned to Miller's unit that had crashed with Burke on board.[7] But it was hard to prevent determined junior officers from flying, and the Army, which had far fewer pilots assigned per aircraft than did HA(L)3, welcomed the young and avid Navy flyers eager to fly with their experienced pilots.

Weseleskey himself began to fly Army style, even though he was the safety officer and never forgot his famous safety briefing at MACV. But he was also aggressive in his pursuit of mission accomplishment and flew very confidently, having already flown on heroic missions earning him two Distinguished Flying Crosses. However, he did not feel any discomfort with his execution of the two somewhat conflicting roles.

It was not just on combat flights that Weseleskey stepped into harm's way while serving as the detachment's Assistant OINC. On December 29, 1967 shortly before noon, two UH-1C gunship helicopters of the Army's 235th Aviation Company (one of several Army units operating out of the airfield) returned to Vinh Long after carrying out a mission in their operating area outside of Vinh Long. After parking the helos in adjacent revetments on the north side of the runway, the pilots departed for lunch, leaving it to their crews to manage the refueling and rearming process.

The first of the two aircraft was refueled by its crew chief, Specialist 5 James A. Duncan.[8] During the process he noticed a moderate leak coming from between the trigger guard and the two-inch spout of the fuel hose. Seated inside the cockpit, Specialist 5 Ralph Pelliccio (the crew chief of the second helicopter) was checking the fuel level by cycling the battery and inverter switches, which (according to Duncan), was standard operating procedure for the refueling evolution. After the hose was returned to the fuel truck, which had been parked in the revetment, the truck moved to the adjoining revetment, just west of Pelliccio's aircraft.

Specialist 4 Freddie Stratton, the fuel truck driver, then proceeded west to the adjoining revetment in order to fuel the second helicopter. At the same time, Pelliccio walked over to his aircraft, opened its fuel tank, grabbed hold of the fuel nozzle, and "stuck it into the aircraft's fuel tank,"[9] with Stratton remaining seated in his truck, operating the tank's main pump.

This time Pelliccio noticed a leak coming from where the nozzle is attached to the fuel hose. During this procedure, the aircraft's other crewmember, Specialist 4 William E. Bradfield, having just returned from picking up a few hamburgers, sat in the Huey's cockpit. This time it was he who periodically cycled the battery and inverter switches in order to check the fuel level.

Stratton, not having seen anyone ground the aircraft to prevent an electrical spark, observed the nozzle being placed into the fuel tank opening in the side of the fuselage and watched the refueling begin. Within seconds, the nozzle backed out of the opening and fell to the ground. Pelliccio instinctively backed up, but after a few seconds, he picked up the nozzle and put it back into the side of the aircraft. Stratton saw that during the nozzle's fall, it had splashed JP-4 over a two-foot by three-foot area around the fuel tank opening, with some fuel residue draining to the ground. The refueling continued.

A few minutes later, when the process was nearly completed, Bradfield again recycled the switches. This time the side of the aircraft suddenly burst into flames momentarily engulfing Pelliccio in smoke and fire. Immediately and instinctively, he pulled the nozzle out of the aircraft and tried to unlock its trigger. He was unsuccessful. Interested in his own survival, he dropped it to the ground and kicked the nozzle to try to unlock the trigger. Again unsuccessful, he backed off, leaving it ablaze.

Stratton, hearing the explosion of the igniting fuel, immediately disengaged the fuel pump by stepping on the clutch and shifting the transmission out of 4th gear and then throwing the drive lever into gear thereby disengaging the pump lever. In a panic, he jumped from the truck cab. Momentarily dazed and weakened by the flames, he ran west along the runway. He recalled, "I was scared and panicky."[10]

As Bradfield recalled, as soon as he heard Pelliccio yell "fire," "without thinking, I jumped out of the ship leaving the battery and inverter switches on."[11] On seeing the fire's intensity, he then ran from the immediate area to escape the impending disaster.

At 1215 hours, LCDR Weseleskey had just returned from a morning reconnaissance mission. He hovered the UH-1B gunship helicopter into one of the three assigned Seawolf revetments on the south side of the runway and set its skids down on the ground. After shutting the rotors down and securing the engine, he had planned to conduct the flight debriefing in the operations shack located just behind the Seawolves' parking area and then head for lunch.

This shack consisted of two metal CONEX boxes conjoined and heavily sandbagged for protection against shrapnel from enemy mortars. Inside was the detachment's office, where flight crew briefings and debriefings were held and where maps and notices were hung from the inside bulkheads. It had air conditioning running continuously, providing a temporary respite from the scorching midday sun.

With Lieutenant (junior grade) Everett Miller as his copilot, Weseleskey was preparing to exit the helicopter when he heard a muffled explosion coming from across the runway where a number of Army helicopters were parked, including those UH-1Cs of the Army's 114th Aviation Company's Cobra Platoon. Shortly after the explosion Weseleskey observed a sudden burst of flames coming from a refueling hose alongside one of the Army helicopters. It appeared to him that both the fuel truck and the UH-1C helo it was refueling were on fire.

Weseleskey immediately realized the emergency and impending calamity. Without an iota of hesitation, and while still wearing his flight helmet, he grabbed the aircraft's small fire extinguisher and ran across the runway to lend a hand. He saw that Army personnel were fighting the fire, also with small handheld extinguishers. However, they seemed to be in shock and frozen in their flight boots. As soon as he reached the helicopter, Weseleskey grabbed hold of and yanked the nozzle spewing flaming fuel away from the aircraft. Watching the driver running from the fuel truck, Weseleskey shouted at him and ordered him to return to the truck and drive it away from the scene of the expanding conflagration.

Stratton, still running, heard Weseleskey yell at him to "get that truck out of there."[12] He returned to it and climbed back on board, but the engine was dead. At the same time, Weseleskey unloaded the contents of his fire bottle on the truck, extinguishing the flames. Stratton tried again to start the engine, but it stalled, further aggravating the situation. Stratton then jumped out of the truck, running in front and picking up a fire extinguisher. After another crewman entered the driver's side, Stratton went back in through the passenger's door. On a second restart attempt, the truck moved about 40 feet before stopping again, this time on Weseleskey's orders, as it was dragging the still-burning hose. Stratton again jumped out of the truck and started to unload the contents of his extinguisher on it.

By this time, airfield firefighters were arriving on the scene and beginning to douse the fires. Weseleskey grabbed one of their hoses and finished extinguishing the flaming hose. And, fortunately, the fuel truck was now far enough away from the burning aircraft to permit Weseleskey to focus his attention on saving the helicopter.

Preceding the arrival of the lumbering water tanker, the first of two airfield fire trucks had arrived. But JP-4 fuel continued to seep from the fuel hose nozzle onto the ground. Fire hoses were laid towards the burning aircraft. Weseleskey attempted to secure the open fuel hose nozzle but was unsuccessful. He called out to the fuel truck driver to secure the main fuel valve to cut off the flow of aviation fuel in order to start containing the fire. The driver replied, "I'm trying Sir, but I don't know where it's at."[13] (Apparently, Stratton, now seated in the passenger's seat, did successfully secure the pump minutes earlier, but residual fuel continued to flow from the open nozzle.)

Now everything seemed to Weseleskey to be unreal: a bad dream. He thought that at any moment everything might blow up. At the same time, the fire hose he had just used to extinguish the flames coming from the helo's fuel tank suddenly went limp. So now the fire truck engine had broken down, and with its power off, he was unable to finish extinguishing the burning fuel line. At the same time, he was nearly knocked down by a sudden flash of flames and intense heat. (Never talk to Weseleskey about Vietnam's blistering midday sun.)

Just as he regained his equilibrium, Weseleskey observed the burning JP-4 fuel, now mixed with water, streaming towards the next revetment, which housed another fully armed and fueled UH-1C. He dropped the useless fire hose, ran towards the other helo, and while boarding it calling for help. Responding to his calls, Warrant Officer Charles A. Hardin, Jr. (watching from nearby) ran over and jumped into the aircraft alongside Weseleskey. They were able to start the aircraft, with Hardin manning the controls while Weseleskey helped with the switches and radios he advised the tower of their plans to move the aircraft. By the time they lifted off, the burning fuel had spread beneath them, and they were temporarily engulfed in smoke and flames. Weseleskey took the flight controls and hovered the helicopter across the field to avoid the fuel truck and fire. Then he gave the controls back to Hardin who safely landed the aircraft. By the time Weseleskey had left the aircraft and run back to the scene, the fuel truck fire had been brought under control.

The first helicopter continued to burn uncontrollably, and now the foam hoses of the second fire truck were being pinched under its rear wheels. Weseleskey grabbed one of the hoses and ordered the driver to move the truck off the hose. Although the firefighting personnel seemed to finally have complete control of the apparatus and were starting to contain the fire, the helicopter was still engulfed in flames. Weseleskey became alarmed that there might be only moments before the 14 rockets armed with high-explosive warheads cooked off. Already, 7.62-millimeter ammo rounds were popping like fireworks.[14]

Responding to Weseleskey's call for assistance, the second fire truck arrived, and now there seemed to be plenty of personnel to contain the fire. Not taking any chances, however, Weseleskey ran back to the aircraft, helping to organize the positioning of fire hoses in order to extinguish the undying flames. The fire was continuing to blaze, now to the top of the helicopter. Then Weseleskey, along with an airfield firefighter, climbed to the roof of the aircraft and hosed it with foam. As the inferno was starting to subside, there was a sudden explosion inches from where Weseleskey stood, nearly jolting him off the helicopter. Luckily, it was the dying cough of the fire, and he was able to descend without being scorched.

Only after the fire was extinguished were the personnel able to remove the helicopter's mini-guns, the live rockets, and the thousands of rounds of 7.62-millimeter ammunition in the cabin. Under Weseleskey's direction, the men gently placed the ordnance on the ground in a separate revetment.

For this action Weseleskey was awarded the Navy's highest non-combat award for heroism, the Navy and Marine Corps Medal. The main excerpt from his citation follows: "Weseleskey promptly took command of the explosive situation and ordered the flaming fuel truck moved. Pulling the flaming fuel hose from the aircraft and then protecting the driver with his own body by standing between the truck cab and the burning aircraft he successfully directed the truck's removal. With full knowledge that a fuel or rocket explosion was about to take place Lieutenant Commander Weseleskey ran through the fire, obtained a fire hose from an arriving fire truck, knocked down the flames, and cooled the gas storage tank on the fuel truck. When a valve on the fuel truck failed causing LCDR Weseleskey to be caught in a back flash of fire, he rushed through the fire to a nearby revetment pit that sheltered another armed helicopter about to be consumed by the fire. He succeeded in flying the helicopter to safety despite dense smoke and intense flames that enveloped the revetment pit as he took off." Weseleskey "continually exposed himself to the fire and explosions with complete disregard for his own personal safety. As a result of his heroic conduct, the fuel truck, several aircraft, and many lives were saved from a fiery destruction."[15]

Every six weeks, Weseleskey attended the OINC meetings in Vung Tau, serving as the guiding light in the safety department. Weseleskey deserved a great deal of credit for bringing a sudden halt to the squadron's casualties. After he became safety officer, no casualties occurred during the period of his watch, until his tour was completed and he rotated out of country in April 1968.

Gradually, over the next several months at Vinh Long, Rosenthal started to fit in with the detachment, and both he and Weseleskey were able to synergize their efforts on behalf of the squadron and the men whose service and dedication meant so much in achieving success. Each of them flew and led effectively in his own way, both in support of the riverine forces and, when called upon, to provide assistance for the U.S. Army.

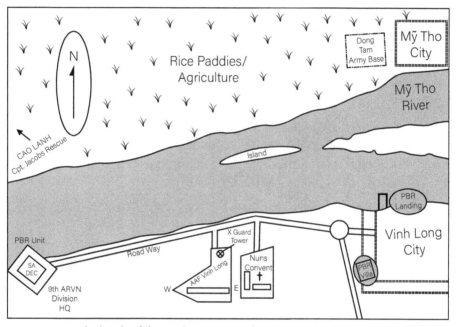

A rough sketch of the Vinh Long area. (Courtesy of A. E. Weseleskey)

Vinh Long runway. (Courtesy of A. E. Weseleskey)

Aerial view of Vinh Long Airfield, June 1967, showing the inverted helicopter in the pond. (Courtesy of Joseph Bouchard)

CHAPTER SEVEN

Tet Offensive Surprise

General William C. Westmoreland: "The enemy is presently developing a threatening posture in several areas in order to seek victories."

General Westmoreland visits Nha Be Naval Base. (Author's photo)

In early January 1968 more than 500,000 U.S. military personnel were stationed in South Vietnam. At this point in the war, 16,000 American servicemen had been killed in action while serving there. Battles being waged at the Marines' northern firebase at Con Thien and at several small border outposts had been underway since September 1967 and so far were being viewed as nothing more than as North Vietnamese Army infantry incursions.

But it was the later battle at Khe Sanh and its surrounding hills commencing on January 21, 1968, that drew alarms from Military Assistance Command Vietnam about the possibility of a Dien Bien Phu style, all-out North Vietnamese offensive. No one could ignore the powerful artillery round that scored a hit on a bunker that instantly killed nineteen Marine defenders.

Striking back at the dug-in artillery sites, the Air Force unleashed a series of aerial bombardments, including a huge unloading of some 60,000 tons of explosives around the base by B-52 bombers during the campaign, battering but never neutralizing the three divisions of NVA soldiers in the surrounding hills. This battle would continue during the Tet Offensive and for months thereafter.

The Tet Offensive of 1968, recalled as the Year of the Monkey (*Tet Mau Than*, for the Vietnamese), would be remembered for many reasons. It was a surprise attack that staggered the American military leadership, it brought about the short-lived but dramatic siege of the U.S. Embassy in Saigon, and it caused the enormous civilian catastrophe in Hue, one of the most beautiful cities in the country. And it demonstrated the ability of a determined enemy to completely surprise and, in the first week, nearly overwhelm a beefed-up American and allied force.

Throughout the country, military readiness to respond to the Tet Offensive seemed to vary depending on intelligence, intuition, experience, and luck. In early January, General Westmoreland, commander of all forces serving in Vietnam, had received intelligence indicating enemy movement toward the cities, and shortly prior to Tet, he believed that the enemy was preparing to take advantage of the Tet cease-fire in order to launch an offensive.[1] On January 20, 1968, Westmoreland transmitted a message to U.S. Army Chief of Staff General Earle Wheeler stating that "the enemy is presently developing a threatening posture in several areas in order to seek victories.... He may exercise his initiatives prior to, during, or after Tet."[2] Westmoreland sought cancellation of the customary Tet cease-fire but was rebuffed by South Vietnam President Nguyen Van Thieu. Even if the president had reservations about the sincerity of the North's commitment to holding a cease-fire, he did not allow it to thwart the nation's most important family holiday, for the sake of its citizens.

But as Tet approached and even though he would be vacationing with his family at his wife's villa in My Tho, Thieu, receiving intelligence and the advice of his advisors, suddenly changed his mind and, according to Westmoreland, in mid-morning of January 30, he announced the cancellation of the cease-fire. After being notified of Thieu's decision, Westmoreland "sent a priority message to all American units, announcing the cancellation and directing that troops will be placed on maximum alert with particular attention to the defense of headquarters complexes, logistical installations, airfields, population centers and billets."[3]

Whether this alert was passed on to the front-line soldiers and sailors serving in III and IV Corps is doubtful, as later evidenced by their lack of preparedness. In I Corps the U.S. Marines were nearly always engaging the enemy, and since there were ongoing battles at both Con Thien and Khe Sanh, any elevated concern for a possible new attack around the start of Tet would thus have been purely academic.

Just after midnight on the 30th, there was a series of coordinated attacks in eight different towns and cities in II Corps, all located in the Viet Cong's Military Region Five. Since the order from the NVA command was for the attacks to begin in the early morning hours of January 31, this was later concluded to have been a premature initiation of the Tet Offensive by the enemy. Hanoi's General Staff were aware of their blunder, and although the element of surprise was lost, the allied forces failed to take advantage of it in order to go to full alert.[4] At the Nha Be Naval Base (where the author was stationed), just 25 kilometers southeast of Saigon, there were rumors of possible attacks, but since there had frequently been intelligence-generated rumors of pending strikes that never materialized, these rumors were discounted. Furthermore, there would always be some occasional attacks occurring without warning. But on the night of January 30, based on a little intuition, the base was placed in a state of slightly elevated readiness for an attack. On this night, the HA(L)3 Seawolf helicopter gunship fire-team crew, who were always on five-minute scramble alert, were dressed in flight gear and decided to remain in their well-fortified sandbagged bunker adjacent to the helipad, instead of cat-napping in their bunks.

Their close proximity to their aircraft would enable them to lower their response time to launch from the helipad to just a few seconds, rather than the standard five minutes.

In Saigon, the South's capital and Westmoreland's front yard, it is doubtful whether the intelligence was passed down to the American military police who were responsible for the security of many of the military's government buildings, billets, and other installations. The fact that many of the men of the 716th MP Battalion were not dressed in combat gear, and were wearing their glossy black plastic helmet liners with their red-and-white painted band and unit insignia, clearly indicated a lack of serious preparation for any type of enemy engagement. If there was any word even hinting at a possible attack, why wouldn't the MPs be adhering to their unit policy of wearing steel helmet covers when engaging the enemy? So Westmoreland's earlier warnings that afternoon either were not passed on or were ignored. Tragically, the 716th's Headquarters Company suffered more than 20 fatalities during the first 24 hours of the offensive and the 716th MP Battalion suffered 72 casualties, of which 27 were fatal during the week of January 31 to February 6.[5] However, one lucky Army private scheduled for MP jeep patrol was approached by some children whom he had befriended. They advised him not to report for duty that night.[6] He took their advice and lived.

It seemed that there was an unwillingness to accept the unpredictable and unimaginable; a "not in my backyard" mentality, a denial of what was being reported. This is evidenced by the fact that General Creighton Abrams was at home, asleep; Generals Kerwin and Davidson were also at their respective homes. Major General John Chaisson, chief of MACV's combined operations center, having returned from leave, was asleep. (At MACV's Tan Son Nhut's headquarters compound, an intelligence staffer's report to his senior officer of a bar girl's warning of impending attack was scoffed at.) Colonel Daniel Graham, then a senior intelligence official, was also asleep in his bunk. Even Marine General Robert C. Cushman in Danang was in his quarters. Equally unprepared, were Ambassador Ellsworth Bunker home at his villa (it was probably fortunate that he was not on duty at the embassy, which received the brunt of the assault), and Ambassador Robert Komer, MACV's deputy for pacification operations, asleep. Also unprepared was senior CIA official Colonel George Jacobson, living on the embassy grounds, whose only weapon to defend himself from the Viet Cong commandos attacking his house was a sidearm.[7]

At the city of Sadec, home of ARVN's 9th Infantry Division and more than 100 kilometers to the southwest of Saigon, Brigadier General Lam Quang Thi, commander of the Vietnamese Ninth Infantry Division, lived with his family. General Thi recalls being advised by IV Corps commander General Mang, the evening prior to Tet, that the Viet Cong had been staging attacks in a few cities in II Corps. Taking measure of this now, General Thi canceled leaves and ordered units to be on high alert. (Since these orders seem to have been given less than six hours before the Tet attacks, it is doubtful whether they could have been acted upon.)[8]

At Vinh Long Army Airfield, a few kilometers west of the city of Vinh Long and 35 kilometers east of Sadec, there were also rumors of an impending attack, but the information was not disseminated to all hands, leading to a lack of a cohesive plan of preparation for defense.

Located at this airfield in Vinh Long, which had formerly been a Japanese dirt landing strip, was the Army's 114th Assault Helicopter Company. It had arrived there in May of 1963 as the 114th Air Mobile Company and by 1968 had been the core unit responsible for the evolution of the airfield into a major airbase. Vinh Long was in the heart of the Mekong Delta, and the Army airfield was one of the most important strategic bases, providing air support for military operations in the heavily populated geographical area designated by the Army as the IV Corps Tactical Zone.

The base became home to the personnel of the 83rd Medical Detachment of the 114th, the gunship platoons of the Cobras and Lancers, and the slick helicopter platoons of the Red Knights and the White Knights, also of the 114th. In September 1964 more units received their assignments to Vinh Long, including the 175th Assault Helicopter Company, consisting of the Mavericks gunship platoon and the Outlaws with their UH-1D Huey slicks, used for transport. Other units arrived, including Army signal, transportation, and maintenance detachments. Initially, in 1963, in Army fashion, everyone lived in tents.

By 1968, at the base there was an improved 3,500-foot runway, revetments providing protective enclosures for helicopters, wooden barracks with cement floors, Quonset huts, and large fabricated steel maintenance hangars. There were wooden guard towers, a small base control tower, and other, smaller structures. Although not too elaborate or sophisticated, it had become a fully operational base providing support for mostly ARVN ground operations.

In March 1966, the Navy's PBR sailors were first given their assignments to patrol the Mekong River's downstream offspring—the Song My Tho, Song Ham Luong, Song Co Chien, and Song Hau Giang (also known as the Bassac) rivers—as part of Operation Game Warden. This newly conceived River Patrol Force, designated as Task Force 116, was to become a vital tool in preventing enemy infiltration and in keeping the rivers safe for transporting rice and other cargoes necessary to sustaining Vietnamese commerce. In support of these patrols, the Army was ordered to expand its mission.

As these operations continued to grow in number and intensity during the spring of 1966 U.S. Navy headquarters in Saigon decided to begin utilizing Navy crews to man Army helicopters in support of the riverine operations. This would relieve the Army of having to continue working on the development of specific operational procedures for naval support and at the same time enable the Navy to interface with the LSTs, PBRs, and other riverine and ship-borne units. It was clearly understood that although the Army had been successful in its initial support of riverine units, having Navy support Navy would not only pay tribute to its own traditions, but enable it to attain maximum efficiency in its role of supporting its fellow seagoing counterparts. In addition, it would enable the Army to concentrate on supporting the ever-growing Army ground force operations as well as the operations of ARVN troops.

The Navy had recruited its first pilots and crews from HC-1 (Helicopter Combat Support Squadron One) at Ream Field in San Diego and designated three different detachments. The detachment assigned to Vinh Long in the summer of 1966 was called HC-1 Detachment 25. Initially lacking their own aircraft for the assignment, they were provided with two Army UH-1B gunship helicopters. Within a year, the Navy decided to expand its riverine operations with the commensurate expansion of helicopter support by commissioning Helicopter Attack (Light) Squadron Three. The Vinh Long fire-team, having received its own two armed UH-1Bs, was then transformed into HA(L)3 Detachment Three.

By January 1968, HA(L)3's Detachment Three had had a year and a half of operational experience, with pilots and crews accumulating a respectable amount of combat flight time—perhaps more combat hours than any of the squadron's other seven detachments. In order to better service the detachment's two helicopters, the squadron decided to send a special maintenance team to Vinh Long to enable the detachment to achieve a higher level of readiness. The crews lived in their own barracks, had their own operations center, and even augmented the base defense with assignees for perimeter guard duty. Many of the maintenance personnel interfaced so closely with the aircrewmen, that, after receiving training and experience, they were able to get themselves assigned as door-gunners.

Even though Vinh Long's Army and Navy units had separately designated missions, they often provided support for each other. But in the context of being prepared for the Tet Offensive, the soldiers, sailors, and airmen at the Vinh Long Army Airfield were like most other military personnel serving throughout the country; they were left to their own ingenuity, energy, spirit, and sense of survival to defend their base against the surprise attack that was to come in the predawn hours of January 31, 1968.

CHAPTER EIGHT

Tet Attack at Vinh Long

Dick Martz: "Incoming."

Mortar explosion at "hero hooch" at Vinh Long Airfield at start of Tet Offensive. (Courtesy of A. E. Weseleskey)

By the end of January 1968, Weseleskey had immersed himself in his duties as Assistant OINC, and having already proven himself with his heroic accomplishments, spent a great deal of time instructing and providing guidance for his young charges. He encouraged first-tour pilots to fly in the right-hand seat as aircraft commanders and as fire-team leaders to enable them to gain confidence and experience. For Lieutenant (junior grade) Tom Crull, this was what he had aimed for, as he enjoyed flying in the operating area and was eager to become a true professional. He had already amassed hundreds of flight hours with the Army's 175th Assault Helicopter Company, the Mavericks.

The Navy's first-tour pilots were unique: one read the Bible most of the day but when flying was intent on killing. Another excellent and aggressive aviator was intent on shooting water buffaloes in order to keep the farmers from feeding the hungry Viet Cong fighters. On one mission as fire-team leader, with Weseleskey flying in the cabin as a gunner replacement, this same pilot received clearance to sink a barge carrying rice in a free-fire zone. Bent on its destruction, he prepared for the attack and began a coordinated firing run. However, with so many civilians present on the craft and at the shoreline, Weseleskey, who had been listening in, exercised his command authority and ordered him to break off the attack, most likely saving the lives of a lot of friendly civilians.[1]

On the eve of the Tet Offensive, Weseleskey, like most other Vinh Long Airfield denizens, had no clue of any impending attack. There had not been any intelligence briefing as far as he knew. He does not recall there even being an intelligence specialist assigned to the base, though occasionally, Wes recalled that base commander Lieutenant Colonel Bernard Thompson might give a casual briefing to a few individuals, including him. So he retired to his small room for the night at the usual hour of 2300, unaware of what was to occur.[2]

After reporting to Vinh Long as its OINC in October, by the end of January LCDR Rosenthal had become familiar with both the aircrews and the mission requirements.[3] The earlier friction that had arisen between Weseleskey and Rosenthal had been reconciled, and they respected each other's strengths and weaknesses. Still, each had obviously different and somewhat polarizing approaches to their primary job: "leading and training crews in one of the squadron's most combat-active detachments."[4] Even though his junior Seawolf pilots flying with the Army got accustomed to flying at lower altitudes, Rosenthal tried his best to be accommodating. Nevertheless, somewhat conflicted by feeling strongly about their safety, he tried his best to encourage everyone to follow the squadron's SOP. Without any doubt, Rosenthal began to feel proud of the detachment's terrific esprit de corps and wanted very much to keep it that way.

On the eve of Tet, Rosenthal was as unprepared as anyone else for the surprise assault that would begin while he slept in his bunk at the Seawolf officers' Quonset hut.[5]

Major Lee Sheider was a career Army officer assigned as Operations Officer of the 235th Assault Helicopter Battalion headquartered in Can Tho, 20 miles south of Vinh Long. Sheider recalls there being a warning at the afternoon briefing about an impending attack. The warning had come down directly from MACV and called for an increase in base security, a doubling of the guard, an increase in overall alertness, and having aircraft prepared for evacuation.[6]

The highly distinguished platoon leader of the Army's 114th Assault Helicopter Company, nicknamed the Cobras, was Captain Robin Miller. He had earned the Distinguished Service Cross two months earlier for executing a daring rescue mission and was on his third Vietnam tour of duty. He felt doubtful about the likelihood of a successful mutually agreed cease-fire that had been broadcast through the media. Early in the evening, at the Officers' Club bar, he was advised by Lieutenant Colonel Thompson of a broadcast from Saigon warning of a possible surprise attack by the Viet Cong. After hearing this, he passed the word to several of the platoon's crewmen. Ominously, before he went to sleep, Miller prepared his tape recorder to be activated with the touch of the "On" switch.[7] But he also felt reassured for the base's security, knowing that the 114th's assistant platoon leader, First Lieutenant Jim Williams, and his fire-team crew were manning the "hero hooch" at the east end of the airfield runway, with their two UH-1C gunship helicopters parked nearby in a revetment and prepared for launch.

First Lieutenant John Morris, a 1965 graduate of Bucknell University, served as a UH-1D "Slick" pilot for the 114th's White Knights. He had heard warnings of a possible attack and went to sleep with his .45 caliber Grease Gun loaded for action.[8]

First Lieutenant Jim Williams, educated in Raleigh, North Carolina, rose from the rank of E-5 to First Lieutenant and had just completed his instrument training before being assigned to the 114th Assault Helicopter Company in Vinh Long. As a fire-team leader, he was assigned to fly during the cease-fire period on the 30th. Early in the day, with disregard to the cease-fire, he was directed and cleared to engage and destroy a large fleet of sampans moving in the direction of the town of Sadec, 15 miles west of Vinh Long and the home of the ARVN 9th Infantry Division. On two passes, his fire-team and another from the 175th Assault Helicopter Company unloaded their ordnance on these boats, creating a scene of chaos and carnage with the river turning crimson red. This outward display of enemy confidence, to move along the river so openly, made for a feeling of unease amongst the crews. So, when he went to sleep in the hero hooch that night, Williams was not very confident of a peaceful night's sleep. He climbed into a steel-framed bunk bed wearing just his T-shirt and skivvies.[9]

Gunners Specialist 4 Richard Oliva and Specialist 4 James A. Maestas, and Private First Class Jimmy Reed, a "hangar rat" of the 544th Maintenance Company, had no idea there would be an attack and went unprepared. Reed spent the evening at the movie theater, one of the few alternatives to drinking at the "Fifty-Stater" enlisted club.[10]

Specialist 5 John Cahill had earlier in the day flown as a gunner in Williams' aircraft during the sampan shoot-em-up; he went to sleep feeling ill at ease.[11] His fellow gunner, draftee Eugene Schwanebeck from Baltimore, recalls being mentally prepared for action as he lay down on his bunk for a night of rest.[12]

John Keller was drafted into the Army in 1967 and trained as a radio-teletype operator. He was assigned to the operations center adjacent to the base control tower. Since there were no scheduled operations during the dark hours before Tet, he "sat with my feet up on my desk listening to an audio tape which had been sent from home."[13]

Specialist 4 Lauren "Buck" Jones, blond, 18 years old, and a self-confident Texan from the small town of Nazareth (population 250), voluntarily entered the service in Amarillo, Texas. Although he had not planned it this way, his life and his maintenance work on CH-21 helicopters was so boring at his assignment in Fort Wainwright in Fairbanks, Alaska where "there were so many people in maintenance that we took turns putting bolts in," he decided to volunteer to serve in Vietnam.[14] When he got to Vinh Long in early January, he was assigned to the 114th Assault Helicopter company's night maintenance team; another "hangar rat." Jones remembers feeling a certain resentment that, as the young new recruit, he had been treated disrespectfully by his sergeant. He recalls that on his day off on the 30th he roamed around the base exploring the unoccupied bunkers before going to church to hear Mass. When he returned at 1800, he observed the company's first sergeant issuing ammo to a group of mechanics who had been chosen because they had some infantry background and who were being assigned to perimeter duty for the coming night. He was curious about this. When he asked the sergeant what was going on and was told "you don't need to know," and when he then asked him for some 7.62 mm ammo for his M-14 rifle and was turned down without any explanation, Jones felt dejected and started to be apprehensive about the coming night. So he went wandering off by himself. Because earlier in the day he had seen a bunker containing a pile of ammo cans, he decided to revisit it and snatch 100 rounds, enough to load his five clips. And for the same reason, he also decided to strip and clean his rifle and his sidearm. Since he believed that something big would be happening that night, "I laid all my web gear on the floor and went to sleep with my clothes and my boots on. I just dozed off." Officially though, he was never advised of any warning, "which really aggravates me to this day."[15]

Captain Dick Koenig was the platoon commander of the Army's 175th Assault Helicopter Company, located at the Vinh Long Airfield and also a unit of the 13th Combat Aviation Battalion. Commissioned upon graduation in 1964 from the Army's ROTC program at John Carroll University as an aviation cadet under the larger Army transportation corps, he spent six years on active duty and would later spend another 16 years with the National Guard.[16]

When he arrived in Vietnam in September 1967, he had already had a non-flying tour in Danang with the 565th Transportation Company. Since there had been new and urgent requirements for Army combat helicopter pilots, it was upon his return to the states from Danang that he was sent to Huey gunship flight school. Returning to Vietnam in September, he selected the Mekong Delta area because he had heard that "it was a real good place to fly."[17]

By the time of his arrival in Vinh Long, Koenig had over 250 hours of experience flying "B" and "D" model UH-1 helicopters. With this background, the requirement for 3 months' experience flying UH–1Ds was waived and he went right into the 175th Assault Helicopter Company as leader of the Maverick gunship platoon.

Captain Koenig recalls that prior to Tet his unit had engaged and been shot at by the enemy on nearly every mission. Nevertheless, he felt that "you couldn't find the bad guys unless they wanted to be found." He recalls his fire-team flying the "Big Y" (a section of the Mekong as it appears from the air) alongside Jim Williams at 1400 on January 30 when a FAC spotter aircraft directed them to a large parade of enemy sampans. Within ten minutes the combined efforts of Williams' and Koenig's fire-teams had all but destroyed the entire fleet.[18]

Koenig recalls being told "that there was some sort of heightened alert status"[19] before retiring to sleep that night. However, since it was normal procedure for the 175th to fly the "bug-ship" mission on nights that the 114th manned the "hero hooch," his platoon's second in command, First Lieutenant Mark Goldmark, was airborne in the early morning hours with his 3-aircraft night illumination fire team.

The Navy's Aviation Electronics-man Third Class Jimmy Farrell, from Brooklyn, New York, originally assigned to work in maintenance at Vung Tau, got himself orders to Detachment Three to see some combat. He had resented the pointless standing at attention in the scalding sun for daily musters in front of the squadron hangar. Not long after arriving in Vinh Long, he was assigned TDY with the Army. On the eve of Tet, he went about his business as usual, and he does not recall any briefing about a possible attack. "Nobody said nothing. Nobody knew nothing" [sic], according to Farrell. It was shortly before midnight that he drifted off to sleep in his bunk.[20]

Ronald Pickett joined the naval service in 1957. He wanted to learn to be a barber. After spending four years as a seaman and going nowhere, he decided to try medical training as a corpsman. He passed the required tests and then received comprehensive training in San Diego. After several years of experience, he found himself being sent to serve in Vietnam. By this time he was a first-class hospital corpsman: HM1. He was assigned to HA(L)3's predecessor squadron, HC-1, at its detachment in Vinh Long and, since there was no Navy medical service facility there, he was tasked to work with the Army at the base's 83rd Medical Dispensary.

When Pickett reported there, its director was Army surgeon Major John Hilegas, who ran the small dispensary very efficiently. It had no permanent beds, and it had an X-Ray room with no X-Ray equipment. Nevertheless, it provided enough space for triage and patching up the wounded. If necessary, the more serious cases were airlifted by medevac to the U.S. 9th Infantry Division's MASH unit (Mobile Army Surgical Hospital) at Dong Tam. On the night of Tet, Pickett was preoccupied treating some Vietnamese casualties. Although not warned of an impending attack, Pickett felt uneasy that something was coming.[21]

Nineteen-year-old U.S. Navy Airman Jack Williamson reported to HA(L)3, Det. 3 not long after graduating from high school in Ohio and completing his Basic Training. On the eve of Tet, he had been assigned to fly as a gunner with the Army's 114th Cobra platoon. He recalls being told to be on a higher alert status. He went to sleep before midnight in his lower bunk before midnight in the Army barracks under the protective mosquito netting suspended from the bottom frame of the upper bunk.[22]

Lieutenant Commander Joseph Bouchard, from Montana, was as vital as anyone to HA(L)3's success. He was serving in Vung Tau as Maintenance Officer when he decided to escape from what he felt was going to be a "year of liberty" and got himself relocated to Vinh Long to become the head of helicopter field maintenance. As sharp with his sidearm as he was with the squadron, he was believed to be able to shoot a snake in the eye. He recalls being briefed on the eve of Tet that the Viet Cong were 23 kilometers from the base and "advancing in its direction." He decided to take a walk on the runway before retiring for the night.[23]

In March 1967 Chief Petty Officer Chuck Fields, a tall redhead from Athens, Georgia, arrived in Vietnam, where he served as a crew chief and as assistant to Bouchard. On the night of Tet, he would be completely surprised by the attack.[24]

Master Chief Petty Officer Francis D. Smith had enlisted in the Navy on July 16, 1946, just after reaching his 18th birthday. After many years of shipboard experiences, he eventually became a jet mechanic leading him to volunteer for HA(L)3, where he was sent to receive advanced training at UH-1 Bell Helicopter maintenance school in Fort Eustis, Virginia. He ultimately became a key member of Bouchard's maintenance team at Vinh Long. As with many of the squadron's maintenance personnel, his quarters were at the "villa" a few miles from the airfield. His success as a leader was partly due to his having been an all-Navy boxer. He had blondish hair groomed in a crew cut, and he stood strong and erect at 5 feet, 8 inches, and 180 lbs. His serious look commanded instant respect. Smith had no warning of a looming Tet attack.[25]

ADJC Jim Catling grew up in Pennsauken, New Jersey and enlisted in the service right after graduating from high school in 1955. He arrived in Vung Tau in June 1967, just after the squadron was formed he got assigned to the maintenance detachment at Vinh Long in August and, along with more than 20 other personnel, was berthed at the "villa" located between town and the airbase. There were comfortable bunkrooms on two upper floors, shared with both PBR and heavily armed SEAL sailors. Wisely, the Viet Cong kept a distance from the facility. Catling does not recall it ever having been attacked. He recalls that on the eve of Tet, in celebration of the Lunar New Year, the town was lit with flashes and with the sounds of fireworks popping.[26]

LTJG Tom Crull enlisted in the Navy, was trained in helicopters at Pensacola, Florida and upon graduation from flight school, volunteered to fly with HA(L)3 in Vietnam. After completing five years of active duty in 1971, he finished his 30-year career in the Naval Reserve in 1995, retiring as a Navy captain. Crull recalls that he was completely unprepared for the Tet attack. On the afternoon prior to Tet, he hung out on the base, before retiring to his hooch in the evening.[27]

Lieutenant Everett Miller (Ebb) was a second-tour pilot with experience at Helicopter Utility Squadron One (HU-1), the unit that in 1948 had become the Navy's first operational helicopter squadron and which was later re-designated as HC-1. Coincidentally, he grew up as a shiny blond-haired kid in the heart of the coal mines of Allegheny Township, Pennsylvania, not far from Weseleskey's hometown. He also attended the same Arnold High School as Wes's wife Sally attended. While a student at the Naval Postgraduate School in May 1967, Miller was recruited to fly with HA(L)3. He had been in Vinh Long since November and, with so many pilots competing for flight time, he was able to accumulate flight hours only by flying medevac and supply missions with the Army's Outlaws. Housed in the same hooch with Crull and Weseleskey, Miller remembers his bunk as being in the extreme rear of the Quonset hut.

Miller was not prepared for Tet and, since he was a very heavy sleeper, he often wondered whether he might possibly sleep through a mortar attack.[28]

C. J. Roberson enlisted in the Navy in 1950 and worked his way up to chief petty officer and ordnance man. After returning to the States from a carrier deployment with VF-14, to his surprise, he received a call from his detailer asking for him to volunteer for Vietnam. He responded with "I don't think so." But, because of Roberson's vast experience and strong leadership qualities, the detailer persisted, "Well Chief, it would look better on your record if you volunteered for this Vietnam assignment, but one way or another … you are going for an in-country tour."[29] In the following months, he received what he felt to be unnecessary Army basic ordnance training, followed later by Navy SERE training at Little Creek, Virginia. Again, this training seemed superfluous since Roberson years earlier had had 18 days of SERE training in Nevada and had become a qualified SERE instructor.

Roberson arrived in Vietnam on July 4, 1967, but he was hardly in the mood for patriotic celebration. He was indoctrinated in Saigon and vividly recalls being shown a poster illustrating a Vietnamese man wearing black pajamas. The caption read, "This is your friend." When it was turned around to the reverse side, the same picture was shown, with the caption reading, "This is your enemy."[30] So Roberson had received his welcome to Vietnam. A few days later he found himself on a flight to Detachment Three in Vinh Long.

Sometime after his arrival, Roberson helped improve the defensive abilities of the Seawolves' airfield position by sand-bagging the two trailers (one for the maintenance gang and the other for the aircrew personnel), that had been set up by the Seabees. He was responsible for having constructed a mount for an M60 machine gun on top of one of the trailers. Roberson even started putting chalk marks on the helicopter fuel tank covers, to enable the Seawolves to detect whether VC saboteurs had dropped a hand grenade into the tank. The VC tactic was to remove the grenade locking pin first, tape the spoon handle down, and then drop the grenade into the tank. After the fuel dissolved the tape, the spoon would release, setting off the fuse and detonating the grenade's explosive charge, which would result in a catastrophic explosion, destroying the helicopter.

Roberson recalls that even with the preparations being made, the mood on the eve of Tet was very relaxed, with personnel sitting out in front of the hooch gazing at the stars and telling sea stories.[31]

ADJ2 Kenneth Williams enlisted less than a year after graduating from high school in Swansboro, North Carolina in 1964, hoping to serve aboard a ship and therefore to avoid being sent to Vietnam. Even though he had learned his jet engine trade and had served with VP-28 repairing P-3A Orion patrol aircraft in the Philippines, he was abruptly issued orders in January 1967 sending him to HA(L)3, thereby becoming one of the many non-volunteers joining the combat squadron.[32]

Soon after completing the required SERE training in July, he was flown to Vung Tau, where he worked until September on the squadron's UH-1B aircraft in the engine shop in its maintenance hangar. In late September, he was sent out to Vinh Long to serve with Detachment Three.

Upon his arrival, Williams was given informal temporary duty orders to work with the Army in the maintenance hangar on the north side of the runway, helping to service UH-1 aircraft. While assigned to the Army, and even though he still lived in the Navy barracks and occasionally mustered with his fellow Navy enlisted men, Williams had the feeling that the Navy had forgotten about him. Williams was one of the very few squadron members never to elect to take R&R in the 18 months he served in Vietnam.

On the afternoon of 30 January, he performed his routine maintenance work on aircraft power plants and the intricate fuel control systems. "There wasn't anything particularly different happening than any other day."[33] Williams does not recall having heard any warning about a possible attack on the base. He went to sleep at his usual 2200 hours. Close by his bunk rested his M-14 rifle and .45 caliber "piece."

ADJ3 Glenn Wilson, originally from the Oakland, California area, enlisted in the Navy after completing high school in 1965. In early 1967, Wilson was sent to Ream Field in California to await assignment. To his surprise, during a routine classroom briefing on duty assignments, he found himself "volunteered" to serve in Vietnam.[34] After arriving in Vietnam and serving aboard the LST *Garrett County* and receiving experience as a door gunner, he was reassigned to the Vinh Long detachment of HA(L)3. Wilson was highly sought after by the pilots as an air crewman, because in just a few months of experience, he had become recognized as one of the most reliable and accurate of the squadron's door gunners. During the afternoon prior to Tet, Wilson recalls himself and a few other crewmen being tasked by pilot LTJG Hal Guinn to fill sandbags in order to beef up the squadron's CONEX boxes and aircraft revetments. At night, Master Chief Roberson, the detachment's most senior enlisted man, assigned Wilson to base guard duty, with his watch beginning at 1800 hours. He recalls snoozing in a rack at the guard house during a four-hour sleep break.[35]

At 0200, Wilson was set to return to his post at the lightly fortified perimeter guard tower near the base's main gate. Although these towers were sandbagged and stood 25 feet off the ground, they did not instill a lot of confidence in him, and he did not feel especially secure being perched up there.

During the late evening hours, Pham Phi Hung (at the time of being interviewed, a retired general and former province chief), the commander of Battalion 857, which included infantry, commando, and artillery companies, had been organizing his forces for a direct assault on the base.[36] Born in the Tam Binh District of Vinh Long Province in 1933, he was one of seven siblings. After his farmer parents died in 1945 and while he was still in primary school, he joined the local army at age 12. During his early service, he was able to complete his high school education. By the time of his retirement, he had been wounded nine times, once by a shell from a U.S. Air Force F-105 fighter-bomber, that injured his abdomen and caused him nagging pain throughout his later years.[37]

Hung received his battle assignment from two-star General Nguyen De, commander of Military Zone Nine, of which the southern general headquarters was located in Tay Ninh Province under three-star General Tran Van Tra. Hung had assembled two infantry companies of four platoons each, with each platoon comprising 38 fighters. (Two other infantry companies were kept in reserve.) His battalion had at its disposal a combination of both American (war booty) and Russian weapons. Included in his arsenal were U.S. 57- and 75-millimeter recoilless rifles, 81-millimeter mortars, and AR-15 rifles. The Russian weapons included CKC rifles and the very reliable RPD light machine gun, which was half the weight of the M-60 machine gun but fired the same ammunition. The range of 900 meters was somewhat less than the M-60, but this limitation was negated by the fact that the required range was usually less than 50 meters.[38]

The single commando company of 40 men assigned to the battalion was directed by Duong Van Ca (later retiring as a colonel), also the son of farmers. Ca was born in 1940 in Chau Thanh District of Dong Thap Province. His men (many of them later discovered to be very young boys) were armed with mines, grenades, and explosive charges varying in size from 1 to 6 kilograms. They wore shorts, but not shirts. To keep them from being impeded by the sloshing and slapping of sandals during their running attack, they would run barefoot through the puddles and ponds. The commandos served as sappers during this attack and carried no weapons; only satchel charges.[39]

Chief of the artillery company Pham Thanh Tu (later retiring as a major), was also the son of farmers. Born in 1940 in Lop Vo District of Dong Thap Province, he joined the army after primary school at age 15. His company of 120 men consisted of two clusters set up on Bo Gon Street (about 150 meters from the airfield) and two clusters of fighters set up in the southwest area of the airfield. They were armed with six mortars, one each of a 75-millimeter and a 57-millimeter DKZ (recoilless rifles), and six antiaircraft guns, including at least one 12.7-millimeter and one 12.8-millimeter machine gun.[40]

Thanh Tu's plan of action during the assault on Vinh Long Airfield was for his company to fire its artillery weapons onto the base, which was to be followed by a coordinated direct assault by the commandos and infantrymen in order to overrun the battlefield. Since they lacked radios, communication was to be by using hand and verbal signals.[41]

As 0300 approached, most of the base personnel were comfortably asleep in their bunks. Both Navy and Army personnel who had been there for any length of time were accustomed to the sound of a few mortar rounds falling, the noise of the helicopter fire-team on alert scrambling their aircraft and the ensuing stillness of the air, and then the comforting sound of the UH-1 transmissions singing and the soft clap of their rotor blades. But this night was different.

At about 0315, Battalion 857 began its attack by unleashing a barrage of mortar shells onto the base. As the first rounds struck the asphalt, First Lieutenant Jim Williams and his crew in the "hero hooch" awoke to the roar of explosions going off only a few feet from the flimsy structure. Rounds had hit within 50 meters on one side and on the other of where they lay. Williams felt that someone was out to kill him. As shrapnel started to splinter the corrugated metal frame, he and the others dashed madly outside and sprinted the short distance to the waiting helicopters. Within a few moments, another round landed right on the small structure, turning it and their steel bunks into twisted, crumpled metal.[42]

First Lieutenant Williams was wearing only skivvies and flip-flop sandals as he climbed into the right-hand seat of the helicopter's cockpit, switched on the battery, and began cranking the starting mechanism. Since the copilot had apparently forgotten to secure the aircraft lighting switch when parking the helicopter earlier in the evening, it suddenly "lit up like a Christmas tree." Immediately, the helicopter started getting pelted with small-arms fire. Without his helmet on and with the aircraft rotors turning, Williams gently raised the collective control, lifted the heavily loaded helicopter, and nudged the nose over in order to pick up airspeed and get airborne. Within seconds he was halfway down the runway heading west, which would take him past the Seawolf parking area.[43]

During the initial mortar attack, it was not known that VC commandos had infiltrated the base and that in this area that the VC had booby-trapped parked helicopters and the small fixed-wing Bird Dog FAC aircraft on the south side of the runway. Williams had barely gotten the aircraft airborne and was starting his ascent, when automatic weapons fire started to hit the aircraft, entering the cockpit from both sides. Suddenly, the copilot, Warrant Officer Brad Duncan, slumped over the cyclic control, causing the aircraft to pitch dangerously forward. Williams, who already had his hands full and not knowing exactly what had happened except that a round had nicked the tip of his nose, now had to pull Duncan back and reposition the controls to avoid crashing into the ground and while trying to escape from the fusillade. Immediately after stabilizing the aircraft and after barely clearing the west end of the runway, he identified an enemy position by seeing a green stream of enemy tracer rounds rising from it. He instinctively fired his entire load of 48 2.75-inch rockets into that position.

Williams immediately altered his flight course and headed to the medical unit at Dong Tam, about 10 miles east, where he left the body of his copilot. He thought ruefully of the round that had grazed his nose and wondered whether it might have been the same one that had instantly killed Duncan.

Shortly after landing, and knowing that he was badly needed back at Vinh Long, Williams took off and flew back to his besieged base. Upon returning, he landed the aircraft and was greeted by Sergeant Swann who had it refueled and rearmed. After getting a set of clothes and a pair of boots and finding a replacement copilot, Williams launched his aircraft and, with intermittent refueling and rearming, flew cover over the base for the rest of the night. He recalls having flown continuously for nearly 18 hours before shutting down the aircraft, after which it was discovered to have 87 holes of varying sizes and shapes.[44]

SP5 Cahill, after being in a deep sleep in his bunk, awoke as soon as he heard the first mortar round exploding. He ran to the bunker just outside the barracks for cover. Following the first lull in the action, he returned to the barracks, retrieved his M14 rifle, and headed directly to the east end of the runway, where he teamed up with other aircrews to safeguard the helicopters in the revetments. He observed enemy tracer rounds coming from more than 100 yards to the south; many seemed to be directed at him. Not knowing exactly where the enemy positions were, he held back from returning fire for fear of harming American defenders. Although the hero hooch occupants were long gone by the time of his arrival, Cahill recalled seeing the hooch get hit by a recoilless rifle round that caused a huge explosion. He was amazed at the enemy's tenacity, and as many incoming rounds continued landing throughout the night, he feared that the base was going to be overrun. He felt "scared to death and thought that it might be my last night on earth."[45]

Hearing the first incoming rounds, Captain Miller "punched on my tape recorder and ran out to the bunker…which was beside my hooch."[46] After about ten minutes and the impact of more than 40 mortar rounds, repeated machine gun bursts, and the faint sound of a helicopter flying in the vicinity (recorded on his tape recorder), there was a break in the frequency of the explosions. After waiting a few more minutes, he and other Cobra platoon members "went back to our hooches to get dressed and armed." They gathered their personal weapons, and after another ten minutes had passed, Miller gave the order, "Don't shoot unless you have something to fire at."[47] All of them then left the hooch and ran out to the perimeter bunkers, where they began to engage the invading commandos and VC infantry, who had by this time infested most of the base.

There was chaos everywhere. The main tower, about 100 meters from the officers' quarters, was under heavy fire. Enroute to the flight line, as Miller was leading the Cobra pilots, they passed several dead Americans lying on the ground, and they now clearly comprehended the severity of the attack.

Seeing the main hangar ablaze, Miller felt compelled to abandon his position at the flight line to help extinguish the fire and save the aircraft. When he got there, he helped the hangar personnel pile sandbags onto one helicopter to smother the fire and prevent the copter from exploding. Another nearby helicopter had its wheels locked, requiring a group of men to drag it out of the hangar. After the fires had been put out, Miller and his men returned to the flight line to man their defensive positions. Intent on maximizing their firepower, they even set up an 81-millimeter mortar.[48] (Miller's recorder continued playing, taping the ongoing ground action. The recording included sporadic machine gun fire, rifle shots, short bursts of gunfire, and the faint sounds of machine guns firing in the distance, all the while with the sounds of at least one helicopter circling overhead.)

As soon as he heard the first rounds explode, SP4 Jones, fully clothed and as ready for battle as any seasoned infantryman, sprang into action. "I just rolled out of bed and strapped my stuff on … and I left the hooch (observing people 'just going nuts'), ran down towards the hangar seeing guys just firing into the night. I went into the hangar, and there was just chaos, with several aircraft burning and people running around. So I said to myself that I am going to go on my own, went past the helicopter wash rack (just to the east of the 114th hangar) and I ran down to the Seawolf line. I saw sparks bouncing off of some construction material down there. There were bullets coming from the south side of the runway. So I did a low crawl and just past the Seawolf line…stopped and waited."[49]

Jones sighted two defenders appearing from nowhere and starting to fire across the runway. Since Jones did not see any clear enemy targets in the direction in which they were shooting, he asked them to hold their fire. Then an E-5 or E-6 came over, followed shortly by a lieutenant colonel. The colonel asked for volunteers to cross the runway in the direction of the attackers. "Since I was a newbie, I didn't say anything. Not hearing anyone volunteer, I scooted up beside him on my knee and said 'I'm ready to go.' The colonel grabbed the sergeant by the arm and said to him 'You're going along.' But the sergeant didn't want to go. When things got split-second quiet, we started across the runway, and suddenly some mortar rounds hit just to the west of us. We survived that and made it into a bunker at the base's southern perimeter where some of the guards were and had been wounded. The colonel then took off with them to seek medical attention."[50]

In the bunker, Jones observed an M-60 machine gun with a can of linked ammo. After surveying the situation for a few moments and realizing that the two of them were alone in no man's land, the sergeant said "they're going to kill us, and they are going to overrun the base, I'm leaving" after which he simply departed from the bunker, leaving Jones alone to defend the position. The machine gun was not loaded, and Jones had never operated one before, but with the help of the glare of the flares falling from the sky, he figured out how to load it. He then pulled the actuator back into firing position. To his utter astonishment and chagrin, the gun started shooting. Quickly, Jones broke apart the links connecting the ammo rounds in order to let it run out of ammo. However, while it was still firing, the bunker was rocked by an explosion. Suddenly he found himself both blinded by the exploding sand and deafened by the concussion caused either by an enemy rocket or by a small grenade. With his eardrums now damaged, Jones was instantly hors de combat. But when he removed his hands from his eyes, Jones realized that he still had his sight even if it was blurry from his tears. But his world was now deathly silent.

Peeking through the bunker's firing slit, he now saw several VC soldiers running towards the bunker and closing quickly. Jones picked up his M-14 rifle and started firing at them, killing them with rounds striking their midsections. "But one VC reached the bunker opening and pointed his AK-47 right in my face." Jones shot him in the chest before he could fire. (It was discovered later that his AK-47 had jammed.) Over the next several minutes other VC attacked his bunker, but unfortunately for them, Jones had recovered from his shock and stopped them in their tracks with bursts from his reliable M-14. After nearly an hour, when things had quieted down, Jones reloaded his magazines and peeked outside. Seeing several wounded VC who were still moving, he decided that to ensure his own survival, his only recourse was to "finish them off."[51]

When Jones thought that all was safe, mortar rounds again began to land in sets of three near his bunker. Planning to extend his survival, he thought it prudent to fill in the damaged areas with sandbags. As he was making the improvements, "a mortar shell exploded directly behind me. The bunker was filled with hot, stinging shrapnel that peppered my back as I lay face down in the dirt." As he looked around, Jones saw another two VC fighters charging the bunker. Instinctively, he fired at them, and they fell dead. "All this took place in just seconds."[52]

Radio operator Keller was at his desk at the Army operations building listening to his audiotapes when he heard the first of multiple explosions followed by the rattle of an M-60 machine gun coming from a nearby guard tower. Being unprepared and without his gear, he immediately dove under his desk for cover. To his surprise, the door opened, and a sergeant entered the room screaming, "Get your ass to the hooch and get your weapon, gear, and helmet." With mortar rounds impacting the ground throughout the base he ran the quarter mile to his room, retrieved his assigned equipment, and ran back to the operations command bunker. He made it through the night at the flight line without firing a single round from his weapon.[53]

Deep-sleeping Ebb Miller had no difficulty awaking during the Tet attack. After the first projectile hit the ground, he ran the entire length of the barracks and out the door and scurried the 25 feet to the sandbagged bunker, shared with officers of neighboring barracks. His quickness and agility enabled him to be first into the bunker, barefoot and wearing only skivvies. He thought about the myth related to him by the prior OINC, Sam Aydelotte, that mortar attacks directed at Vinh Long were not significant. Ebb remained there for a half hour until the explosions became less frequent and then returned to the hooch, got clothed and armed and proceeded the quarter mile to Seawolf flight operations. The heavy gunfire seemed to be in the background. By the time he arrived at Operations, he saw that on the southwest side of the airfield the Army was firing wildly in all directions, so he decided to stay out of harm's way at Operations where there was now a significant force of defenders.[54]

Waking to the booming sound of rounds crashing down onto the base's hard ground surface, Weseleskey recalls young Ensign Richard Martz, jumping up and yelling at the top of his lungs, "Incoming."[55] Wes scooted out from his rack, quickly slid into his flight suit, grabbed the .38 revolver with which he slept, threw his arms into the wide openings of his bulky flak vest and—not forgetting to grab his M16 and a bandolier placed at the door—dashed out the Quonset hut into the sandbagged bunker some ten meters away. In moments, it was packed full with other of the squadron's officers, some barely clad but most armed and ready. Adrenalin began to flow in response to the thunderous explosions, and the aircrews began to transform their night's dreams to actual fighting and survival. Still, initially, no one comprehended what would be taking place on their once-secure base and home away from home.

While the exploding mortar rounds and recoilless rifle shells were getting louder and seemingly being walked toward them, a head count was promptly taken. After more than ten explosions, Wes and some of the other pilots considered the precariousness of their situation and decided that this attack was a great deal more significant than just harassment fire. So they determined that rather than trust the integrity of the overhead sandbags, it would be safer to head out into the darkness. So many of them sprung into action and dashed to Seawolf Operations.

As soon as the rounds started to fall, Rosenthal awakened and darted from the officers' Quonset hut. Moments later he peered out and observed an Army Bird Dog pilot pausing just outside the doorway to his bunker but behind the sandbagged wall protecting the entrance. At that moment a mortar round exploded, peppering the pilot with shards of hot metal. The pilot then disappeared back into the bunker.[56] Rosenthal would remain in the heavily sandbagged operations CONEX box throughout the remainder of the horrific night. He thus avoided getting involved in the ongoing skirmishes, most of which were being fought within 20 yards of Seawolf Operations.

Glenn Wilson had barely awakened from his four-hour sleep break at the watch duty guardhouse when he heard a mortar explosion just short of the base perimeter, barely 70 feet from the base ammunition dump. He recalled hearing someone utter at the same time that "there was movement out there."[57] Along with other Army guards, he ran into a bunker adjacent to the guardhouse. When he realized that it was alongside piles of ammunition, "scared shitless, I say to myself, I'm getting out of here." Without hesitation, he began his 200-foot dash back to the main gate guard tower, along the way retrieving his helmet, which had fallen off during his initial scramble to the bunker. When he reached the fortified wooden tower, he yelled to his fellow guards, "hey it's me, Wilson, I'm coming up" and proceeded up the ladder alongside the 25-foot tower.[58] During the night, the three guards received sporadic fire, shooting back over the sandbags. Knowing of Wilson's reputation as a helicopter gunner, one of the guards volunteered to Wilson, "I'll be glad to load your clips if you do the firing."[59] Not wanting to be the only participant in the fight, Wilson told the guard to load his own clips.

Weseleskey sped to the operations trailer, first passing a bunker from which screaming and the sounds of laughter were emerging, seemingly out of context. (Afterwards, he heard that it was the bunker housing the Army's Bird Dog FAC pilots and that one of their senior officers had in his company a civilian Red Cross "Donut Dolly" girl clad only in a flak jacket.) As soon as he arrived at the operations trailer along the north side of the runway, Weseleskey took up a defensive position alongside other Navy aircrew defenders.[60]

Meanwhile, Martz jumped into a passing vehicle heading toward the Seawolf revetments. One Army aircraft parked nearby was aflame. After seeing that the Seawolf helicopters were secure and observing a firefight at the end of the runway, he ran out on his own to assist in the counterattack. With his M16 in hand, he sped across the runway to the south side of the field in the direction of silhouettes darting about the Army aircraft revetments, assuming them to be those of VC attackers.[61]

"Crouched behind a revetment bunker, Martz noticed some darkly clad figures coming over sand dunes directly behind parked Army Bird Dog aircraft. Others were milling around the revetments."[62] Instinctively, he aimed and shot at four VC, killing one and wounding another before his rifle jammed. While he was holding the weapon across his chest and attempting to clear the chamber, he was struck by an enemy round aimed at his chest that was deflected by the stock of his own rifle. Shortly afterward he was hit by three rounds: one in his right wrist, one in his upper left arm, and another through his thigh. Alone and immobilized and with his body becoming numb, he took cover until he was lifted onto a truck and taken to the dispensary.

Joe Bouchard recalls hearing the sound of "a tremendous mortar barrage," followed by the wailing of the base's attack sirens. After running to his barracks' bunker close to the main gate, he was able to regain his composure and load a bunch of men into his Dodge pick-up and speed it toward the squadron's spaces. "As soon as I turned down the runway, there was a string of 50s (.50 cal. rounds) going by my windshield. I then ran the pickup into the canal and proceeded to set the record for the 400-yard dash."[63] When Bouchard reached Seawolf Operations, since "I forgot the combination to the lock on the armory, I shot the lock off and started passing out weapons."[64] After setting up one position with an M-60 machine gun, he "looked down the runway and could see the colonel's (Base commander Colonel Bernard Thompson) jeep coming down the runway. Charlies were firing from right across the runway from us. The runway was 75 feet wide. I ran out onto the runway, trying to flag down the colonel. He never saw me, as he was opposite me. A Charlie stepped out with an AK-47 and hit the colonel at least nine times. A couple of guys got him out of the jeep and brought him over to the edge of one of the bunkers. I killed the guy who had run out with the AK-47." At this time Bouchard recalls "all hell breaking loose."[65]

LTJG Crull recalls that "as soon as the mortar barrage slowed, along with the others huddling in the hooch bunker, we jumped in our detachment Dodge pick-up truck and headed for the flight line and operations trailer. We then saw that the airfield flight crew's ready-hooch had been hit and as we heard gunfire nearby, we realized that we were in trouble. When we got to the trailer, we jumped out of the truck not knowing that the VC were right across from us, hunkered down in the Bird Dog revetments just 75 feet away."[66]

After Bouchard blew off the lock to the weapon/ammo CONEX box and started handing out weapons Crull recalls that, "he gave me an M79 grenade launcher. I said to him, 'what in hell do I do with this thing?' He yelled back to me, 'shoot it like a shotgun.'" Crull, aware that the 40mm round had a kill radius of five meters and had to travel 30 meters to become armed, decided to take the weapon but use it only if absolutely necessary.

Crull also recalls that "Pandemonium was everywhere. When I witnessed one of the Army gunships that had scrambled, landing nearby to reload and seeing one of its gunners get shot, I realized we were in deep trouble and that the base was being over-run. As soon as Bouchard figured out that friendlies were shooting at other friendlies, he ordered everyone at the trailer to hold their fire. Little did we know that that the VC across from us had thrown some grenades at us that turned out to be duds. We discovered them laying on the PSP after we went out to survey the damage in the morning."[67]

Airman Williamson slept in his bunk with the mosquito net opening on the left side in case he had to scramble and fly with his Army fire-team. At the first sound of explosions, and as prepared as he was, he rolled to the right side and immediately got entangled in the netting, nearly falling over. Embarrassed, he composed himself and dashed out to the hooch bunker in the company of at least 15 Army hooch-mates. Hearing the repeated heavy explosions, accompanied by brilliant flashes of fire, he waited for a pause in the action. After a while, discovering that VC attackers had penetrated the base's defenses and were concentrating their efforts on aircraft revetments adjacent to the runway, he scrambled back to his bunk area and retrieved his M16 rifle and .45 cal. handgun. Instead of returning to the bunker, he and a few other crewmen jumped into their recently dug foxholes. He remained there for some time, occasionally ducking away from bullets whizzing over his head. He readied himself for a direct assault. By this time, aircraft were landing, and one of the lieutenants ordered the crewmen out onto the runway to assist in refueling and rearming. Williamson sprinted more than 100 meters in the midst of automatic weapons fire, brilliant explosions, and the sheer madness of an unexpected enemy assault. He had a mental flash that he was participating in an action movie, an *Apocalypse Now*, years before the movie's script was written. With its rotors turning, he and other crewmen reloaded the helicopter, which had expended its ammo. A wounded crewman was helped off one of the aircraft and taken to the dispensary. The other helo (which must have been the one flown by Jim Williams) was boarded by a new copilot. After it took off, Williamson took up a defensive position near the revetment for the remainder of the night, remaining confounded by his surreal experience.[68]

AE3 Jimmy Farrell was jolted from his sleep when the mortar bombardment began. "All of a sudden, they just hit. I went right to the bunker outside the hooch."[69] After a few seconds of silence, wearing his flak jacket and armed with hand grenades and his M14 loaded with three taped clips of ammo, Farrell turned left and headed to the runway, passing the large Army hangar. As he was turning in the direction of Seawolf Operations, he heard someone say, "they just took the perimeter." Farrell exclaimed "What?" and, realizing the urgency of the situation, quickened his pace. He passed the Seawolf area and crossed the runway to the south side. Almost at the runway's end, he joined up with other Seawolf gunners and started firing to the south side in response to a heavy stream of enemy rounds whistling through the air overhead. He recalls trying to outflank the attackers as they were charging the runway and "confusing the hell out of them. Then we threw grenades at them and chased them into the revetments until they disappeared."[70] At this moment most of the Seawolf personnel were manning defensive positions alongside their revetments to deter any sapper assaults on the aircraft.

Farrell then found a few Army personnel and teamed up with them. Within the revetment area, he saw an American soldier get shot. As he approached one bunker, "all of a sudden a VC comes out, and I say 'stop.' He would not stop, so I shot him in the back. He got up, and I shot him a second time. He got up again, and I fired my rifle on automatic. He then tried to crawl and just stopped. We looked at him and realized he was our 'hooch boy.' We kept going in the dark and got to the last revetment and started to think about how to take out the last bunker, unaware that two soldiers from my own hooch were in it. They were from Brooklyn, NY, and being held captive in the bunker by the VC.

At this point, I was ordered to pull back. I asked 'why?' Again we were instructed to pull back. So we started pulling back. As we were pulling back, one of my fellow card players appeared out of nowhere. He had run out of luck earlier in the day, losing all his money in one of our games. Since he was nearing the bunker, I told him to get down. He turned toward me and was immediately cut down by rounds from an AK-47. After he was shot I went nuts, and took out the bunker with both of my hand grenades and my M14. I covered my guys, and I went and took out the bunker and killed the VC without realizing that two Army guys in it were still alive. I had thought that they were dead."[71]

At just before 0300, with the first sound of incoming rounds exploding near the runway, ADJ2 Ken Williams got up, grabbed his gear and ran into a nearby bunker. As he always had, Williams put on his black beret and wore his .45 cal. sidearm. After about 20 minutes, when the incoming rounds had stopped, and it seemed quiet and somewhat safe, Williams started running south across the runway to his assigned bunker near the southern perimeter (and adjacent to the long-term maintenance hangar). Suddenly there was a resumption of incoming mortar fire, and there he was running in the most exposed area of the base and at a point of no return. Running alongside him was his best friend, Sergeant Donald Smith.

Reaching the bunker, they discovered that the guard had already expended most of the ammunition. Realizing the gravity of the situation and seeing several mortar rounds explode nearby on the taxiway, and without consideration for their own safety, Williams and Smith spontaneously bolted from the security of their bunker and into the uncertainty of the night in order to secure a supply of ammo from the command bunker located 50 meters away. They ran down the parking area between two sets of revetments protecting more than a dozen helicopters. For their fellow defenders, they left behind their own rifles and ammo.[72]

With the staccato of explosions and small arms fire, and with the brilliant flares slowly descending from the now glaring sky that were being dropped by an Air Force Spooky circling overhead, the airfield was in complete chaos. Barely ten meters into their mission, the two men now saw shadows lurking, or was it their imagination? Lying alongside the third revetment were two fellow defenders who had been shot. One of them, barely alive, had been hit in the eye.

Unknown to them, experienced and highly trained VC infantry had infiltrated the base in support of the commandos, who had earlier infiltrated to plant their booby traps on the aircraft. Many of these sappers were now being gunned down by the American defenders: other than their satchel charges, small mines, and hand grenades, they bore no arms and were now out in the open and cut off from escaping. The commandos were unaware of their predicament ... that their fate was foredoomed.

While Williams and Smith were heading toward the command bunker, now with a greater sense of urgency to secure help for their fallen comrades, they were suddenly confronted by lurking shadows that became all too real. Coming from behind the cover of the third revetment, one shadow suddenly lurched out and at point-blank range unloaded several rounds from his Browning into the chest of Sergeant Smith, killing him instantly.

Believing that his fate was sealed and seeing that he would have to abort his mission, Williams looked around and saw a bunker alongside a small structure housing fire-fighting supplies. As Williams cautiously approached the bunker, darting out of the nearby shadow came the same VC who had just killed Smith. Without hesitation, the VC approached him and from within inches, aimed and fired at Williams's head. A single round discharged from the VC's rifle. It cleanly entered right through the front of Williams's black beret, passing swiftly over his skull and exiting out the back. Now facing the attacker, Williams raised his hand and pulled the trigger of his .45 handgun three times, killing the man. Luckily for Williams, the VC's Browning rifle had jammed after firing the one round. Feeling safe for the moment, Williams took a few deep breaths and walked back to the wounded soldier he had seen earlier. When he reached him, he dragged him to a safer area, where he might be able to receive some medical aid.[73]

Williams then decided to return to the nearest bunker where he could have a chance to defend both the base and himself. He entered the bunker, which to his good fortune was unoccupied. Flares were still falling and, although there was sporadic gunfire, the whole weird scene seemed to play itself out over a period of hours. Within 45 minutes another shadow, larger than the earlier ones, was moving around and seemed to have an interest in approaching the bunker.

Realizing that the shadow was a man (and not his imagination) and not sure whether he was a friend or an enemy, he did not dare take any chances. Williams repeatedly yelled, "Identify yourself, or I'll shoot." Without saying a word, the man "dove into the bunker with me."[74] As Williams had warned, he fired several rounds at him. On the ground inside the bunker was the body of a black man—not like any VC he had ever seen. Starting to feel queasy that he had killed the man, he was startled to see a U.S. Army major look up at him in awe. Williams had completely missed his mark. "To this day I cannot figure how I missed him with my .45. He couldn't have been more than two feet from me."[75] When the major had recovered from the shock of being shot at, he stood up and said humbly to Williams "I'm not hit. I'm okay."[76] Williams and the Army major decided to defend the base by remaining in the bunker until daybreak.

Master Chief Roberson and a few of his men were still stargazing in the late hours when they heard the sound of firecrackers, followed by the booms of mortar rounds striking the airfield surface. He scurried into the nearest bunker, which was between his hooch and the small base post office. He recalls seeing an Air Force sergeant who usually coordinated the control tower but was off duty that night, running into the bunker as explosions were occurring nearby and exclaiming, "Oh my God, I forgot my teeth!" "I grabbed him as he was trying to leave the bunker and said to him 'Stop right now—you don't need your teeth, Sarge. What do ya think the VC are doing, lobbing hamburgers?"[77] As soon as there was a pause in the action, Roberson headed to Seawolf Operations. He remembers having received emergency instructions to defend the detachment's helos and the flight line. If personnel were available, they were to defend the base perimeter and as the last resort if the base was being overrun, abandon the base and head to the PBR docks on the river after setting fire to all squadron assets. But this night, even though there were rumors of the American forces abandoning the base while it was being rocked by continuous explosions and the enemy seeming to be everywhere, he and his fellow Army and Navy defenders were able to repulse the attackers.

From the security of the Seawolf Operations bunker, Weseleskey decided to head across the runway towards the south perimeter, which was the side of the base from which the main body of the enemy force had entered. He met up with Staff Sergeant Slaughter, one of the Army corpsmen and together they looked for wounded. Nearing the perimeter, in the darkness punctuated by flashes of light, they saw a grenade bouncing along the ground just a few meters away from where they stood. They dove to the ground and covered their heads but were stunned by the horrific explosion. Weseleskey felt that his own death was at hand as he was lifted a few inches off the ground by the deafening concussion. But with both of them still in one piece, they got up and proceeded carefully to the perimeter, where they had expected to find the ARVNs who had been assigned to provide perimeter security. They were not there, either because they were away on leave or because they might have dodged off into the scary night (as it was conceived by some of the base's skeptics). However, it was reassuring to discover some U.S. Army troops manning an M-60 machine gun. Weseleskey recalls helping them out when the weapon jammed. It was after 0400, and although the incoming mortar fire seemed to be tapering off, the base was still in chaos.[78]

When he felt that he was no longer needed to help the Army protect the base perimeter, Weseleskey returned to the operations shack, where, to his amazement, he faced a visibly angered Rosenthal. "I explained to him that I was helping to protect the south perimeter of the base."[79]

Rosenthal complained to him, "You should have been safeguarding the hooch. How dare you go looking after Army assets when you should have been here protecting Navy assets?"[80]

By daybreak, the attacking VC had broken off the brunt of the attack, and most of the attackers who had survived the counterattack had retreated from their positions at the airfield and headed for safer terrain.

Weseleskey recalls that when dawn broke at 0645 and gunfire along the perimeter had become sporadic, the revetments were searched for any remaining enemy and for survivors. Ten Americans were dead, and many were wounded. Six seriously wounded VC were discovered, all teenagers and one not being older than 14. Mangled VC corpses were strewn about everywhere, two of them those of commandos who had lost limbs as a result of premature detonations of their satchel charges. Enemy wounded were taken to the dispensary for triage and treatment and then turned over to arriving ARVN soldiers for transfer to detention centers. When the fighting had abated, Weseleskey sat down with his men at squadron operations during a moment of respite and shared with them some C-rations for nourishment, after which he flew the detachment's first helo mission of the long day.[81]

"Under the bright morning sun rising from the horizon, the top sergeant from the aviation company started telling me what I did," recalls Jimmy Farrell. "He was going to put us all in for medals, me for the Silver Star." When the bunker that he had attacked just hours before was searched, one soldier was brought out dead and the other with a severely injured right eye. This wounded man looked at Farrell and said repeatedly, "We were alive, we were alive. Why did you do it?"[82] "I told him to no avail that the VC had been shooting at us from within that same bunker. I felt bad. I felt lousy. I then refused any offer of an award."[83] They also discovered the lifeless body of the card player who had nearly been cut in half by the VC. As they lifted him, by his shoulders and ankles, his body fell apart onto the ground.

Upon exiting his bunker, Buck Jones discovered a stack of lifeless or wounded VC bodies, who just a few hours earlier had been aggressors hopeful of overrunning the base. Six or seven of them, including the much younger commandos, were still alive, but barely. With his ears oozing blood he headed to the dispensary but got held up at the hangar. The first sergeant's first act was to tell him to unload and surrender his M-14. Arriving at the dispensary, he could see many badly wounded Americans being treated. Recognizing their greater need for treatment, he decided to go back to his hooch for some personal comfort. After a short while, heading back to the dispensary, he again ran into the sergeant, who wasn't quite sure just how to handle all the bodies that had been discovered. Seeing Jones, he shouted, "Jones, you killed em, you load em" onto the dump truck standing by with its engine idling.[84]

At dawn, Captain Miller rounded up a group of soldiers. "We made a sweep of the flight line, turning bodies over and collecting weapons. Then we decided that we'd continue on to the muddy area on the other side of the runway, across from the Seawolf line. There was a flat sandy area where we ran across the route of withdrawal. You could see a lot

of footprints. So we followed them and came upon a clump of bushes…
there were two guys in there. And they were hiding in there, and so we
called on them to come out. We didn't know if they had weapons. We
couldn't really see them. They wouldn't come out. I ended up firing a
couple of rounds into those bushes. I wounded them really badly, and
they were dragged out, and about that time a South Vietnamese truck
with some ARVNs in it came by. We flagged them down and boosted
the VC up on to the truck, which took them to the dispensary. Both
of them ultimately died from their wounds. After the sweep, I went to
get a couple of hours of sleep."[85]

SP4 Maestas, along with a group of fellow aircrew, gathered bodies of
Americans killed during the attack, transporting them to the dispensary.[86]
SP4 Oliva noticed amongst the dead several base employees including
the young man who had served as the base barber.[87]

Master Chief Roberson and a few of his shipmates conducted a sweep
not far from where Miller searched, capturing a few wounded VC,
including one youngster who had been hit by a round that entered his
shoulder and exited near his buttocks. He was given some water but
soon died of internal wounds.[88]

When the badly shot-up Martz was brought into the dispensary,
Corpsman Pickett was already there, working with four Army medics,
trying to make do with minimal assets. Their supervising doctor, who
had arrived only days before, was gone, sitting frozen by fear in a nearby
bunker. Staff Sergeant Slaughter, nicknamed "Sloe," who had been a
door gunner serving multiple combat tours but was now functioning as
a medic, was able to make it to the dispensary from the fighting on the
airfield to start managing the care of the incoming patients. They were
kept busy with triage and emergency aid. They had never seen anything
like this and had to improvise. One Army door gunner, who had been
struck by shrapnel in the back of his neck, had his head placed on a
40-millimeter grenade round to put pressure on the wound, which was
gushing blood. With more than 40 casualties (mostly Army) entering
the small dispensary suffering mostly shrapnel wounds in legs, arms,
buttocks, and eyes, Pickett directed his fellow medics to "patch them
up and get them out the back"[89] and into the medevac slicks landing
on the helicopter pad, to be evacuated to the Dong Tam MASH unit.

If they were on stretchers with IVs, then they were given first priority for evacuation. As the dead were brought in, Pickett had them put into body bags, which were in good supply, and put into a bunker outside to keep them from the view of the men being treated in order to mitigate their misery.

There was a lot more going on at the dispensary than Pickett was able to recall. Eugene Schwanebeck had taken off soon after the attack began. Almost immediately, his helicopter was hit on the side by enemy rounds that knocked out the hydraulics system and struck one of the 2.75-inch rocket motors. The motor exploded, sending shards of shrapnel into the aircraft that hit his chest plate and slightly injured his wrist. Since the aircraft was flying low and was near the approach end of the runway, it was safely set down. Amid the shelling, he strode over to the dispensary and was upset to see that it "looked like a butcher shop, with guys torn up pretty badly."[90] Like Jones, he left after deciding that he would rather not interfere with the more seriously wounded being treated by the three medical personnel.

SP5 Cahill was one of many people making the morning sweep near the Bird Dog flight line. He came across dead and wounded VC, a few of whom were handed over to the MPs. One had been shot in the groin and was in pretty bad shape. Later Cahill went over to the dispensary. In the outer room were nearly a dozen VC youth waiting to be treated for wounds, one of them having a bullet hole in his chest. Wearing only shorts, they were most likely commandos, shot as they were breeching the perimeter fences. Cahill was appalled at cruelty being administered to one of the enemy, when he observed a base soldier pour the contents of a Coke can into the VC's chest cavity, drowning him. When an MP protested "Get away from these guys, they are my prisoners," one soldier pulled out his .45, aimed it at his head, and threatened "How would you like to be dead, just like him?"[91]

In the morning Ensign Martz was patched up and prepared for evacuation. He made light of his three wounds and wanted to return to the flight line to be with his squadron mates. But that was not to be. After arriving at Dong Tam field hospital, he was brought to the 36th Medical Evacuation unit at Vung Tau for surgery. A few days later he was taken to Japan for further treatment. When ready for release from the hospital more than a month later, he insisted upon being returned to HA(L)3 to complete his tour of duty, which he ultimately did at HA(L)3's Detachment Six.[92]

Corpsman Pickett remained at the dispensary for the next several days, grabbing naps between treating casualties. Throughout his tour he never had time to feel any fear, and he had so much loyalty to his assignment that he preferred going on MEDCAPS with Major Hillegas rather than on R&Rs, which he never took during his one-year tour in Vietnam. In April 1968, he was transferred to serve with the 3rd Marine Air Wing at Cherry Point, NC.[93]

LTJG Crull walked over to the muddy area across the runway, carrying his M16 rifle with the M79 40mm grenade launcher slung over his shoulder. He discovered dead and wounded VC, who looked more like young boys. They were in shock and silent in their misery, having been both wounded and captured. Since they were wearing only shorts and looked so young, they were probably commandos who suffered the greatest losses earlier in the morning. He watched them, feeling mixed emotions. One VC sitting in the mud, who had suffered an internal wound, keeled over and died in his presence. Soon several ARVN soldiers appeared, collected the wounded and took them away. Crull wondered where they were going to be taken and what the likelihood was of their survival.[94]

In the morning LCDR Bouchard discovered why earlier he had seen VC running across the canals by skimming on top of the water. The innovative enemy had constructed sheets of perforated steel plating runway matting and placed them six inches under the water, creating the strange illusion.[95]

Sometime after daylight, Catling and other maintenance personnel went to the airfield, where they would remain. After a few days, when things had quieted down, they made a round trip from the base to the villa to collect their gear. Many of them would not return. After having to share quarters for a few days with base personnel, the maintenance crew decided that they had no choice but to build their own barracks. They were quite capable. After construction was completed, they decided to cut a hole in the building's frame to construct a bunker that during the frequent mortar attacks could be reached without having to exit through the front door.[96]

In late morning on February 2, Weseleskey scrambled his fire-team for a mission in Vinh Long city. Smoke billowed from smoldering ruins. Many parts of the city, especially government buildings, had been razed during the earlier attacks. For many days Vinh Long would remain under siege. It was observed that initially, instead of trying to repulse the enemy, groups of government forces joined in the chaos and looted many targets of opportunity, including homes and businesses.

Weseleskey and his wingman would return to the airbase to rearm and launch their aircraft over and over again.[97] Each time they returned to the city they were met by heavy gunfire coming from different positions, some fortified and some from windows and doorways of small buildings. His fire-team rolled in on one recoilless rifle position, knocking it out. But the relentless VC attackers kept on firing their automatic weapons, even though they were facing superior firepower from the air. It was apparent that the attacks during the Tet Offensive were different from most previous offensives because this time the VC were not running but were staying and hoping to take over the city in order to prove their invincibility. Wes noted, "This was the first time I'd seen such a dedicated VC reaction to one of our attacks."[98]

Being aware of the heavy fighting at Vinh Long in the immediate days following the Tet attack, Commanding Officer Spencer decided to leave the security of his Vung Tau headquarters in order to visit the detachment and provide some relief for the pilots, some of whom "had flown 55 hours in three days."[99] A man of proven courage, he didn't hesitate to take personal risks by flying on some of the most dangerous missions. And since they were at night, he was able to debunk the Navy notion of senior officers flying only during the presence of a "commanders' moon," or only when it was most safe to fly. Spencer recalls that on one night he "scrambled nine times."[100]

Spencer also recalls the city of Vinh Long being completely overrun by the Viet Cong. On one particularly dangerous mission while making firing runs over downtown Vinh Long with Rosenthal as his wingman, Spencer simply "couldn't find him." Although Spencer was greatly disturbed by this, it seems likely that Rosenthal was lying back a little too far while providing cover for Spencer, avoiding the heavy VC fire directed at them from different positions. After a few days of continuous flying, Spencer felt satisfied at having had the opportunity to help the detachment during the heavy fighting. He believed that they had defeated the enemy, stating proudly, "we drove them out of town."[101]

Finally, after six days, when their casualties had mounted and when more attacks would not have been productive, the VC attackers left the Vinh Long Airfield vicinity either to regroup or to melt into the population and avoid annihilation by the now reinforced American and ARVN forces and from the constant threat of helicopter gunship attack.

General Pham Phi Hung had planned to destroy all of the base's helicopters. He claimed that his forces "destroyed 63 [sic] helicopters" so "with no helicopters overhead, the enemy could not stop the attack."[102] However, the evidence is that it would not have mattered, since the helicopters that were airborne (at least during the critical first night) could not have fired onto the base for fear of hitting the American defenders, who were so close to the VC invaders. Furthermore, although there were more than a dozen helicopters damaged during the attack, only a few were documented in the official Army report to have been destroyed.

All three of the former VC witnesses interviewed stated that they usually had communication gear including GRC9 [sic], BR25, and telephone, but it appears more than likely that they did not on this mission since no Americans mentioned recovering any of this equipment in the early daylight hours of the 31st. Actually, it appears that one of the major flaws in the attack's execution—a flaw that led to heavy VC casualties—was the lack of communication. This flaw became evident during the premature artillery and mortar fire that resulted in some of their unarmed infiltrating commandos becoming casualties, and at the same time prevented them from setting all of their satchel charges, booby traps, and other explosives and escaping from the airfield prior to the counterattack by U.S. Army and Navy personnel.

The leader of the commando company, Colonel Duong Van Ca, in an interview in Vinh Long on July 10, 2003, expressed remorse that he had lost 32 members of his company. (Nearly all of those who had been killed, wounded, or taken prisoner by base personnel appeared to be under 16 years of age.) For him, the action was "fierce, terrible, out of my imagination." There were "sounds of heavy gunfire, mortars, and explosives with light flares blazing. The attack was so fierce that I did not think that I would survive. One man was seriously wounded, losing two arms, and another one had been caught by the enemy."[103]

Whatever chaos had occurred during the armed struggle at the Vinh Long Airfield, nothing exemplified it more than the unbridled mischief that took place near the base dispensary. LCDR Rosenthal recalled that sometime during the last few days of the Tet Offensive, he observed a terrifying incident during which two adult VC suspects were being questioned in the presence of their wives and children by some ARVN soldiers. One ARVN officer tried to prevent his fellow officer from pushing one of the prisoners to the back of the dispensary building. Moments later two shots from the officer's sidearm cracked out, executing the man. All the while, the man's family was wailing, as they were aware of what was happening. Rosenthal could do nothing but stand by helplessly in utter disbelief.[104]

To consider the heavy VC losses in the Vinh Long area a stunning defeat and the return to previous harassment tactics evidence of desperation would be in denial of the facts and open to debate. According to official U.S. Army records compiled by the commanding officer of the 164th Aviation Group, during the period from February 1 through February 28, the Viet Cong continued harassing the airfield almost daily. From February 1–4 there was sniper fire, and mortar rounds were coming in nearly "all day and night." On the 9th and 10th of the month, there were a few mortar rounds and light sniper fire. On February 17, one of a barrage of mortar rounds fell on the command post bunker, killing two ARVN and one American. On the night of the 18th, even though there was intelligence of an impending attack and many aircraft were sent to from Vinh Long to Vung Tau for the night, no action was taken that was able to thwart the enemy's plan. Approximately 30 mortar rounds struck the base, hitting the same targets as during Tet: the Cobra flight line and the Red Knight (slick helos of the 114th AHC) ramp. One American was killed and 18 were wounded, with two aircraft destroyed and six others damaged. Just as everything seemed to be quieting down for the rest of the month, on the 20th, both in the afternoon and in the late evening, mortar fire struck the base.[105]

During the period of the report, at Vinh Long, the combined U.S. Army and Navy losses numbered 11 killed in action with around 27 wounded. The base commander was killed and was replaced by the commanding officer of the 175th Assault Helicopter Company. The air base would recover, but the big losers were the townspeople of Vinh Long, who suffered hundreds of casualties. The VC had holed up in pagodas and churches, calculating that this tactic would provide safe shelter for them and their munitions. Reluctantly, Weseleskey could no longer resist firing on such buildings with rockets and machine guns. However, he derived some satisfaction from seeing large secondary explosions. Homes and business would take weeks, if not months to return to a semblance of normality. The local government was slow in organizing itself and in providing aid and food to the population. No matter how much pressure was being applied on the enemy by American helicopters, pilots, and crews, it was imperative that the ARVN forces get back into the field and sweep the surrounding area and blow up VC bunkers and fortifications and destroy their mortar positions. Mortar shells would continue to rain sporadically onto the base for days until the ARVN forces returned to their perimeter assignments.[106]

After spending the week at Vinh Long, Spencer returned to Vung Tau, almost collapsing from exhaustion. He recalls, "My eyes were going bad, so bad that I could not fly the lead ship, only the trail ship. I had to take my gloves off and soak my hands to alleviate the soreness from all the blisters that had developed while holding the cyclic control during so many hours of flying."[107] Spencer had accomplished his goal: to demonstrate his leadership at the detachment level in the worst of combat circumstances and inspire the crews. With three months of his Vietnam service tour remaining, no one could denigrate him with the accusation that he suffered from the "short-timers" syndrome. The citation for the Bronze Star Medal he had received for his earlier Vietnam service period (May 9–December 1, 1967) read: "Mastering the overwhelming problems of organization. Supply, and utilization of forces, Commander Spencer displayed outstanding tactical acumen and command decisiveness."[108]

After the siege ended, Weseleskey went on R&R in Tokyo. He felt it was time "to climb on the first available plane and go wherever it takes me. I'm going to soak in a tub, sleep and eat good hot food for seven days—and then I'll be ready to come back and finish up my tour."[109] From the start of the Tet Offensive on January 31, he had flown every day (except for February 5) through February 18, completing 46 separate missions.[110]

Weseleskey left for his R&R on February 20. It would be his second trip to Japan. The first one had been in December, when he went to Atsugi on assignment as Naval Forces Vietnam's air safety representative and met to exchange ideas on accidents, safety stand downs, and helicopter flight limitation envelopes with people from air group squadrons, staff officers and marines who flew there from Okinawa. When his wife Sally was told about his trip and a return to Tokyo for "Hotsi Baths," she was miffed that he would have such a desire or need. But for Wes, the straight-arrow character who never drank more than iced tea at any Vietnam bar, there was no pleasure greater than the steam room, a scrub-down, soaking in a hot pool, and then a long rub-down, all lasting an hour at the bargain price of a dollar fifty.[111] He returned on the 26th and was right back in the air over the Delta on February 27.

Since Weseleskey had already received orders to HS-1 in Key West, he had the opportunity to become one of those combat "short-timers" and ease off a bit to ensure his safe return to CONUS. But his dedication to his assignment and his loyalty to his charges, without any doubt, set him apart from many others. He would continue to fly missions after his replacement had arrived and even on his next to last day in country: April 6, 1968.

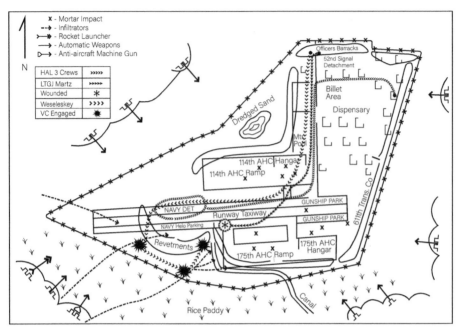

Vinh Long Airfield Battle Area sketch during Tet Offensive, January 1968. (Modified by A. E. Weseleskey)

Explosions at Vinh Long. (Courtesy of A. E. Weseleskey)

CHAPTER NINE

Bystanders Trapped During Tet

Sister Joan Gormley: "I felt like the world of the Good Shepherd Sisters Convent was collapsing before my eyes."

Good Shepherd Sisters: Anne, Mary, and Joan standing next to Good Shepherd Statue in Vinh Long, 1967. (Courtesy of A. E. Weseleskey)

A month later, as the Tet Offensive began to wind down to a series of ongoing skirmishes, MACV, in its calculation of enemy losses, concluded that the enemy's offensive had been poorly executed. The goal of bringing about a general civilian uprising was not attained. Even more encouraging to MACV was the decimation of so many main NVA and NLF units, leading to the belief that most of the Communists' fighting resources had been exhausted. It was estimated by the allied body count experts that nearly half of the 84,000 fighters committed had been lost, as compared to the loss of 1,000 American lives.

But in the eyes of the American public there was no way that the huge NVA losses compensated for the American loss of life. No mercy would be given to the American leadership by the American public after the widespread publishing of a few horrific photographs—one in particular being, the perfectly timed photo of the national police chief, Brigadier General Nguyen Ngoc Loan executing a Viet Cong prisoner with a round from his personal, silver-plated snub-nosed revolver. With his arm extended straight, the executioner's single bullet traveled just inches before piercing the side of the head of sapper commander Nguyen Tan Dat. The distorted grimace as the bullet entered the brain of this small man standing in his torn plaid shirt and dark shorts, with hands tied behind his back, appalled millions. And with the clicking of the shutter of Eddie Adams's camera and the simultaneous recording of Vietnamese cameraman Vo Suu's NBC newsreel footage of the execution, showing the details of Dat crumpling to the ground with blood bursting out of his head, the war began its own death throes.[1] The date was February 1, 1968. Saigon and most of the rest of the country were in utter chaos, and it was only the beginning.

Could anything fruitful have resulted from the huge loss of civilian life and destruction of property in the Mekong Delta towns of the prosperous My Tho, Ben Tre, and the important central Delta city of Vinh Long?

The Good Shepherd Sisters convent, training facility, and dormitory was located less than one kilometer northeast of the Vinh Long Army Airfield on a piece of property provided them in 1958 by the Diem government and blessed by President Diem's brother, Archbishop Monsignor Ngo Dinh Thuc. Its buildings ordinarily housed about 100 girls and young women between the ages of 9 and 25 "in need" of professional guidance.[2] Many of the young women had been referred to the convent by the local government and were engaged in providing laundry and sewing services to the Vinh Long base personnel. According to Pham Phi Hung, the leader of the VC battalion responsible for the attack on the airfield, the convent was recognized for its humanitarian nature and respected by the Communist forces and left alone.[3] Still, the large property would occasionally be hit by a short round aimed over the facility in the direction of the airbase. Sister Mary recalled that on occasion the VC would harass the convent's half-dozen guards, beseeching them to join the VC. But since a few of the guards were originally northerners and had migrated south after the Geneva Accords, these offers were never accepted, as the guards were especially leery about being discovered and suffering recriminations.

By January 30 many of the convent's occupants had gone home to visit and celebrate Tet with friends and relatives. This was fortunate since during the assault on the city there were far fewer than 100 girls remaining with the eight, mostly Irish, sisters.

Although they had some interaction with townspeople, the sisters were not aware of any impending attack. According to Sister Mary, "Nobody knew anything. Everybody thought there was going to be a truce. Period."[4]

At the convent, the Good Shepherd Sisters and their young charges were awakened at about 0200 hours on January 31 by three massive explosions. Immediately, they knew their lives were in danger. The nuns and the girls rushed into the dining room, where they huddled together and prayed. They were even more frightened when they heard the continuous firing of automatic weapons and more explosions coming from the direction of the base. They felt helpless, knowing that their lives were going to be forcibly affected by events beyond their control.[5]

As the day passed and with the sight of so many refugees passing on the road just outside the convent property, Sister Mary, although blessed with hope and charity, grew increasingly concerned for the safety of the girls and for the lives of her fellow sisters. The sisters heard that the VC had taken control of the city and that, to avoid becoming victims of the enemy assault, many of the residents were simply evacuating. Any hope they held for an early end to the attack had been dashed.[6] As evening neared, Sister Joan recalled feeling "overwhelming fear, followed by numbness. It seemed that our whole world was collapsing around us. All we could do is flow with the events, which seemed so surreal." So they decided to call on their American friends at Vinh Long for help.[7]

Later in the day, at 1700, LCDR Bouchard, a close friend of the convent sisters, received a call for help from Sister Mary. He was told that the nuns and 70 of their charges had survived the earlier attack but that with some of their guards having deserted them and the Viet Cong marching down the narrow streets, they had become terrified for their safety. Sensing the urgency of the moment and hearing the despair in Mary's voice, Bouchard decided to act. Assured that he was not needed at Seawolf Operations, he recruited Chiefs Francis Smith and Chuck Field, grabbed some M16 rifles and two M79 grenade launchers, and got a ride to the convent to reassure and protect the nuns and the other innocents living there. It was dusk when he and the two others climbed onto the roof adjacent to the parapet and decided to remain still so as not to attract fire but to stay vigilant in case there was a VC assault.

The three Seawolf maintenance men remained balanced on the roof for the entire night while observing flames shooting skyward from the burning buildings in the city. They kept their cool when enemy bullets seemed to pass over their heads. Some of these rounds struck the compound, perhaps as a test of its defenses, but since their presence had been concealed, more than likely they were errant rounds. After many hours of tension and apprehension, the sun finally rose and, when all seemed secure, Bouchard and his chiefs returned to the base.[8]

When the three men reappeared at Seawolf Operations on the morning of February 1 and it was discovered by LCDR Rosenthal that they had left the base for this mission, Bouchard was threatened with court martial for deserting in the face of the enemy. Understandably, Bouchard felt insulted at this absurdity and became incensed at his accuser. Weseleskey was there at the time to witness this flare-up, and he wisely intervened by convincing Bouchard to fly to Vung Tau to get away for a few days and allow for the men's tempers to cool off.[9]

Later that morning, the nuns, seeing smoke billowing in the sky from fires burning in nearby Vinh Long city, again felt despair. So they placed another call, this time to Captain Robin Miller, another of their close friends at the nearby airfield.

Miller fully understood Sister Mary's heightened concern for the safety of the innocent Vietnamese girls. He was aware that she had never forgotten her World War II experience in occupied France nor the experiences of one of her closest sisters in a Japanese war camp in a jungle just outside Singapore.

When Mary called Miller in a state of panic, and the phone line went dead, Miller sprang into action; he got hold of an available but unarmed UH-1C from the maintenance hangar, assembled a crew, found Lieutenant Jim Williams to fly cover and flew the short distance to the orphanage compound. By the time they got there, the VC were attempting to climb the southeast stucco wall of the building, which, with its high flat roof, would have been a perfect location from which to fire both at aircraft and directly upon the airbase.[10] (According to battalion commander Pham Phi Hung, the VC would not have intended to harm the orphanage occupants. Nevertheless, achieving such a vantage point inside the orphanage would have exposed the occupants to counter fire and would still have imperiled their lives.)[11]

Another aircraft, flown by Army pilot Robb Munroe, teamed up with Williams to help prevent the VC from gaining access to the property. The VC obviously knew that if they succeeded in entering the convent, they could then fire upon the gunships, which would not be able to return fire during the evacuation. So in a "daisy chain," the helos circled the property in a tight right-hand turn, leaving it up to the door gunners to fire on the pesky VC climbers. Miller's aircraft was able to land adjacent to the swimming pool, where there was adequate space for the girls and sisters to board the helicopter for evacuation. After landing the first time, Miller exited the helicopter and walked into the building, where he recalls seeing a group of girls "standing in a big circle, holding hands and praying."[12]

Joan recounted that "during all the confusion while they were hiding in a small room in the back, one of the girls told her that the VC were already in the outer dining room." Thinking that it was going to be over for them, Joan pondered "Should I go first and get it over with or see it through with the others and go last? So I went first, and there was Miller. What a relief it was!"[13] After landing his helicopter by the swimming pool, he stepped out and on his way to the convent went into the dining room.

Mary recalls being "on the steps looking out from the convent, nearly overcome by the acrid smell of burning coconut trees coming from private property across from the convent. I observed VC running around in black shorts and armed with AK-47s rushing towards the convent and, as the gunship door gunners fired on them, they would disappear into neighbors' houses, setting them on fire. It was from these positions that the VC fired on the helicopters."[14]

Mary recalls that most of their Vietnamese guards stood by as they were very loyal and never abandoned their gate positions. But it was Miller she vividly recalled. "There was Miller with his helmet on, visor down and sidearm in his hand. I hardly recognized him." His first words were "There's a helicopter here to take your people out. If you have any money or other valuables, bring them with you."

During this flurry of activity, groups of girls scurried out to the swimming pool area and were lifted onto the helicopter. Mary recalls that "there was no order. Paper was flying upwards into the rotor wash, birds were flying helter-skelter, and smoke and embers from the flaming coconut trees were being sucked up into the air." The helicopter lifted off and minutes later returned for another pick-up. Altogether, there were more than a dozen trips: "75 girls and six nuns [sic], dressed in their white habits. There were Ursula, Patricia, Anne, Mary, and Joan, all experiencing an eerie sense of bewilderment. Mary was fatalistic about their immediate future. Joan "felt numb and I felt like the world of the Good Shepherd Sisters Convent was collapsing before my eyes. It was all too surreal."[15]

With Mary on board the last evacuation flight from the convent, as the helicopter landed at the airfield, she felt comforted by observing the dozens of Army and Navy personnel standing by the runway taking pictures and clapping their hands with excitement as they witnessed the conclusion of this amazing rescue.[16]

A few days later, after the fighting had calmed, two of the sisters returned to the convent in order to transfer supplies to the base. During this trip, they also stopped by the badly damaged house of the Bishop of the Vinh Long Cathedral. They passed through the town, which was now a charred mess. Property owners returned to their homes only to discover masses of smoldering rubble. Around the cathedral were thousands of refugees looking for friends and loved ones and seeking comfort. Upon the bishop's return from visiting his parishioners, he discovered that his house had been looted, not by the Viet Cong, but by the ARVN soldiers who had been tasked to protect it. Several refugees lay dead in the basement. The safe, which had contained money and documents, had been smashed open. Amongst half-burned papers strewn about were a pack of playing cards and empty beer bottles, testament to the soldiers' lack of respect and decency.[17]

The complete disruption in the lives of the sisters would last for more than two weeks, after which they returned to the heavily damaged property. But life never completely returned to normal, and by the end of the Vietnam War on April 30, 1975, they were expelled from the country, to whose social welfare they had contributed so much, particularly in the improvement in the lives of so many innocent young girls caught in the turmoil of war.

There were many other cases whereby unsuspecting and unwary civilians bore the brunt of the Tet fighting even as the fighting seemed to have begun to calm down. Barely two weeks later, on February 13, 1968, while the author was flying an administrative mission with his crew in a UH-1B gunship to Tan Son Nhut Airport, he was also trying to film some of the ongoing fighting down below with a Nikon Super 8mm camera. We had already passed over the smoldering ruins of the Cholon district of Saigon, where VC had been holed up and which had been so heavily bombed by the South Vietnamese Air Force that it seemed to have been turned into a large junkyard. It would not have taken very heavy munitions to raze this predominantly Chinese area since the houses were typically constructed of mud, straw, and corrugated tin roofs. By the time we had flown over the area, it had been all but abandoned. Not even the invading Viet Cong had any reason to hang around.

Off on the horizon, 10 to 20 kilometers north of the city, there seemed to be an unusual visual eruption rising from the ground. From the distance, and through the bright haze, this disturbance looked like a forest of tall trees. For years I had wondered about the strange events that I had witnessed during my duty tour. However, this particularly odd view and seemingly insignificant detail remained recorded in my subconscious.

More than 30 years later, during an interview with Mr Bay Nguyen of New York, I learned that when he was 14, being the seventh-born of ten siblings, he was living on a farm in Nhi Binh, a small village in the Hoc Mon District, just north of Saigon. He related that in the middle of January 1968, his father and his uncle had disassembled their thatched house and moved it using sampans to another town ten miles north. In the interest of the family's safety, the house was reassembled adjacent to a small church. Traveling with them were his mother and nine brothers and sisters. This unusual project was undertaken because his father, Mr An Nguyen had observed a sudden increase in the number of ARVN patrols and fighting nearby. He also had a feeling of heightened concern for the family because he had been tipped off by friendly Viet Cong soldiers, who had frequented his farm during the night for food and sanctuary, of a forthcoming battle. So as the patriarch of this large family, and as a survivor of the 1954 war with the French during which he lost a brother, Mr An became dedicated to its survival.[18]

Among the many residents who did not have the same knowledge as Mr An and who remained in the village during the period, going about their normal business, were two neighbors of the Nguyen family, Mrs Anh, and Mrs Bay. As described by Mrs Anh, "It was in the early afternoon of February 13, when looking up into the bright hazy sky, I saw at least eight very big airplanes. Suddenly and "without warning, the airplanes began to drop their load of bombs over my village." Mrs Anh was thrown into a state of panic but could do nothing but remain in her house.[19] It became the most dreadful day in her life.

Mrs Bay was selling groceries out of her house when she heard unusual sounds coming from the sky. Suddenly, her house shook violently from the vibration of bombs exploding everywhere. She immediately became concerned for the safety of her 14-year-old daughter, who had been husking rice 200 meters off in a small field. After the bombing had stopped, everyone Mrs Bay knew ran to the small local post office and gathered there. Moments later, as they were catching their breath, a second wave of bombers appeared, and they too dropped their bombs. For many villagers, it was already too late to escape. They were now either dead or wounded. After the bombing stopped, Mrs Bay began to fear that her daughter, Tran Ngoc Anh was among the dead. She was, indeed, and Mrs Bay would never again see her daughter or even find her remains in the smoldering field. Mrs Bay miraculously survived the bombing, but her small house and store suffered the same fate as did many of her neighbors; they were obliterated.[20]

During the ensuing silence, the village's survivors began to panic and fled the area by rowing their boats upriver toward the village of Lai Thieu in the adjoining province. But another flight of B-52s flew there, dropped their bombs, and then flew away. At the sound of these new explosions, the villagers in the boats again panicked, leaped out of the boats, and swam to the shoreline.

B-52 bombers flew in cells of three aircraft. Since there were three different sets of explosions in Nhi Binh that day, it is assumed that there were three cells that unloaded their bombs during this not unusual Air Force mission, named ARC Light, comparing the bombing run to the arcing of electricity between two nodes, as observed in a bolt of lightning.[21] If each of these eight-engine airplanes had been carrying its normal payload of 108–500 lb Mk. 82 conventional bombs (60 in the airplane's belly and 24 under each wing), then in less than 30 minutes time, close to 486,000 lbs of explosives were dropped on this small friendly Vietnamese village.

Since B-52s had been assigned to fly so many thousands of allied support missions during the war, and in places like Khe Sanh, assigned to drop their huge ordnance load as close as 1,500 feet from its marine defenders, I wondered how it was possible for there to have been such a mistake, or whether it had been a mistake or an accidental bombing.

According to retired B-52 bomber pilot Lieutenant Colonel Stuart Hughes, who had served as a pilot with the Army Air Corps earlier in World War II, the B-52 navigation system was flawless and during his two tours flying over Vietnam (in 1966 and 1968) and he never heard of a B-52 off-target bombing accident. Even though the bomb load was usually dropped from 33,000 feet, and the pilots never saw the targets, the RIO (radar intercept) officer was able to deliver the ordnance within extremely precise parameters by using ground radar tracking or by being directed to the target by ground operators who often instructed the crew as to the exact time to release the bomb load.[22]

When the three airplanes salvoed their ordnance load nearly a half-mile from the target, it was referred to as "dropping in train" or "carpet bombing." Airspeed and altitude factors resulted in a two-mile-long swathe of destruction, which is probably what I had witnessed during my helicopter flight to Saigon.

A few days after the bombing, representatives of the United States government and the Republic of Vietnam came to the village to meet the returning villagers. They explained that the air strike was an accident: the bombs were intended for a target in Binh My, not Nhi Binh. (The village of Binh My was located a short distance north of the nearby Bien Hoa Airfield and earlier in the month had been a staging area for guerillas attacking the airfield.[23] This information dispelled any doubts that I had as to the bombing accuracy record of the B-52 flight crews.)

The dazed villagers were given 5,000 dong (at rate of 1 cent per dong: equal to $50.00) for each dead family member), one can of rice for each villager, and one liter of cooking oil for each family. At the time, this was the normal amount of compensation given to accidental civilian casualties.

According to Mrs Bay, "the villagers were very angry at the U.S. government for the disaster and terribly saddened by the great loss of life." She recalled that they had not supported either side in the war and had no interest in politics. "They only wanted to work and go about their normal lives. There were no Viet Cong known to be in the village. The residents of Nhi Binh only wanted to celebrate their most important holiday, the Lunar New Year, Tet."[24]

The only official explanation ever offered was by the Command Center Duty Log dated February 16, 1968, recorded the incident as:

IN GIA DINH PROV (XT8405) EIGHT KM N OF SAIGON AT 131400H LATE ENTRY: ARC LIGHT STRUCK CIVILIAN POPULATED AREA OWING TO ACCIDENTAL DELIVERY OF ORDNANCE OUTSIDE TARGET AREA. RSLTS: FRD. 44 KILLED (CIV), 57 WOUNDED (CIV), 72 STRUCTURES DEST. INVES. UNDERWAY.

This accidental bombing report was later coded as "PINNACLE," designating it with the Air Force's highest level of secrecy.[25]

When the Nguyen family returned to Nhi Binh after Tet, once the fighting had quieted down, they discovered for the first time that their village had been struck by B-52 bombers. Looking up, they were horrified to see that in the trees there were still body parts of their neighbors, blown up there during the errant air-strike. The family resettled back onto their small farm, rebuilt their house, and would try to get back to their normal routines, always being cognizant of the disruptive nature of the ongoing war.

Throughout the country, the hardships and tragedies suffered by so many people meant that no one would again feel secure, whether it be on military bases, at places of work, or while raising a family in a big city or a small village, until the war had ended seven years later. Nevertheless, it seemed that after the Tet siege had been broken in the northern city of Hue at the end of February, there would at least be a period of calm.

Buddhist nuns (Nico) Sister An and Sister Bay. (Author's photo)

CHAPTER TEN

Rescue at Cao Lanh

Glenn Wilson: "You ever been hit with a .50 caliber?

Det. One Gunners: Standing, left to right: Christopher Maher, Tom Olezeski, Jack Ordner, unknown. Kneeling: Beach, Glenn Wilson, Doug Leaf. (Courtesy of A. E. Weseleskey)

By the second week of March 1968, the ferocity of the Tet Offensive had mostly petered out. Both sides needed some rest. American veterans could flock to R&Rs in Bangkok, Tokyo, Sydney, and even Honolulu. Viet Cong might return to their farm families in the Delta or just hide out in the jungle forests. Neither side could claim victory.

Years later, American historians would concur in the magnitude of the military defeat of Communist forces throughout the country during Tet, but what was not always mentioned was that for months afterward, Vietnamese Communist fighters continued to wage battle and inflict serious allied casualties.

Weseleskey returned on February 27 from his well-earned Tokyo R&R, taken after flying every day except one from January 30 through February 18. Although his one-year tour was nearing completion, he continued to fly his alternating day flight schedule, doing more than his share of leading the detachment in both combat missions and flight hours. He continued to train the new arrivals and never backed off engaging the enemy during scrambles to aid allied forces.

Officers and enlisted men who had arrived in-country along with Weseleskey in May 1967 as plank owners of this unique Navy combat helicopter squadron had already secured their orders for their next duty stations and were preparing for their return to CONUS. Many had calendars prominently tacked to their barracks bulkheads marking each passing day with a large "X." It was the final countdown for return to the land of the "round-eyes."

March 9, 1968 was a typically hot, uncomfortable day for Weseleskey and his fire-team. It was an anniversary date: the first United States advisors had joined the fight in Vietnam on March 9, 1962. At Vinh Long, new aircrews assumed the watch at noon, which was not exactly the most pleasant time to be climbing onto the aircraft rotor head and engine deck and inspecting their components for damage or hydraulic lines for leaks. It was also time to walk around the aircraft and check the armament, ensuring a full load of 14 rockets and properly linked and belted 7.62 ammo for the four side-mounted machine guns. And most important for the crew chief and the gunner was to make sure that their hand-operated M-60 machine guns were in superb operating condition. Other serious concerns were for the ammo boxes to be filled and the rounds neatly aligned and for there to be extra gun barrels in case overheating damage occurred during firing runs. Weseleskey and copilot Lieutenant (junior grade) Bill Mackey adjusted their seat-height positions, looked over the cockpit switches and felt reassured that the old UH-1B would be able to get off the ground and would be safe to fly. Depending on the wind strength, this underpowered aircraft might have to have its skids dragged on the tarmac to make a successful take-off.

Crew chief and door-gunner Aviation Ordnanceman Third Class (AO3) Bolton and door-gunner Aviation Jet Engine Mechanic Airman (ADJAN) Wilson, each barely over 20 years of age, had responsibilities much more significant than their pay grades implied. When the going got tough, if the flex guns malfunctioned, or if the rockets had been expended, the young men in the cabin would be there to serve as the lifeline of the mission. They were also in the most vulnerable positions, sometimes hanging outside the aircraft while tethered to the cabin bulkhead with a two-inch-wide gunner's belt. On the other hand, with the pilots focused on what was going on at 12 o'clock and at their 3 and 9 o'clock positions, the gunners were able to see almost the entire spectrum of the landscape. But the risk they took was necessary for mission accomplishment and for crew survival.

The crew of the wing-ship also performed the preflight inspection of their helicopter. Pilot Lieutenant (junior grade) Hal Guinn (whom the author had befriended since they met at flight school), copilot Will Simpson, and gunners Tom Conklin and Cliff Wimer signed off on their aircraft's readiness for their day's assignments.

By 1300 the preflight process was complete, and both aircraft were ready for flight. Later, when the equatorial sun dropped somewhat in the sky, Weseleskey would launch his fire-team and patrol the rivers in support of the squadrons of PBR boats that, to interdict enemy movement of personnel and supplies, were keeping an eye on the small flotillas of sampans and junks traversing the rivers and canals. For now, the crews would wait in the air-conditioned ready room. It would also be a good time to discuss tactics and review maps for coordinates of friendly outposts and ongoing operations.

Unbeknownst to Weseleskey, a Vietnamese ARVN operation was being conducted in an area six kilometers southeast of the Vietnamese town of Cao Lanh—an area very familiar to him. Several downsized companies of the ARVN 9th Infantry Division's 2nd Battalion, 16th Infantry had been inserted in the morning by boat with the intention of making contact with a small force of VC.

While still in the ready room, Weseleskey received an urgent call from the Tactical Operations Center (TOC) to scramble his fire-team and contact call-sign Duet Charlie on board one of the PBRs, which had been serving as a blocking force on the small river adjacent to the ARVN patrol, when it had walked into an ambush, suffered massive casualties, and was in the process of being annihilated. As if from a written script, he and the other crewmen, with rushes of adrenalin, dashed out to their aircraft and were instantly airborne.

It was 1440 hours, and Navy Lieutenant Paul Huchthausen was the OINC of River Patrol Section 513. After nearly an hour trying to conduct a close-in fire support mission for the embattled ARVN troops, he decided that his PBRs could barely sustain the onslaught of fire from the same enemy battalion that was in the process of overwhelming the two lead ARVN companies.[1] And since his position was immediately below the riverbank, he felt that just loitering there would be exposing his crews to a risk that was unnecessary. Frustrated, he simply could not provide effective fire support for the ARVN soldiers. While withdrawing to the safety of the main river and seeing that no Army air support was available, he decided to call for help from the Seawolves. (Apparently, Huchthausen was either unaware of or not inclined to pay attention to the HA(L)3 policy restricting Navy Seawolf helicopters from supporting Army operations, or providing medevacs for which the heavily laden, under-powered helicopters were not designed.)

In contact with Weseleskey—Seawolf 35—and his wingman, Guinn—Seawolf 30—Huchthausen briefed them on the serious situation occurring on the ground. By now a couple of Vietnamese Air Force A-1 Skyraiders, flying out of the Binh Thuy Air Base, had lobbed some ordnance at the enemy, but they were driven off by heavy VC firepower. One of the aircraft had been struck by large rounds, probably 12.7-millimeter. Their mission was probably wisely aborted since the friendly troops were not only extremely close to the VC, but they were being attacked from several positions. Therefore, there was a risk of the soldiers being struck by friendly fire.

Another friendly force involved in the ground mission, the ARVN 41st Ranger Battalion, was in coordination with the ARVN patrol. It had earlier been airlifted into the area with the intention of having its troops move along a tree line perpendicular to the movement of the infantry battalion, now under fire, in order to serve as part of a pincer tactic in the planned assault of the suspect VC force. But at the moment when they were needed, they were not in any position to come to the aid of the beleaguered soldiers.

The American Army officer serving as deputy advisor to the ARVN 2nd Battalion and now trying to command the two besieged lead companies, First Lieutenant Jack Jacobs, was a 1966 Rutgers University and Army ROTC graduate. He had originally volunteered for airborne duty in order to support his wife and young daughter with the additional hazardous duty pay. But a year later, he was transferred from his 82nd Airborne assignment to be an advisor so that the Army could benefit from his college degree.[2]

So here Jacobs was, in Vietnam since September 1967, employing the lessons of his training more than a month after Tet. According to his morning briefing, it was anticipated that his battalion would encounter a smaller enemy force, surprise them, engage them, and defeat them. At the briefing, Jacobs was even provided with a likely location of the VC adversary.

Jacobs had already been involved in numerous skirmishes with VC fighters, including one encounter a couple of months earlier during which mortar-round fragments seriously wounded the ARVN battalion commander standing next to him. So now Jacobs was advising the battalion's former executive officer, who had been promoted to battalion commander and was not known for strong leadership, in what would be the fight of his life.

As the patrol commenced, Jacobs (whose call sign was Newport Capone 32A), was uncertain whether the new commander had ordered the company's scouts to position themselves on the perimeter and during the advance, to secure their flanks, or if they had followed up on the order. His concern was not too heightened in undertaking this mission because even though the ARVN battalion's strength had been reduced to less than half of its pre-Tet 350 men, the enemy force strength was estimated to be much weaker.

But at the precise moment when the lead company was most exposed in an open field, the VC fighters let loose with a fusillade of mortars, small arms, and automatic weapons fire from a number of different locations, directed upon at least two flanks of the advancing troops. Immediately, Jacobs' company suffered a significant number of casualties. One of those casualties was Jacobs himself.

The enemy force that was to be engaged by the ARVNs that day was not there just by happenstance. Sitting in wait were nearly 300 fighters from VC Battalion 857, which five weeks earlier had nearly overrun the Vinh Long Airfield. Although their number had been depleted (from 500), as the ARVN's number had been, they were given a new assignment to expand their operations towards Sadec, home of the ARVN 9th Infantry Division.

Again led by Pham Phi Hung, the VC leader of the Tet Offensive assault at Vinh Long Army Airfield, his command had received intelligence (from a spy at ARVN regimental headquarters) of the ARVN operation and planned an ambush in an area that would likely be patrolled. In addition to being armed with an assortment of weapons, his fighters prepared themselves to oppose any air support or helicopter rescue with two below-ground 12.7-millimeter tripod-mounted Russian heavy machine guns equipped with both armor-piercing and incendiary rounds. Pham Phi Hung positioned himself in the northwest corner of the field where he would be in the best position to direct and monitor the ensuing surprise attack. Monitoring a PRC-52 radio, he was pleased not to hear of any air support planned for ARVN operation. So his fighters prepared themselves by manning fortified bunkers, having their weapons loaded, and waiting for the order to fire.[3]

Weseleskey's briefing was short. Duet Charlie gave him the rough position of the action just inland from a small river in the Kien Van District of Vietnam's Kien Phong Province. He headed northwest to arrive over the scene at about 1500 hours. It was one of those typically hot days, with a bright sun beaming down through the broken clouds and with a light wind out of the northwest. He climbed to 800 feet, an altitude high enough for him to get a clear picture of the battle area upon his arrival. As he flew past the PBRs, he could see the heavy VC mortar bombardment and green tracer rounds (indicating VC armament) headed in the direction of the overwhelmed ARVN battalion. But because of the heavy foliage on the perimeter of the open field, he could not exactly determine the location of the enemy gunners. He thought to himself, "Holy hell, who would want to fly into that?"[4]

Just before Weseleskey's arrival, Jacobs and his superior, the battalion's senior advisor, Major James T. Nolen, were on the airwaves with forward air controller (FAC) Captain John Lewis who was flying overhead with his artillery observer in an O-1 Bird Dog aircraft trying to coordinate air and artillery support for the beleaguered ARVN battalion. There was not much in the offing. A USAF F-4 Phantom jet came by and dropped some ordnance along with the Vietnamese Air Force's A-1s that had unloaded bombs onto and strafed the enemy positions with 20mm cannon fire before being chased away. But no gun-ships and no UH-1D medevac slicks would come, even though there were several airbases within 25 miles of the scene. This was the nature of the war: if helicopters had other commitments and there were no aircraft on standby for this operation, they would try to flag down a passerby on guard channel of the UHF radio.

A pair of AH-1G Huey Cobra gun-ships were in the area flying a test flight, but one of them had to set down at the Cao Lanh airstrip with maintenance problems. The other Cobra, piloted by Army First Lieutenant James Kenton (call sign Death Dealer 21) of the 235th Armed Helicopter Company, was returning to its base at Can Tho to have its UHF and VHF radios replaced. Captain Lewis was able to flag down this aircraft and have Kenton connect to Weseleskey on UHF guard channel and on FM radio, enabling them to try to coordinate their efforts even with Kenton's avionics problem.[5]

At this moment Jacobs was too preoccupied with getting air and ground support for the troops still able to fight to be concerned with the wounds he had just suffered. Jacobs, his sergeant, the battalion commander, and others in the lead group had just been shredded by mortars and heavy automatic and small-arms fire while traversing a rice paddy.

Many ARVNs were either killed or wounded on the spot. This was no simple hit-and-run attack. The VC fighters had them in their sights from multiple positions within 200 meters, and the firing was relentless. Worse, those ARVNs not put out of action had panicked and had begun to scatter to escape the murderous fusillade. Immediately, and ignoring the severity of his own wounds, Jacobs ordered those men not incapacitated to scramble over to a tree line to set up a defensive perimeter. This was absolutely necessary for their survival and in order to enable them to suppress some of the incoming rounds being directed at the wounded, already immobilized on the ground. Jacobs then thought of one thing. "I must get these wounded guys to the tree line, or they will certainly die." There was also an abstract thought which entered his mind. The words of the great Jewish philosopher Hillel jumped into his mind: "If I am only for myself, what am I? And if not now, when?"[6]

There was no cover fire coming from the retreating ARVN soldiers and no overhead air cover to strafe the enemy who were being sheltered in multiple dug-in positions and were trying to kill him. So, with his head peppered by multiple shrapnel wounds and with blood oozing over his eyes and impairing his vision, using all his remaining energy, Jacobs ignored the continuous enemy fire and returned to the casualty area 13 times to carry and drag away the wounded ARVN soldiers, the company commander, and his American sergeant. As several VC closed in on his exposed position, he found the strength to change his focus, dispatch them with rounds from his M-16, and resume dragging the wounded to the perimeter, until nearly exhausted.

Weseleskey recalls someone at one point uttering on the radio, "We've been hit; we're in dire straits; not sure we're gonna make it."[7]

Moments later, it was Weseleskey's calm voice that the exhausted Jacobs propitiously heard over the radio, which was completely unexpected. "Understand you've got wounded soldiers there."

To which Jacobs answered, "Yeah. We do." Jacobs was surprised by the sudden appearance of two Navy Seawolf helicopters. He later recalled that during one of his supply runs to Vinh Long Airfield he had observed them "taking off and barely getting in the air." He felt that they were terribly underpowered aircraft. And he was right. "And on previous engagements we'd get some Navy gunship support. These things lumbered over the area since they had no power."[8]

Carefully considering whether to go ahead with the rescue, Weseleskey was aware of the necessity of asking the beleaguered troops to clearly identify their position by setting off a cylindrical-shaped smoke grenade that field units carried with them. Since they were of different colors, he would leave it to Jacobs to identify the color, which would prevent the enemy from using one of its own to set up a trap. It would also help him determine the wind direction to assist in the helicopter's approach to the rescue site.

Weseleskey then answered back with, "Pop smoke."

"So I popped a purple smoke grenade and identified the color to him. So he asked me where the bad guys were in relation to the smoke. I told him that I was in the middle of it. I had brought some wounded guys back to the tree line, and my recollection is that Weseleskey said, 'Well, there's a clearing.' He then said, "I'm going to come in and get these guys."[9]

Jacobs told him, "I don't think you want to do that…it's a mess here…there are bad guys everywhere" as the clearing was brimming with VC and he then said, "No I gotta get in there and get those guys out."

Weseleskey recalled replying, "How many U.S.?"

Jacobs returned, "Two alive that I know of."

Weseleskey recalled that after hearing this, "I decided to have my fire-team go in for the pickup."

Weseleskey stated that, in order to better understand what he might be getting himself into, "I made a quick, counterclockwise circle of the battlefield, and it was apparent that there was a superior enemy force hitting those guys."

Weseleskey recalled, "I started my steep descent from about 800 feet. Not far behind was Seawolf 30. I asked my crews to hold their fire until they can see where the enemy fire is coming from because we are aren't sure where all the friendlies are."[10]

During the approach from the south, "I took some hits from the tree line to the north. They were shooting at the length of the helicopter due to our direction of flight." At this point Weseleskey started to wave off, banking his aircraft to the right.

A few seconds later, his wingman yelled out, "I've been hit. I'm hit in the leg and in the hydraulic system."[11] Following Weseleskey at the 8 o'clock position in trail, Seawolf 30 was hit from the northwest after almost flying directly over one of the enemy positions.

Watching a disaster unfolding before his bloodied eyes, Jacobs radioed, "Wave off, wave off; you're under extremely heavy fire." Jacobs did not want them to make this dangerous approach and get shot up, even though his head wound made it feel like "it was nearly it for me."[12] Witnessing the helicopters come in and getting shot up, Jacobs felt badly, especially so because "it was what I had expected. It was predictable."

Gunner Tom Conklin recalled that after Seawolf 35 was hit during its approach to the LZ and began his wave-off, Seawolf 30, following closely behind, was "hit when it was at treetop altitude. It received multiple hits as Guinn got hit first and gunner Wimer got hit second as the ammunition in his door box blew up. The aircraft started rolling to the left, and we were in the trees."[13]

Conklin recalled that seconds later, Seawolf 30 copilot "Simpson blurted, 'I got it, I got it' as he took control of the helo. He rolled us out of the trees and banked starboard. We were at between 70–80 knots (of airspeed). I started shooting out the left side, down under the tail boom, since we had just flown almost directly over a 50-caliber gun and I tried to silence its fire."

Conklin "…realized it was a 50-caliber incendiary round when, as it penetrated through the underside of the aircraft, it blew up the ammo box. After it was pointless to shoot anymore, I got back in the cabin and wrapped up Wimer's hand, which had its fingers dangling in the glove, and put something on his groin area, which was probably injured from the shrapnel of the explosions of the ammo rounds."[14]

At the controls, Simpson immediately steadied the disabled helicopter, which without hydraulics powering the flight controls boost system that assisted in handling the primary flight controls, was no simple accomplishment. He then smoothly added power, commencing a steady climb out away from the enemy fire to gain some friendly altitude. With numerous enemy rounds having penetrated the frame of the aircraft, one after the other, not only with accuracy but with maximum velocity, Simpson's instincts and his calm handling of the stiff controls were responsible for saving the helicopter and the lives of the crew.

While Guinn continued taking care of the wound to his right leg, Seawolf 30 headed toward the Co Chien River for the 20-minute southeast flight back to Vinh Long.

Weseleskey asked Guinn if was able to control the aircraft. He recommended that Guinn use a belt to tie around his leg.

Simpson got back with, "I have control of the aircraft. Guinn is taping his leg with a tourniquet."[15]

Weseleskey asked if there were any other injuries.

Simpson responded with, "The gunner took shots in the hand; pretty bad."

"Can you control the aircraft?"

"Yes. We can control it."

"Can you provide first aid?"

"Yes. We can control the situation."

"Can you fly the aircraft back to base?"

Weseleskey recalls flying behind Seawolf 30 in a corkscrew pattern to determine the extent of damage to the helicopter. "I could see some pretty big holes and streaming hydraulic fluid. But otherwise, they were okay."[16]

Huchthausen, on the PBR, recalls hearing Weseleskey direct Seawolf 30 to return to base with the wounded.[17]

As he headed back to base, Simpson radioed, "Are you going to come with us?"[18]

Weseleskey replied, "No. I am going to go back. Can you fly the aircraft by yourself?"

Simpson: "I can do it."

Hearing this, Weseleskey felt assured for the safety of their flight.

According to Weseleskey's door-gunner, Glen Wilson, the wounded Guinn transmitted over the radio, "Hey, what are you guys going to do?

Weseleskey got back, "We're gonna…I told those guys we're gonna go get 'em out, so we're gonna go get 'em out."

Somewhat disconcerted, Guinn blurted out, "What the fuck! Aren't you going to escort us home?"

Wilson thought, "Jesus Christ, here I'm with John Wayne or somebody. And I mean I said 'holy shit.' We're gonna go back down there and get 'em out? Shit." Wilson was uncharacteristically scared. He recollected his fear with, "You ever been hit with a 50 caliber-round?"[19]

As Seawolf 30 departed Guinn asked of Weseleskey, "Well, do you know that you got some other people in that aircraft?"

Weseleskey: "Yeah. Wait one."

He then asked the crew one of those questions that are difficult to turn down, "You guys want to go in there?"

Wilson and Bolton gave a "Roger that," by double-clicking their microphones. According to Wilson, "Mackey didn't say anything. He was just scared shitless like the rest of us."[20]

So with his feeling of approbation, Weseleskey answered Seawolf 30, "I got a full volunteer crew here."[21]

Guinn's closing words were, "Good luck."

Alone after Seawolf 35 broke off, Seawolf 30 called on guard frequency for additional helicopter fire-teams to be sent to the area. A ground evacuation of the wounded advisors to nearby Cao Lanh had been briefly considered, but since the Special Forces base of Cao Lanh was manned by only a single doctor and had very limited facilities, its value was negligible for dealing with severe wounds. So it was obvious to everyone that a helicopter would have to make the pick-up and evacuate them to a fully equipped field hospital.

So at about 1530, when AH-1G Death Dealer 21 was airborne in the area and alerted to the situation on the ground by the FAC pilot, he was contacted by Seawolf 35 on his FM and barely audible UHF radio frequencies. Weseleskey briefed the Cobra crew on the battlefield status, now being able to identify the enemy positions more accurately. Weseleskey asked for suppressive fire cover during his next attempt at the rescue.

The Cobra pilot Kenton advised him that since it was a single aircraft, they would not be able to provide continuous fire during the entire time he was going to be in the LZ. Furthermore, his attack helicopter had enough ammo for only one pass. Kenton understood the urgency of the medevac as Weseleskey radioed him that if the American advisors were not immediately evacuated, they would most certainly die from their wounds. Kenton eagerly awaited the opportunity to assist in this rescue.[22]

Weseleskey flew back over the PBR towards the battlefield still seeing mortar rounds being lobbed onto the ARVN positions. Weseleskey "tried to make it back from the south and every time I tried to make an approach, I would receive heavy fire. I tried this twice, unsuccessfully." Finally, Weseleskey made up his mind to "go in try to get the Americans out." He radioed to Death Dealer that "I was going to skim along the tops of the trees" in order to avoid being sighted by the VC.[23]

As Weseleskey was getting set for the approach, he asked the advisors where the enemy was. The answer he heard was, "They're all around us. They're right on top of us." Being cognizant of the second rescue plan, Major Nolen, who by now had joined up with Jacobs and the other wounded, had them dragged to a point about 100 meters south of the original area that was shielded by some small trees and somewhat out of the line of all the incoming enemy gunfire. But upon hearing Weseleskey telling Nolen to move the wounded so he could come in and pick them up, Jacobs aired his opinion—as he had done prior to the first attempt, saying, "This whole area stinks. You're only 50 meters away from where the first helicopter came in."[24] But Jacobs was not able to dissuade Weseleskey's determination to "get in there and save them."

Clearly, focusing his sights on the new evacuation area, on this approach Weseleskey planned his flight track to avoid the enemy gunners completely. He again asked for a smoke grenade enabling him to be 100 percent certain of location and to determine exactly the wind direction at the LZ. Confident, but cautious, approaching from the south with a slight crosswind condition, Weseleskey flew below the tops of the trees, rendering the aircraft invisible to most of the enemy guns.

During the initial descent, Mackey screamed out that he was hit. "I've taken one in the leg," he exclaimed.[25] With adrenalin rushing through his body and mind, Weseleskey thought of aborting the mission and of the dire consequences.

Amazingly, Mackey blurted over the intercom, "I see the bullet." Apparently, the round had penetrated through the port side of the aircraft and almost fully spent, struck Mackey's boot and dropped harmlessly to the helicopter's deck.

It was at this moment that Weseleskey reminded Mackey, "If I take a hit, you're going to finish this mission."

"We were both scared," Weseleskey admitted. "All of us were scared."

Having waited for this second approach, Pham Phi Hung, who positioned himself at the apex of the L-shaped ambush, and his men were ready and eager to unleash their 12.7-millimeter guns, shoot down the helicopter, and accomplish their objective by wiping out the rest of the ARVN soldiers. He let off a smoke grenade that, because it was of the wrong color, did not deceive the aircrew. When he could just see the helicopter's rotor, he had his men fire their weapons. A few rounds found their target, but since the pilot was flying the helicopter at such a low altitude and in a flat trajectory, the VC heavy weapons team was unable to lower the 12.7-millimeter guns to the necessary angle to destroy it. (The emplacement of the heavy guns in bunkers below ground, while making them effective as anti-aircraft weapons, conversely, prevented them from being lowered to the correct position to hit the low flying helicopter).[26]

Death Dealer 21, who had considered making a run on enemy positions, decided to circle the area and perhaps draw fire during Seawolf 35's approach to the rescue area. He reasoned that if then he saw Seawolf 35 in peril he could swoop down into the thicket and cover him with his last rounds of ammunition.[27]

Making the approach, Seawolf 35 was pelted with small-caliber rounds coming from different directions. Weseleskey recalls making a fast approach and then "flaring the helicopter sideways (so the aircraft's nose would be into the wind) and raising the nose high almost standing on its tail, and plopping it into a small depression in the ground."[28] Not seeing the helicopter hidden behind the small trees, but hearing the "WHAP, WHAP, WHAP" of its rotor blades, the enemy's rounds were aimed in its general direction, but too far overhead to do any damage.

Immediately upon landing there was scurrying about the helicopter and voices coming from the cabin. One after another, the ARVN soldiers, with Major Nolen's help, shoved the two American advisors into the helicopter's cabin.

Wilson reported to Weseleskey, "I've got one of 'em; he's in bad shape." In the next instant, Wilson picked up his M60 and started to return fire.[29]

Wilson picked up another man by his collar, handed to him by Nolen, who appeared to be either Mexican or Spanish. In the crowded cabin, he piled him on top of the first guy. Blood was all over the place.

During the loading of the wounded it seemed like an eternity to Weseleskey even though it was less than five minutes. He saw a third soldier, a critically wounded Vietnamese, who was bleeding from a partially severed thigh artery. He was still alive. With the helicopter now on the ground, sheltered from the bulk of the enemy's fire, Weseleskey decided to hover the helicopter just slightly to see if he had the available engine power to take on the weight of the third man. As he slowly lifted the aircraft off the ground, Wilson fired at the perimeter to keep the VC's heads down.

Wilson couldn't believe it. "He hovered up, I don't know, five, six, seven feet. And I hear him say, 'I can take one more guy.'"

Getting ready for liftoff, Wilson saw that "everybody wanted to jump on board. And I was fighting these guys off, telling them that they could not come." Wilson felt badly, but that was the hard reality; there was no more room for anyone.

Jacobs recalled the chaos at the scene just prior to the liftoff. "A bunch of Vietnamese who were not wounded were trying to climb onto the helicopter...and then I think there was an explosion, with more shrapnel hitting us, perforating the skin of the helicopter. I got dinged on the leg. As we were getting stuffed onto the helicopter, you could hear the rounds hit the helicopter. I don't think it was my imagination."[30]

Wilson recalled that, after they set down again and the wounded Vietnamese was put on board, the whole scene was unbelievable. "I was hoping to get outta there then."[31]

Now weighted down with a total of seven men on board, Weseleskey had to swing the aircraft around and start his take-off heading to the southeast: downwind. "I had to take off with the enemy behind us."[32] However, just as he lifted the aircraft, before turning the helo, with enough altitude for a clear shot, he fired all 14 rockets that he felt would relieve him of some extra weight and at the same time, keep the enemy's heads down.

Wilson recalled that Weseleskey "hovered on up and then he says, 'How's my tail?'"[33]

So Wilson "looked over, checked out the tail boom and the rotor and cleared him aft as far as we could go. I said, 'That's it' because he was trying to get enough 'runway' [room to take off]. And then he nosed it over, and we started coming out of there, and we were scraping, and we were hitting some trees and then got some altitude."[34]

Weseleskey recalled having to "make a running takeoff to get out of there heading east with the enemy behind us. They (the enemy) picked us up again after I reached 300 feet, but we were able to evade from receiving further hits. We also headed in the direction of the medical unit at Dong Tam ... a good 20-to-25-minute flight."[35]

Jacobs recalled the aircraft being struck by enemy rounds during the takeoff. "It was like somebody hitting the helicopter with a hammer."[36] Faintly, he heard the unmistakable sound of a crack of a round being fired, almost instantly followed by a clunk, which was the round striking the aircraft.

Watching the helicopter make the evacuation and depart the area disappointed the Viet Cong fighters. For General Hung, the missed opportunity to shoot down the helicopter returning to make the second rescue attempt left him with a bitter feeling "because I had been in many battles (since 1964) where my forces had become casualties as a result of being struck by allied aircraft, and I would have liked to have gotten back at them. Seeing the helicopter come in so low to the ground was a complete surprise, as my men were not able to adjust the aim of their weapons to effectively hit it and bring it down. It flew very low under the tops of the trees, and we were not prepared to shoot it down."[37]

After reaching a safe altitude, Wilson and Bolton put down their M-60s and started to apply compresses to both the sergeant and the officer (Jacobs) to try to stanch their heavy bleeding.

With his bandaged head wound and the racket going on all around him, although somewhat muffled by his state of semi-consciousness, Jacobs was in awe that he was laying on the deck of this Navy helicopter … not a medevac helicopter … but a gunship. "Somebody in the helicopter was trying to tend to my wounds. Maybe it was the crew chief; I can't recall. There were a lot of people inside the helicopter. There was somebody lying on top of me, sort of."[38]

Wilson recalls one of the Americans asking, "Are you guys in the Navy?"[39]

Wilson replied, "Yeah. We're in the Navy."

And he said, "What are you guys doing here?"

Wilson recalled saying to the bleeding and barely conscious soldier, " 'We're all in this thing together, man?' And the soldier hung his head down and started crying. He was just one happy camper."[40]

Weseleskey then headed east, bypassing Vinh Long, to the MUST (medical unit self-contained, transportable) unit at Dong Tam: the Army's 3rd Surgical Hospital, housed in a gigantic reinforced synthetic inflated bubble. Knowing that the 60-bed facility and its team of doctors and nurses were capable of handling serious injuries and wounds, Weseleskey calculated that emergency treatment at this facility would mean that his rescue efforts would not have been made in vain.

Set up at Dong Tam, seven miles west of the prosperous Delta city of My Tho in 1967, the hospital was erected in support of the U.S. Army's 9th Infantry Division. However, its doors were, of course, open to any service personnel requiring serious medical attention. Whether anyone would notice or care that a U.S. Navy Seawolf helicopter gunship was inbound carrying two wounded American Army Rangers and one ARVN soldier for life-saving care is anybody's guess.

Within 25 minutes Seawolf 30 had landed on the helipad adjacent to the hospital's entrance. Waiting for them was ground transportation, onto which the three wounded soldiers were loaded and whisked away to the preoperative and resuscitation shelter where they would receive their initial medical care prior to surgery.

As the wounded were being removed from the helicopter cabin, Weseleskey looked out to see that "everyone was still alive." Shutting down the helicopter for refueling, the crew regained their composure and prepared for the 20-minute flight back to Vinh Long. They all felt gratified by their accomplishment. For Weseleskey, he wasn't quite prepared for the reception he would receive upon his return to the base.[41]

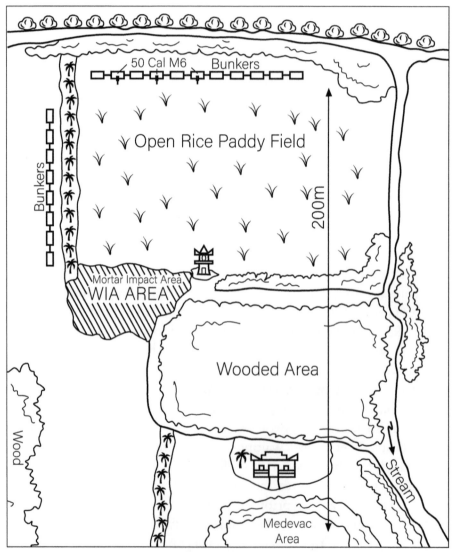

Rescue area sketch submitted for award write-up in 1968.

Typical open field in the Mekong Delta. (Author's photo)

Jack Jacobs. (Courtesy of Jack Jacobs)

CHAPTER ELEVEN

Picnic at Vinh Long;
Return of the Seawolves

C. J. Roberson: "The lead aircraft…looked like it had been used as a battering ram."

Master Chief C. J. Roberson. (Courtesy of A. E. Weseleskey)

At Seawolf Operations, a gathering of off-duty aircrew and maintenance people had begun soon after Seawolves 35 and 30 had scrambled for their mission to rescue Army personnel. The men were indulging themselves at the big squadron picnic—the first such party since the Tet attacks on the base had subsided. And even though it was such a close-knit group of personnel, any friendly face was invited to attend and share in the camaraderie.

No one really cared about the heat from the bright, scorching sun, as there was plenty of Budweiser, San Miguel, and Schlitz to go around and there were soft drinks for those on duty and for the very few who abstained. The crews made creative culinary use of an empty 55-gallon drum. It had been torched in half and loaded with charcoal, and just below its top was placed a metal grill. Rows of hot dogs, cuts of chicken, hamburgers, and a few slabs of steak lay smoking on the grill top. There was some space for the buns, and although they were placed on the grill last, they still started to smoke and turn brown. For anyone inclined to eat C-rations, there were dozens of cases stacked inside the crews' ready shack. Uniform of the day for this event was a potpourri of creative attire: working jeans, khakis, white or olive green T-shirts, or chambrays. A few sailors wore cut-offs. Petty Officer First Class Jim Catling, one of the maintenance personnel under LCDR Bouchard, recalls a line immediately forming for cold beer and soda.[1]

One guest showing up was the commander of PBR COMRIVRON/ CTF 116.7, LCDR Arthur J. Elliot II. He had operational control of five river divisions, two detachments of HA(L)3 fire teams, and two SEAL teams.

As the crowd of 35 sailors assembled for their nourishment, a helicopter landed on the runway across from Seawolf Operations. It was an Army slick helo on a transportation run from the Seawolf headquarters at Vung Tau, and it had come to deliver two new squadron arrivals: replacement pilots Lieutenant Vince Przybyszewski and Lieutenant (junior grade) Tom Patterson. Off-duty Seawolf pilot LT Everett Miller walked over to them with a cold beer in each hand, making it seem to them as though the picnic had been planned in honor of their arrival. As with all new squadron arrivals, their early observations and experiences would form lasting impressions.[2]

While Weseleskey was rescuing the Army advisors, Simpson was doing his best to fly the disabled helicopter and plan his approach to the airfield. He realized that he would have to execute a no-hover run-on landing, utilizing the aircraft skids to touch down on the runway that would enable him to come to a gradual stop. This procedure would somewhat mitigate the loss of hydraulics and avoid the likelihood of over-controlling the helicopter, and thus bring about an end to the debacle that the four air-crewmen had just endured.

While inbound, Simpson called ahead and advised the tower of his difficulties and of the wounded crewmen on board so that the base could prepare for the landing with emergency and fire trucks and have an ambulance standing by. Medical personnel needed to be ready to provide immediate first aid to Guinn and Wimer.

Catling recalled hearing an announcement that a Seawolf helicopter was on approach for a run-on landing. The picnic-goers looked out towards the east end of the runway. One sailor blurted, "There is something wrong!"[3]

Now holding a beer in one hand and a burger in the other, Miller observed the arrival of Seawolf 30. "It wasn't pretty." Miller and the other partygoers witnessed the "helicopter approach the runway fluttering like a falling leaf." At this moment the emergency vehicles arrived at the scene.[4]

Still holding the beer given to him by Miller, Przybyszewski, standing alongside the smoking barbecue, stood frozen; he couldn't believe what he was witnessing. He thought, "What in the world have I gotten myself into?"[5]

The sailors watched in awe as the landing was made with the helicopter skidding along the tarmac and coming to an abrupt screeching halt. As soon as the engine was shut down, the helicopter was surrounded by a bunch of nervous and curious sailors, eager to learn the nature of the problem. They didn't have far to walk since Simpson's extraordinary handling of the aircraft had it placed just opposite the squadron's two trailers. But what the sailors saw was horrifying.

As reported by the observant Miller, it was "discovered that the pilot commanding the helicopter was hit and bleeding severely from a calf wound, while one of the gunners (Wimer) apparently had a serious hand wound and injury to his groin." A corpsman helped Wimer from the helicopter into the waiting ambulance while the wounded "LTJG Hal Guinn, much concerned about his wingman, exclaimed, 'Where's Al?' Guinn related (to Miller) getting hit during the (rescue) approach followed by both aircraft waving off." He also recalled being asked by Weseleskey if he could get home safely. Guinn further stated, "Al said he would stick around to see what he could do."[6]

Gunner Conklin was not initially aware that Wesleskey had returned to make the rescue. "When I heard that they went back in and got those guys out of there, I was amazed."[7]

Guinn was helped into the ambulance, joining Wimer. With its occupants on board, the vehicle sped to the base dispensary, dropping off Wimer and Guinn, who had their wounds cleansed and bandaged before being airlifted to Dong Tam to be given more extensive treatment. Guinn would have his leg wounds successfully treated and rehabilitated, enabling him to return to duty at HA(L)3 a few months later, while Wimer was eventually evacuated to Japan and returned to CONUS.

As things began to calm down, Catling went over to the damaged aircraft and with some assistance had the helicopter's tail boom lowered, set a wheel under each skid and rolled the aircraft into a revetment. The helicopter had more than 15 bullet holes including several .50-caliber-round entries in the tail boom. The whole aft section of the aircraft exterior was covered with red hydraulic fluid. On the right side of the cabin, the bulkhead was scorched with black powder. Pools of blood had already dried in the cockpit and on the cabin floor.[8] There was no doubt in anyone's mind that this helicopter had been through a meat grinder.

Observing all the activity was LCDR Elliot. He wasn't sure what to make of it. When Bouchard approached the helicopter; he asked, "What about Weseleskey?" At that moment it was a question that no one could answer.[9]

It was not long before there was a call over the radio in the maintenance shack announcing that Seawolf 35 had made a rescue with a Cobra helicopter flying overhead, standing by. Elliot got on the phone with one of the Cobra pilots informing him that Seawolf 35 had made one of the most courageous rescues he had ever seen.

However, Elliot, as the task force operational commander and the person most responsible for approving awards for heroic actions, was aware of the many awards that Weseleskey had garnered for his crews and himself. He was not alone in sensing that there had been an over-submission of award write-ups, several of which he had been compelled to turn down. (However, Weseleskey never wrote himself up without including each crewman of his fire-team. According to one Seawolf officer, one of the detachment copilots had already called for an officers' meeting with Weseleskey to complain of what he felt were many frivolous and unsubstantiated award write-ups.)

Elliot was observed pacing up and down and probably wondering whether Weseleskey would indulge in another award write-up. But after speaking to the Cobra pilot, he began to understand the degree of heroism displayed in this rescue and decided to actually sponsor Weseleskey for a write-up for the Medal of Honor. However, as a responsible and influential task force commander, he was heard to stipulate three conditions: 1. "Al is not to know about it." 2. "I will need help to gather information to submit it." 3. "If Al writes himself up, the deal is off." According to Everett Miller, Tom Crull was summoned to go to Army headquarters to gather information.[10]

Most of the picnic-goers had either finished consuming the barbecue offerings or had lost their appetites by the time Seawolf 35 returned to the base. Upon landing, Weseleskey, now exhausted, as were his courageous crewmembers, recalls being approached by OINC Gene Rosenthal, whose first words were, "What the hell did you do?" He then reproached Weseleskey: "You risked eight people's lives to save two."

Weseleskey replied, "They were Americans, and they were pleading for help. I was not going to abandon them."[11]

He recalls Rosenthal lecturing him, "Well, you made a bad judgment. You broke all the standing orders by not escorting your wingman back after he was wounded and the aircraft was damaged. Further, you flew into a mortar attack, and you flew the mission alone. Consider yourself under arrest. You're grounded. You will go to your quarters, and you are to remain there."[12] Weseleskey recognized that Rosenthal was all wound up. But Weseleskey, now drained of energy, kept his cool.

Rosenthal recalls being concerned with the notion that Wes deserted his wounded wingman and flew directly into the enemy's strength, making a landing with his crew for the risky pickup. He felt that being surrounded by the VC, they were "sitting ducks." Disregarding his anger of the moment and showing a bit of compassion, Rosenthal recalls asking Wes, "Are you hurt?"[13]

Tom Crull was within earshot of the two lieutenant commanders. He recalls hearing a Rosenthal's tirade that "the Army should have made the rescue" since the wounded soldiers were U.S. Army grunts that needed help or that they should have utilized USAF attack support aircraft. Crull felt embarrassed by the whole episode and the idea of grounding Weseleskey and placing him under "house arrest."[14]

LCDR Bouchard was also there to observe Seawolf 35 during its approach; he was amazed that the helicopter and crew had survived the ordeal. He observed the normal approach and air taxi into the revetment. "I could see the ship had taken many hits. The windshields were a mess, and the rotors whistled from all the holes in them. As they shut down and secured the helicopter, all four crewmembers seemed to be intact, despite all the blood inside the cabin left by the wounded U.S. Army advisors."[15]

Bouchard and the others were interested in hearing the flight debriefing, but they were interrupted by the shouting of the OINC, "Wes, you're grounded. We'll see you at court-martial!"[16]

Bouchard observed the exhausted and wide-eyed crew. "I saw holes in Weseleskey's flight suit. A ruined service .45 handgun which he wore strapped over his groin had taken a direct hit. Where had this crew been?" he asked himself.[17]

Crull recalled that during the informal debriefing it was discovered that the round that Mackey had thought had penetrated his leg had actually entered the aircraft through the pilot's side, through the leg of Weseleskey's flight suit and through the center console before it hit Mackey's right boot. Having lost its energy, the enemy round fell to the deck of the aircraft, completely spent. The other round that had hit Weseleskey's handgun had actually entered the aircraft through the chin bubble, which had several holes and long scratches and was covered by dirt and rubble. Crull recalls Weseleskey telling him, "it felt like he had been hit between the legs by a baseball bat."[18]

Ordnance Chief C. J. Roberson, also the senior combat aircrewman, walked over to the helicopter and was flabbergasted at what he saw. He observed that "The lead aircraft...looked like it had been used as a battering ram." He imagined that the aircraft's "external damage and traces of blood" must have been caused by a "frontal assault made directly into the enemy."[19]

Guinn called the next day from Dong Tam hospital saying that he would be okay. He also related that "the army guys might make it."[20]

Weseleskey recalls meeting privately with Bouchard, who was charged with restoring the two aircraft to flying condition. He said, "Rosenthal is serious about court-martialing you."

Weseleskey intuitively knew that Rosenthal had called and alerted Vung Tau (squadron leadership) for their guidance, which enabled him to make these threats confidently.

Bouchard recommended to Weseleskey, "The only way for you to counter any (court-martial) proceeding against you is for you to go and get statements."[21]

Avoiding a confrontation with Rosenthal, Weseleskey retired to his room to think things over. He also wisely took Bouchard's advice: "So a couple of days later I called LCDR Huchthausen (whose PBR patrol providing the blocking force had called for Seawolf assistance). Then I went to the Special Forces camp at Cao Lanh and asked if they had information. Major Nolen was there and told me that the Army advisors were going to recommend me for the Medal of Honor. I asked for statements regarding the action and was told that they would write up the rescue and send the paperwork to Vinh Long." With the statements they included a sketch of the battle scene.[22]

Crull recalls hearing the discussion between Bouchard and Weseleskey. He also remembers that within a couple of days an Army FAC pilot arrived at the barracks looking for Weseleskey. He came to lend his support for a medal recommendation by handing Weseleskey a write-up stating that not a single aviation unit had responded to his calls for air support except for the Seawolf fire-team. Later, the PBR officer arrived with a write-up for a Medal of Honor and carried with him a souvenir AK-47 rifle as a gift to Weseleskey. (This kind of war trophy was the most sought-after souvenir in the land.) Then on a subsequent day, the Army Cobra pilot and copilot showed up, each with a written statement supporting Weseleskey.[23]

Weseleskey wrote up the awards for his crewmen. He felt that he wasn't going to receive anything but that he had to cover himself for any potential court-martial proceeding. He wrote up the gunners for Distinguished Flying Crosses and Mackey for the Silver Star. According to Weseleskey, he did not write himself up for either the Medal of Honor or the Navy Cross. He stated that "I was not aware of being awarded any medal until June 1968 when it was awarded to me in Key West."[24]

Miller recalled that a few days after the rescue, Weseleskey's copilot Mackey received a call from the Seawolf staff to fly to Vung Tau while maintaining secrecy. It had been rumored that when the HA(L)3 CO heard that Weseleskey was writing up the awards for the rescue, he hit the roof, going berserk. Everyone in his office had to dive for cover. And CO Spencer was quoted as saying, "I'll either court-martial him, or he'll get the Medal of Honor."[25]

Mackey's arrival did not at first reduce the tension in the air. He was shocked to feel the hostile atmosphere and felt belittled when, in the presence of Spencer's staff, he was ordered to stand at attention. Mackey truthfully related the details of the story and expressed his opinion of the courage it had required to accomplish the rescue of the Army advisors.[26]

Mackey, not known to be one of Weseleskey's strongest admirers, was unaware of the progress of the Article 32 Investigation, which had apparently already been requisitioned by the squadron. But he then noticed a change in Spencer's demeanor. Spencer, a little more relaxed, paused and started to ponder. He was observed to look around and then over to Mackey, saying that he would consider forwarding the write-up as a recommendation for a Navy Cross.

One of the beneficiaries of the rescue, advisor Jack Jacobs, would have been dismayed to know of the cataclysm that had been taking place within the Seawolf organization. He had barely survived the helicopter ride to the Dong Tam Hospital, during which his shattered head was wrapped in makeshift bandages, and he was being cradled in the arms of gunner Wilson.

One morning, before being transported to 93rd Medical Evacuation Hospital in Saigon, Captain Jacobs was startled to discover a naval officer dressed in his "ice cream suit" (Service Dress Whites) standing over him. Although he was still in pain from his wounds and was being stabilized in the intensive-care ward, he wondered if the guy was in the wrong room. Jacobs thought, "maybe my mind is playing tricks on me."[27]

Extending the officer professional courtesy, Jacobs allowed him to begin an interview regarding a particular action. "I said yeah and asked him what this was all about." The courtesy ended after hearing him declare, "We're conducting an Article 32 investigation on the pilot" who came to pick you up. At hearing these words, "I got really irritated, as you might expect."[28]

"I was in the bed," Jacobs recalled (with his head bandaged and being fed intravenously) "and felt really irritated by the fact that the guy who saved my life and the lives of a bunch of other guys was being investigated. It was ridiculous. And in those arduous combat conditions. Then I recall yelling for the hospital crew to come drag this guy away."[29]

The naval officer hadn't been there for very long. Although he seemed surprised by Jacobs' hostility, he had to have understood the absurdity of the interview for which he had been tasked. The staff officer went to the hospital ward to fulfill a tasking from higher authority, realized the futility of his assignment, received the response that might have been anticipated, and left the hospital. And that was the last Jacobs or anyone else ever heard concerning the Article 32 or court-martial for the March 9 rescue mission.

CHAPTER TWELVE

Returning Home

The U. S. Army awards LCDR A. E. Weseleskey the Bronze Star for Valor for Ground Actions during the 1968 Tet Offensive at Vinh Long Army Airfield, at Key West Naval Air Station. (Courtesy of A. E. Weseleskey; Official U.S. Navy photo)

Weseleskey and Spencer checked out of the squadron within a week of each other in April 1968. Wes flew to Virginia Beach for a 90-day leave with his family at his Thunderbird Drive home (where he still lives today) before heading to his next assignment as an instructor pilot at Helicopter Anti-Submarine Warfare Squadron One (HS-1) at Key West. Sharing the flight with him back to CONUS was Lieutenant (junior grade) Dick Martz, the other Detachment Three pilot who fought the VC on the runway during the first night of Tet.[1]

Commander Spencer reported to his next duty assignment at Quantico's Command and Staff College as an instructor specializing in carrier strike force operations. He felt disappointed in receiving this job, since it was not the kind of assignment that would enable him to get placed on the highly competitive list of potential candidates to be executive officer of a CVA aircraft carrier, or for that matter, any other deep draft navy ship, leading to command at sea, which is a prerequisite to command an aircraft carrier, the most cherished assignment of career naval aviators.

There was further disappointment for Spencer as he had to wait for more than one promotion cycle to receive his fourth stripe. Being passed over for promotion (probably as a result of being held solely accountable for the tumultuous first year at HA(L)3) would in effect take him out of the running for the most sought-after assignments in the Navy. Not being promoted at this stage of his career would also prevent him from ever being screened for command at sea.

Spencer's next assignments reflected his loss of opportunity. After Quantico, he was assigned as the executive officer of NAS Ellyson Field. Then in 1973, a year after finally being promoted to captain, he was given orders to be the assistant chief of staff in Saigon (although most of the U.S. forces had already left Vietnam). Luckily for him, these orders were canceled at the last moment, and he was assigned as assistant chief of operations in Puerto Rico. Spencer's next and final assignment was as assistant chief of staff at Naval Station Charleston.

Spencer was proud of the fact that he was one of the very few naval officers selected for a command as challenging as Vietnam's Seawolves. The squadron became a legend in the annals of riverine warfare and being assigned as its first designated leader was certainly something to be proud of. In August of 1978, Captain Robert W. Spencer, USN, retired with 31 years of service. More than 20 years later, on June 24, 1999, Spencer was inducted into his Baton Rouge High School Hall of Fame.[2]

LCDR Eugene Rosenthal departed Vietnam along with the other HA(L)3 squadron plank owners, in May 1967. After completing 29 years of military service that included serving during World War II and Korea, and earning numerous Air Medals and a Distinguished Flying Cross, LCDR Rosenthal retired to his home in Pensacola, Florida. For many years he ran a home improvement business. He passed away in March of 2016 at the age of 93.[3] His goal of wanting all of his squadron-mates at Detachment Three at the Vinh Long Army Airfield to "come home" safely was achieved as no aircrew fatalities occurred during his watch as Office in Charge of the detachment. Furthermore, his detachment of airmen distinguished themselves with extraordinary bravery during the Viet Cong assault that had nearly overrun the base on January 31, 1968.

Captain Jacobs returned to the states, mostly recovered from the wounds he suffered at Cao Lanh on March 9. A little over a year later, on October 9, 1969, at a White House ceremony, Jacobs, for his extraordinary bravery on March 9, 1968 was awarded the Congressional Medal of Honor by President Nixon. During the next 15 years, he advanced his career with various assignments including serving on the faculty at West Point, instructing cadets in comparative politics and international relations. In 1980 he commanded the 4th Battalion, 10th Infantry Regiment at Fort Davis in the Canal Zone. After more than 20 years in the Army Jacobs retired in 1987 as a full bird colonel and entered the world of business, resulting in successes as a partner in real estate, investment banking, and equity.[4]

Presently Jacobs serves as an ambassador of the Medal of Honor Foundation and speaks to and supports veterans' causes throughout the country. However, he is mostly known for being a highly respected military analyst on one of the prime TV networks.

In 2011, Jacobs returned to Vietnam to visit the site of his 1968 ambush and speak with the retired Vietnamese general, Pham Phi Hung, who had been identified as the leader of that ambush. They discussed that fateful day with Jacobs learning that his South Vietnamese unit's patrol plans had been learned about from a VC spy at the ARVN provincial headquarters that resulted in the well-executed ambush that nearly led to his demise.[5]

During his visit to a field he discovered using old map coordinates, he was able to recognize the ambush area except that the field had been flooded and turned into a large fish farm. When asked by the interviewer, he excitedly recollected, "This is it, this is it. This was all open field back then." Then he recollected the moment his life changed. "The crack of rifle and machine-gun fire and the explosions, that one of them wounded me. You don't even hear it; it is so close—feel a rush of warm air and get lifted up. I was surprised, initially, and thought that it was a mistake. I wasn't supposed to be wounded; it always happens to someone else."[6] For Colonel Jacobs, it seemed to be a complex and emotional moment of rediscovery.

During Weseleskey's flight home, he was tired but felt relieved at having his Vietnam tour behind him and slept soundly. For nearly all Americans completing their Vietnam tours, the long flight home to CONUS gave time to reflect on the experience of having been at war, for good or bad. Arriving home in Virginia Beach for his planned 90 days of leave, Weseleskey had looked forward to a great family reunion with Sally and their four sons, who had already prepared for his arrival and his household concerns: homework assignments, yard work, and other help around the house. But he felt mentally and physically wasted and considered that his weight loss, which had taken him down to 128 pounds from his normal 175, might have resulted from more than simply flying combat missions up to his last day in country.

After a couple of days at home and while in the middle of unpacking his luggage, Wes suddenly felt dizzy and began to pass out. Seeing him in this unusual condition and fearful of losing her man after such a long and worrisome wait for him to return, Sally helped her groggy husband to the car and drove directly to the emergency room at NAS Oceana, where he was immediately placed on a gurney.

When Wes awakened, he found himself in Portsmouth Naval Hospital in the officers' ward on the 12th floor. The first things he noticed were the nurses, looking as dumbfounded as he was feeling. Surrounding his bed were trays of test kits, and there was an intravenous bottle and a translucent tube filled with a liquid hanging over his side with its needle taped into his forearm.

After several days of testing and questioning by hospital residents and inquisitive interns, there was still no diagnosis. Wes thought, "Did I become infected with the same bug as the one that had incapacitated my copilot Tom Crull (who had suffered from a debilitating case of amoebic dysentery) in January? God help me." Over the next few weeks and after batteries of tests conducted by the hospital staff, there seemed to be no consensus as to the nature of his condition, which although stabilized, had still not significantly improved. Nothing could fully explain his blood chemistry imbalance, wobbly-kneed weakness, and jaundiced eyes and skin.[7]

During the first week of his hospitalization at Portsmouth, an older man wearing hospital pajamas and a robe shuffled into his room. Without any prompting, he began sharing some of his combat experiences, including several wars and many battlefield campaigns. It was retired Lieutenant General William "Chesty" Puller, the most decorated Marine in the history of the Corps. During his active service, which spanned 34 years, he had earned four Navy Crosses, a Distinguished Service Medal and an array of other medals. Having retired in 1951, he felt some bitterness at not being allowed to volunteer for Vietnam. But the future had not yet revealed itself. Puller's son would be seriously wounded in Vietnam five months later, in early October 1968, losing both legs and fingers of one hand after stepping on a booby-trapped mine while leading a patrol of a platoon of marines.[8]

Chesty had earned the reputation as an aggressive fighter, a Marine's Marine. But as with Weseleskey, he had his share of critics too. It was at Peleliu in the Pacific during the week of September 15, 1944, that the 1st Marine Regiment of the 1st Marine Division, commanded by Puller, "lost 311 men killed and 1,438 wounded out of a total of 3,251."[9] He was not entirely blameless for the carnage, and a number of veterans and authors labeled Puller "a butcher" for what they considered to be a prematurely ordered direct assault on a heavily defended Japanese position on Umurbrogal Mountain.

After a few days of their exchanging sea stories, the staff locked the doors to Weseleskey's ward. Would-be visitors were then put on notice that he was "quarantined" and was to be kept in isolation. Day and night, more tests, including sonograms and "scopes" were performed on the former Seawolf pilot, but at a more frenetic pace. He might as well have been relocated to the laboratory.

After 18 days in the ward, there was finally a diagnosis: highly infectious gastrointestinal Shigella parasitic infection. Although awed by the complexity of his ailment's description, Weseleskey was greatly relieved to finally learn the nature of the bug that had been eating away at his organs.[10] He continued his struggle to survive and prayed that after having persevered through an entire year of sometimes life-threatening combat and near career-ending personal challenges, he would not now succumb to the powers of a mysterious microscopic bug.

Finally, with this revelation, the hospital's medical team prescribed for him mega doses of antibiotics, and within a week the symptoms of the former mystery disease began to moderate. Weseleskey began to regain some of his lost weight and stand on his feet without assistance. After another week of treatment, and being free of symptoms, he was able to return home to celebrate his delayed homecoming. It was on May 27 that he received his official discharge and change of duty orders from the hospital.[11]

With all the hospital time having consumed so much of his planned leave, he had much less time to spend with his family, but at least it was quality time, talking to his boys, going to the beach, barbecuing with some neighbors, and passing private moments with his wife. But when he started to receive phone calls from HS-1, demanding his presence at the training squadron to begin his new assignment, he reassembled his sea bag and personal belongings and before the Navy had the chance to cancel his orders, got on a plane to Key West to begin the next phase of his career.

Not long after his arrival and indoctrination at the Navy's premier fleet anti-submarine warfare training squadron, Weseleskey was eager to try to inspire Pentagon military leaders with an idea to set up a stateside training facility for helicopter pilots being sent to HA(L)3 in Vietnam. While immersed in his instructor duties, he reminisced about his old Vietnam-based squadron. He began to feel that something should be done to improve the training of UH-1 gunship pilots and enable the Navy to set up and structure the training within the Navy's command vis-à-vis that of the Army, which had custody of the UH-1 helicopters and great numbers of the most experienced pilots returning from the war zone. But now, with all the seasoned Seawolves returning to the States, there were certainly enough Navy aviation personnel available who were capable of training prospective combat aircrews, even though most of them wanted to put the year in Vietnam behind them.

Despite Weseleskey's mixed feelings about his own experience, he firmly believed in the future of the rapid-response, close air support of Navy attack helicopters. An article he had submitted earlier in the year, "The Seawolf Helo Pilots of Vietnam," published in the *U.S. Naval Institute Proceedings*,[12] stressed the value of the squadron's efforts and what it had accomplished for the Navy in Vietnam.

In February 1969, Weseleskey sent the Chief of Naval Operations a letter outlining his opinions encouraging the use of the close air support function of Navy attack helicopters.[13] One of its enclosures was a letter he had received in November 1968 from the commanding officer of Seal Team Two in Norfolk lending its support and endorsement for a Navy helicopter attack squadron to "be established within the Atlantic and Pacific fleets."[14] Considering the amount of support the Seawolves had provided to SEALs relying on them for rapid response during moments of extreme peril, Weseleskey expected that he would receive a return letter indicating interest. But none would arrive, thereby implying that the HA(L)3 Seawolves squadron would be a one-war phenomenon. Nevertheless, Weseleskey was glad that he had at least made an earnest effort to help his former squadron.

The HS-1 leadership, headed by Commanding Officer CDR. Robert E. Schock was pleased to have Weseleskey on board, an experienced aviator with an aviation safety background and recent service with HA(L)3 in Vietnam. They very much needed a pilot like him to be a productive member of their instructor team. And it was not unexpected that awards would be showing up to be presented to him. Still, they were greatly surprised at the numbers of awards being routed through to HS-1 for presentation to their new squadron member.

The first presentation took place at 1000 on July 15, 1968, in the large HS-1 hangar. The ceremony was a long one, as it coincided with the squadron's change of command. Standing at attention or parade rest for nearly two hours in the tropical heat and high humidity in the hangar, the squadron's personnel had to survive the obligatory uniform inspection, the change of command, and the presentation of awards to Weseleskey and to Lieutenant (junior grade) Martz and another recent Vietnam returnee, Personnelman Second Class Marlin S. Tarr. The presenter of the awards was the distinguished Rear Admiral Frederick J. Brush, Commander Fleet Air Key West.

Weseleskey, as were the other officers in his squadron, was wearing his highly starched dress white uniform, with its two-inch stiff collar covering his neck and propping his head up high. Admiral Brush recited the award citations for two Distinguished Flying Crosses for heroic flights, the 31st Air Medal for combat flights over hostile territory, and the Navy and Marine Corps Medal for his actions in helping to extinguish the flames consuming an Army helicopter.

Martz was awarded the Bronze Star (with "V" for valor) for helping to repulse the VC attackers at the Vinh Long Airfield during the first night of the Tet Offensive. Since both he and Maintenance Officer Bouchard had been chastised by the OINC for leaving the Seawolf bunker and taking the fight to the other side of the runway, where there was the heaviest concentration of enemy, it was Weseleskey as the Assistant OINC who held them in high esteem and wrote up their awards for the recognition they so deserved.

Within three weeks of this presentation, Weseleskey's HS-1 squadron-mates had to climb back into their formal whites and stand through another awards presentation and uniform inspection, which began to cause Weseleskey's popularity to fade. Since his final HA(L)3 Officer Fitness Report had been somewhat mediocre, it was to his pleasant surprise that Commander Spencer had decided (on May 7) to submit a recommendation along with powerfully persuasive witness documentation for a Navy Cross. When he was informed of it by the HS-1 command, it jolted his memory of the rescue experience. He thought of the wounded air crewmen flying in his wing-ship and sending them back to base alone as he felt compelled to carry out the rescue alone. But he still felt as convinced as ever that he did the right thing.

The award papers had been routed from HA(L)3 to the Commander in Chief Pacific Fleet, the Secretary of the Navy via the Chief of Naval

Operations, then for execution by the Chief of Naval Personnel. And in fulfillment of Navy Regulations, Commander Kamrad and his executive officer were obligated to locate a suitable presenter of flag rank. They were fortunate to have discovered that Rear Admiral Christensen, a former World War II submariner who had himself earned the Navy Cross for sinking a Japanese battleship in Tokyo Bay, was serving at Naval Base Key West.

During the Admiral's introduction by his Flag Secretary, Admiral Christensen's own citation was read to those in formation and to the onlookers, many who for the first time began to understand the rigors of a submariner's life and the sacrifices made by those volunteers that were repeatedly sent back out into the vast Pacific to face the mighty Japanese fleet.[15]

It was the first Friday in August, and even hotter than the July presentation, but at least it took place in the afternoon and the big benefit to be shared by everyone was that there was going to be early liberty that day. Still, it was a full-dress inspection this time with officers adorned with their swords at their sides. The hangar doors were kept open to enable the light breeze to waft through the open space.

In one corner of the hangar was a Soviet helicopter with Cuban markings, testament of Cuban servicemen escaping with their families to the welcome mat of America's most southern shore. In an opposite corner was a SH-3 Sea King ASW helicopter. On this day, the hangar was filled to capacity with the presence of the extra staff of the Admiral and the CAG staff in addition to the HS-1 and VS-30 personnel and their dependents. It was a "sea of white" with all the splendor of a school homecoming.

Standing at attention, Weseleskey was proud to be honored but also was aware of his good fortune in having survived numerous engagements with enemy fighters and being able to return home in one piece. His recent brush with the infectious parasite seemed now to have been just one more threat to his ability to remain alive.

His thoughts began to wander during the silent gaps between speeches, as is common when a serviceman is standing at attention or at parade rest. For many of those who are required to stand still during these formalities, it takes much effort and concentration not just to remain awake but to also avoid locking knees, thereby cutting off circulation and passing out. Weseleskey reflected on unforgettable images that haunted him: the faces of pilots and crews he knew so well, and of others with whom he had only chance encounters, who had not been lucky enough to make it back alive across the big pond. In particular, he recalled one of his fellow plebes at Valley Forge Military Academy in Pennsylvania: Bob Toal, now lying in repose at Arlington National Cemetery. His initial image was of them playing their brass instruments in synchrony during performances of the school band: Toal played the trumpet, Weseleskey, the tuba.

Major Robert Alonzo Toal, a career Army officer, was the American Advisory Team's operations officer at Vinh Long. While returning to his base on a dark road on January 6, 1968, after a day in the field with his ARVN troops, his small convoy was ambushed by a company of Viet Cong fighters. After a short firefight, Major Toal lay mortally wounded.

Weseleskey recalled his gunship fire-team scrambling in support of Toal's team of ARVNs, but by the time he got there, the skirmish had ended. It was over for the good major. At mid-morning the next day Weseleskey was summoned by the medic, Sergeant Slaughter, to identify his former schoolmate's remains shrouded in a rubber black bag in the bunker adjacent to the small infirmary, awaiting transportation to Long Binh, just outside of Saigon.

So now, during the minutes leading up to his medal presentation, he saw the haunting images of his friend's stone-cold body, his disfigured face, with bandages covering his right temple where the bullet had entered into his brain. It was obvious that the tape covering his head was placed there by the crafty enemy, to hide an explosive booby trap for the unwary. He recalled asking Slaughter for his personal effects: "Did you find his glasses? Did you find his snub-nosed .38?"[16] There was no answer to be had.

During the silent moment prior to the presentation, he thought to himself, "Why did Bob get nailed? Why did I have the good fortune to survive?" And finally, having a more positive thought as he was approached by the admiral, he thought, "Who was the Army guy whose life I saved six months ago on March 9?" For Weseleskey, this awards ceremony bordered on the surreal.[17]

Weseleskey's last medal presentation was for combat achievement during the first night of Tet. He received a Bronze Star with a V for valor, for the same action as Martz. Since he had also been scorned by the former OINC for not remaining at the Seawolf bunker, it was the Army people, who, appreciating his efforts at fighting the attackers, wrote him up for the medal. And since it was an Army medal, a senior Army officer had to drive to Key West from Miami in order to make the official presentation, the last one received by Weseleskey that was attributed to his service in Vietnam.

CHAPTER THIRTEEN

Retirement and Fulfillment

Admiral John Henry Towers Memorial Award: "For outstanding leadership and heroic performances during his Naval career."

Weseleskey receiving award for heroism and outstanding leadership at dinner. *Left to right:* C. J. Roberson, Brian Chase, Ed Olezeski, Author Shay, Wes, Matte Gache. (Author's photo)

After completing his instructor assignment at HS-1 as the officer remembered best for receiving the most medals while on board the command, Weseleskey went on to complete a successful Navy career.

He was finally able to put his Vietnam service into perspective. But it was not the case that the March 9 rescue mission would not reappear again many years later.

Weseleskey's next assignment was at the U.S. Naval Postgraduate School, where he earned a Master of Science Degree in Personnel Management. Weseleskey served as a detachment officer-in-charge and operations officer at Helicopter Combat Support Squadron Six (HC-6) from 1970 to 1972. He then was advanced at HC-6 to serve as executive officer, finally commanding the squadron from 1973 to 1974. At the time it was the largest helicopter squadron in the Navy. During his tenure, the squadron had 14 detachments, and the aircrews flew 12,000 accident-free hours. For this assignment, Weseleskey earned the Meritorious Service Medal.

From 1974 to 1976 Weseleskey was assigned as air officer on the USS *Tarawa*, LHA-1, during its construction in Pascagoula, Mississippi. From there he was transferred to the USS *Inchon*, LPH-12, where he served as its air officer—responsible for the largest department on this type of ship - during its deployment in the North Atlantic.

On June 1, 1978, Weseleskey received his promotion to captain. He was given command of the Navy's amphibious assault ship USS *Guam*, LPH-9, from 1980 to 82. This assignment proved to be a most challenging one, for he was given the ship as it was completing major repairs at the Philadelphia Naval Shipyard. On its first day out of the yard on its way to Norfolk, it broke down in the Philadelphia River, causing it to limp back for additional work. After a few more major breakdowns occurred that were publicized in the local Norfolk media, the *Guam* began to receive the attention and scrutiny of the local congressional representative, who considered it to be un-seaworthy.

Weseleskey was unfortunate in that more problems began to manifest themselves, impacting the ship's performance so that by the time the *Guam* steamed out of Norfolk for a three-month cruise to Northern Europe it had been considered by Virginia Congressman C. William Whitehurst as "marginally combat ready with major deficiencies."[1] In the interest of his district, Whitehurst would have preferred that the overhaul of the ship had been accomplished at the local Newport News Shipbuilding Company. He went on to call for a congressional investigation, describing the overhaul program as being so poor that it "poses grave questions about our country's ability to continue as a dominant seapower in the world."[2]

Once Weseleskey got out to sea, he would have sole responsibility for managing the ship, in spite of its earlier problems described in the media and despite the congressman's efforts at maligning its premature release from the shipyard. Predictably, this tour of duty did not go well for him, especially since the *Guam* was Amphibious Squadron Two's flagship and the task force commodore was not at all sympathetic to the new captain's ordeal in managing the ship. Commodore McCaffree was unmerciful in documenting his observations in Weseleskey's fitness report.[3]

As Commander Spencer had discovered 15 years earlier with HA(L)3, a commanding officer had no recourse but to try to manage with the sorry state of equipment he was issued. And, not unlike Spencer, Weseleskey had problems with personnel. Only one of 12 junior officers assigned was qualified as a senior watch officer. The operations officer was ordered in with a retirement date. Three of the LCDRs assigned had been previously passed over for commander. Finally, there were numerous gaps in important billets, including combat cargo officer and air boss. By the time his *Guam* command assignment was finished, Weseleskey's nearly impeccable record was tarnished, taking him out of the running for promotion to admiral.

This assignment was followed by a successful tour at the Military Personnel Command, for which he received his second Meritorious Service Medal. Weseleskey always considered that his major strength was looking after his people. During this period Wes also acted as Ombudsman of the Navy, during which time he was able to support the cohesiveness of Navy families and at the same time becoming an advocate for all service personnel.

Finishing up his 30-year career, Weseleskey served as Director of Navy Command Center at the Pentagon, which was classified as a flag assignment. Acting like a classified news editor, Wes was tasked with delivering morning briefings to the Secretary of the Navy, Chief of Naval Operations and other flag officers.

During this assignment from 1983 to 1985, it was a hectic period that was of heightened concern for the Armed Forces. On September 1, 1983, the Soviets shot down KAL 007 that had wandered off course, reigniting tensions of the Cold War. Less than two months later on October 23 (while the author was sitting at a café in Southampton, LI sipping coffee), the barracks housing American servicemen in Beirut, Lebanon was bombed, killing 241, mostly Marines. Two days later on October 25, acting to protect Americans from a hostile Marxist regime, President Reagan ordered the invasion of Grenada. Then, in the summer of 1984, there was a shock to the international community when more than a dozen ships were either damaged or sunk in the Red Sea at the approach to the Suez Canal, with Tehran's Supreme Leader Ayatollah Khomeini's regime bragging that its heavily influenced Islamic Jihad was responsible for all the terror at sea.

Needless to say, the near cataclysm of these events required constant vigilance on the part of the Navy and in the thick of it was reliable Wes Weseleskey, working to manage not only the Command Center staff but a reserve unit as well, that had been activated in support of all the ongoing cascading events. Often, feeling obligated, he practically lived at the center, catching short naps during intervals between crises. At some point, when Wes realized that the physical and mental demands of this assignment were increasing his anxiety levels and blood pressure he decided that it was time to hang it up and retire.

On his day of retirement on February 28, 1985, Wes was awarded the Legion of Merit for his exceptional performance of his assignment and his achievements while leading the Command Center staff during numerous crises.[4] His superior, Admiral James (Ace) Lyons (whose next assignment was Commander, U.S. Pacific Fleet), and other flag officers tried unsuccessfully to have him withdraw his retirement papers. But he knew when enough was enough and to leave the Navy while he was still in good health. Since Wes had been serving in the capacity of a flag officer, he was relieved of his assignment by a rear admiral.

After retiring back to his home in Virginia Beach, Weseleskey, thinking back to the early sixties when the Navy had lost two nuclear submarines, *Thresher* and *Scorpion*, and was caught off guard when it was discovered that few if any of the crews had prepared wills for their families, he decided to establish himself as a financial consultant to serve officers, sailors, and their families and next of kin. He managed to self-study and pass exams for the required licenses for financial planning.

Privately, and magnanimously, Wes expanded his interests in helping veterans who felt that they had been treated unjustly by the Veterans Administration or by the bureaucrats assigned to the myriad of different offices in DC. Several had difficulty in receiving benefits for injuries that occurred while on active duty. One of his most successful pursuits for adjudication was for a U.S. Marine who received a back-payment check for $156,000, plus a disability rating of 100% for an old combat-related injury.

While serving as Ombudsman Wes became very familiar with the workings of the Board for Corrections of Naval Records (BCNR), enabling him to pursue remedies for servicemen who felt that they had not received proper recognition for combat actions they felt worthy of awards. He was therefore cognizant of following specific procedures in doing investigative research and in locating long-lost eyewitnesses in order to compile a dossier to present corrected facts to awards boards. He helped veterans regardless whether they had served as Sailors, Marines, or Airmen. Awards pending as of 2017 include two Medals of Honor and one Silver Star.

After retirement Weseleskey worked as a financial consultant, providing services to many veteran friends and other people in his Virginian Beach community. He discovered how gratifying it could be to help others with their financial planning, and he enjoyed the social context of the work, meeting with his clients' relatives and friends.

Weseleskey occasionally wondered about his daring and controversial rescue mission, but he was never able to discover the name of the Army advisor he had rescued. And conversely, the advisor never knew who it was who had risked his own life and the lives of his crew, although he had been equally curious.

Amazingly, the Army advisor whom Weseleskey had rescued was discovered 34 years after the mission, not at an Army banquet, but at a Navy dinner in New York. While acting as master of ceremonies at a Naval Aviation Commandery dinner at the Seventh Regiment Armory in New York in the spring of 2002, the author was introduced to one of the evening's guest speakers, retired Colonel Jack Jacobs, serving on the board of the Medal of Honor Foundation and himself a recipient of the Medal of Honor.

Jacobs had been invited to the occasion by Bruce Whitman, one of the Commandery's board members (and a benefactor of the Medal of Honor Foundation), to present the Commandery's Admiral John Henry Towers Award to the evening's honoree, Navy Captain Richard O'Hanlon, who had just returned from a record-breaking cruise of 159 consecutive days at sea in the northern Arabian Sea, commanding the USS *Theodore Roosevelt*, CVN71, during Operation *Enduring Freedom*. At the dais, before presenting the award to O'Hanlon, retired Colonel Jacobs spoke to the audience modestly about himself, noting his somewhat shorter than average 5-foot-7 inches height, but not as though it were an impediment to his own accomplishments.

Colonel Jacobs wined and dined with the evening's guests and the Commandery membership, a flock of mostly aging Navy "flyboys." Just after hanging his glorious medal around his neck, Jacobs spoke with sincerity, saying, "Although I served in the Army and am here amidst a group of naval aviators, I don't feel the slightest bit out of place. As a matter of fact, I must tell you that I owe my life to the Navy Seawolf crew who saved my life in Vietnam after I had been wounded and who evacuated me to a nearby field hospital. If not for them, I wouldn't be alive today. I wish I knew who it was who flew that helicopter."

After the dinner ended, the author, introducing himself as a former Seawolf pilot, approached Jacobs, asked him for the date of the rescue, and promised an answer in a few days. Jacobs seemed eager to learn the rescuer's name. Without much difficulty, it was discovered that the pilot who had earned a Navy Cross on the same date, March 9, 1968, that Jacobs had earned his Medal of Honor was retired Navy Captain Allen E. Weseleskey.

A query was made to Weseleskey the following day. When he heard of the discovery, there was hoarseness in his voice. He was flabbergasted. He felt deeply relieved. After so many years had elapsed, he was again reminded of his successful mission and of the subsequent ordeal he had to wade through.

The members of the Commandery board recognized Weseleskey's accomplishment as an extraordinary one. Without giving it second thought, they decided that Weseleskey would be nominated for the

Admiral John Henry Towers Memorial Award for his outstanding leadership and heroic accomplishment.

On May 11, 2004, at the Seventh Regiment Armory site where the Naval Aviation Commandery had its meetings and dinners for the past 50 years, it almost seemed to be a repeat performance of Jacobs presenting the Towers award. But on this occasion, Jacobs was going to have the opportunity to extend his personal thanks to the man who risked the lives of himself and his crew, and who risked his reputation and career to proceed on a rescue mission that he himself had warned was going to be too dangerous to accomplish. It was going to be a rare moment indeed, as it almost never happens that rescuer and war casualty ever meet; the system was just not designed to be that way during wartime. It wasn't due to the lack of courtesy. It was because most rescues resulted from aircrews simply doing their jobs. It was purely professional, and "thank yous" were not part of the military equation, even in cases of extraordinary and daring feats.

In celebration of this moment of personal victory and redemption were more than three dozen of Weseleskey's friends and relatives and several Seawolf veterans. Also taking part in the ceremony via phone conference was former gunner Glenn Wilson, accompanied by several of his former aircrew pals at a Cottonwood, California post of the Veterans of Foreign Wars. Over many years, the loyalty of Wilson's former squadron-mates—Rick Meussner, Barry Waluda, Art Stoneking, and Dave Frazier—gave both hope and comfort to this man, suffering from a degenerative bone disease. Patched through over a phone in the armory dining room, Wilson asked one question to the man whom he last remembered cradling in his arms while the man lay crumpled in the cabin of a shot-up Huey trying to escape from a barrage of enemy fire. "Are you alright?"

This Commandery event was one of the most successful dinners in the past dozen years, with more than 100 guests attending. And, of course, Jacobs was not only accorded the opportunity to meet his rescuer but was able to express his gratitude during the award presentation in a more formal setting than at his hospital bedside in 1968. The plaque Weseleskey received was engraved with the following words:

Presented To: Captain Allen E. Weseleskey, United States Navy, Retired.

The Naval Aviation Commandery takes great pride in honoring Captain Weseleskey for his outstanding leadership and heroic performance during his naval career. After his second sea-duty tour, he volunteered to serve in the Republic of Vietnam with Helicopter Attack (Light) Squadron Three. During his one-year tour of duty he flew more than 400 combat missions, earning the Air Medal with 31 Strike/Flight Awards. Captain Weseleskey garnered respect and admiration as an officer who never hesitated from flying a mission, however hazardous. He was also honored with two Distinguished Flying Crosses, Bronze Star with Combat "V," the Purple Heart and the Navy–Marine Corps Medal. On 9 March 1968, he commanded one of the most heroic rescue missions of the Vietnam War. During this daring flight he saved the life of a severely wounded American Army Advisor. For his courageous and successful effort, he was awarded the Navy Cross. We thank and honor Captain Weseleskey for his contributions to Naval Aviation and for his personal sacrifices for America.

11 May 2004, Seventh Regiment Armory, New York

On April 29 and 30, 2005, nearly a year after he received the prestigious Naval Aviation Commandery award, Weseleskey's alma mater, the Valley Forge Military Academy in Wayne, Pennsylvania, held its annual home-coming for alumni from across the country. As one of its military heroes named on the school's Monument of Valor, Weseleskey was invited to be the guest speaker for the Alumni Memorial Chapel Service. It was to be conducted at the school's stately Memorial Chapel of Saint Cornelius the Centurion, located in the northwest corner of the main area and on the highest point of the rambling campus grounds.

This year was to be a special one for Weseleskey; it was the 50th anniversary of his graduation from the academy in 1955. For Sally, it was also special, as she recalled visiting him more than 50 years earlier during one of the academy homecomings as a very shy youngster from her small western Pennsylvania mining town.

They pulled into the main parking lot with their 40-foot mobile home and, as is customary when they travel, opened it to friends and other guests. The homey interior's living room is furnished like a family den, with emphasis on Wes's military career. His medals, Navy shoulder boards, ribbons, and earlier cadet mementos are prominently displayed in a glass case as you first enter, giving the appearance of a small museum.

On Saturday, the day of the service, the sky was lightly overcast yet bright as the sun rose to its high spring position. It drizzled lightly as it had been doing since the day of their arrival, but it did not dampen the spirits of the attendees. As Weseleskey walked with Sally arm in arm towards the chapel, he reminisced about such quiet, rainy, and calming days of his youth during which he would remain in his dorm and tend to his academic work, always striving to stay near the top of his class. The same pink-flowered dogwood trees had been in full bloom; the neatly manicured lawns had the same sweet smell; the extended families of northern cardinals repeated their "whoit, whoit, whoit, whoit," in series of eight repetitions.

At the entrance to the chapel, the cadet herald trumpeters were playing in tune with their songs to add to the pomp. Wes wore his cheerful blue pin-striped seersucker suit with a white, round, high-collared blouse, a style similar to the Navy's dress white uniform blouse. The formal procession of the colors preceded the National Anthem. Although Valley Forge is officially a nonsectarian institution, the chapel clearly pays homage to Christ, and the psalms recited by the Chaplain, Brigadier General Alfred Sanelli from the Class of '39, were of New Testament origin. And in the background was a large painting of Christ ascending to the sunlit heavens.

After his sermon addressed to the alumni, cadets, and guests, the academy's two-stanza Hymn Number 16 was sung. Notably, this hymn was called "Eternal Father, Strong to Save." Being also known as the Navy Hymn, the first stanza's words read:

> Eternal Father, strong to save,
> Whose arm hath bound the restless wave,
> Who biddest the mighty ocean deep
> Its own appointed limits keep;
> Oh, hear us when we cry to Thee,
> For those in peril on the sea!

It was by sheer chance the most appropriate introduction to Weseleskey's speech. As a career Navy officer and former band member, he knew the exact words and their meaning.

Chaplain Sanelli introduced Weseleskey as one of the school's proud heroes and noted to the audience Weseleskey's vast leadership skills and many moments of heroism, "be it on the ground or in the air."

Weseleskey stood erect at the dais before a wall of brass organ pipes that were hanging silently. He showed no hesitation in directing his words to the class of cadets, emphasizing the importance of succeeding in their education, learning technical skills, and becoming future leaders. Not only did he offer words of inspiration for the cadets to achieve success for their personal senses of accomplishment but also to contribute to sustaining America's esteemed position in the world. Poignantly, he reminded the cadets that their education and training at VFMA implied future leadership and would impose on them a sense of "noblesse oblige" which he had learned during his days of youth at the academy. For each of them, the die was cast.

Weseleskey reminisced about his own background at VFMA and how it helped him develop from a rejected "street person" living as the homeless son of a coal miner into a military hero, only because he had been inspired by a mentor who encouraged him to enroll at the school with a music scholarship. Weseleskey exhorted the alumni in the audience, "I challenge each of you to become a mentor, to reach out with your wisdom, experience, and knowledge – to give to others and to help them along the way."

Passionately, he looked into the eyes of the alumni seated in the chapel and said to them, "Give them [youths in need] some coattails; give them some spine, and give them the ethics, the morals, and sense of noblesse oblige that you all learned here. Give them back America, and give them the ultimate in striving for the best. That's your job and that's the challenge I give to you."

Weseleskey went on with his final words, saying, "I leave you with a thought. Take time to work; it is the price of success. Take time to think; it is the source of power. But for golly sakes, take time to play; it is the secret of perpetual youth. Take time to read; it is the foundation of wisdom. Take time to be friendly; it is the road to happiness. Take time to love and to be loved; it is the privilege of the Gods. Take time to share; life is too short to be selfish. Take time to laugh, for laughter is the mission of the soul. May your souls always be happy. God bless you all."

Weseleskey's speech was followed by a long round of applause. The service continued with "Ave Maria," the playing of Taps, and Valley Forge Military Academy's Hymn Number 98, "America the Beautiful."

Weseleskey, Sally, and Jack Jacobs meet at Naval Aviation Commandery dinner. (Author's photo)

Glenn Wilson 2006 at Seawolf reunion. (Author's photo)

Valley Forge Military Academy valor monument. (Author's photo)

Epilogue

When the first year of Helicopter Attack (Light) Squadron Three's operations in Vietnam was over, there would be a legacy of continuous struggle. There was a struggle for airworthy helicopters, a struggle for adequate replacement supplies, a struggle for fitting assignments for detachment officers, and, of course, a struggle to stay alive. Fortunately, the crews in the seven detachments, for the most part, remained focused and had the conviction and fortitude to successfully fulfill their mission.

Unfortunately, this illustrious first-of-its-kind, land-based combat helicopter squadron was destined to be short-lived, closing shop after being decommissioned (in Vietnam) in 1972 following not quite five years in operation. During its period of assignment, HA(L)3 personnel earned 5 Navy Crosses, 31 Silver Stars, 219 Distinguished Flying Crosses, 101 Bronze Star Medals, and 156 Purple Hearts.[1] The awards were shared equally amongst officers and enlisted. Forty-four of the squadron's members lost their lives.

Regrettably, neither in its infancy nor towards its end did the Navy assign for it a home base outside the war zone from which to draw well-trained pilots and aircrews. Instead, it was destined to be an "on the job training" assignment. Thus, nearly all of the squadron's assignees were shortchanged in being unable to enter the combat zone as well prepared as they should have been. And for a Navy deservedly proud of its outstanding ability to train its crews, it ignored the needs of this particular squadron. With the exception of receiving some basic training at Army schools at Fort Benning, Fort Rucker, and Fort Eustis for pilots and enlisted crews, the squadron personnel were sent into the war zone as trainees. In all likelihood, many of the unit's shortcomings could be traced back to a short-term view as to the value of such a land-based combat squadron, the paucity of available resources, and of course its competition for those scarce resources with the Navy's traditional sea-going forces.

If there was to be a legacy of this squadron that had accomplished so much in fulfilling its mission and in saving the lives of so many young men serving both in Navy and Army units, it would remain unfulfilled. Because the squadron's commanding officer felt justifiable animosity towards one of his charges, there would always remain a loss. The loss was not just a personal one for LCDR Weseleskey, but also a deeper one for CDR Spencer. In returning to CONUS with memories of his failed attempt to court-martial an officer and by withholding a recommendation for a Medal of Honor award, he inflicted a loss on the squadron that would have been the hallmark of his naval career. Squadron members would always receive back-patting kudos and toasts at their enlisted and officers' clubs, but never the full recognition they deserved had one of their men received the nation's highest award. After all, the Medal of Honor issued to one man would have actually been an award recognizing the squadron as a whole, and it would have been a symbol of all the squadron's efforts to succeed regardless of its neglect by the larger Navy. Furthermore, a Medal of Honor for Weseleskey would have highlighted the Vietnam War's legacy of inter-service dependency and cooperation between Army and Navy. It would most certainly have led to a continuity of squadron ideals for subsequent crews serving in this unique and highly distinctive organization.

Little more than a year after the Weseleskey medal controversy, there would be a similar incident but with a less successful outcome than Weseleskey's rescue. A Seawolf pilot attempted a daring rescue of a wounded American Marine in the operations area of the Nha Be Naval Base, home of HA(L)3 Detachment Two. Captain Clarence J. Wages was stationed there as both Senior Naval Advisor of Rung Sat Special Zone and Commander River Patrol Group 116.9. Unfortunately, during the rescue attempt, the Seawolf helicopter was brought down by enemy fire, which negated the attempt of LCDR Tommie Thompson to complete the rescue. Fortunately, the Marine survived, and there were no injuries aboard the aircraft. However, within a day, the HA(L)3 commanding officer initiated a JAG Manual investigation of the pilot for the aircraft loss.

Wages recalled being appalled by the recklessness, not of the pilot, but of the commanding officer's bold attempt to hold the pilot responsible. Since the Seawolf detachment OINC reported to Wages as an element of the latter's command, he unhesitatingly recommended to his reporting senior, Admiral Elmo Zumwalt Jr., then the commander of naval forces in Vietnam and the future Chief of Naval Operations, that the pilot be awarded a medal.[2] His intervention not only saved the officer's career but credited him with a heroic act and enabled him to be awarded the Distinguished Flying Cross. So this would be at least the second time a HA(L)3 commanding officer had displayed disapproval rather than approbation of an act of bravery of one of his charges.

Nevertheless, several of the squadron's later commanding officers did fight for their crews to be rewarded for their heroic accomplishments. Besides Weseleskey, there were four other Navy Cross recipients.[3] There was pilot Jim Walker, who made a dramatic rescue under heavy fire of a critically wounded sailor off the bow of a badly damaged small ship, a fuel lighter, upriver from Vinh Long Airfield in September 1968. There was helicopter crew chief Lloyd T. Williams, Jr., who ran across an open rice paddy while under heavy enemy fire to rescue badly wounded shipmates from a downed helicopter in April 1969. Pilot Robert E. Baratko, although his helicopter was badly damaged by enemy fire, was able to provide single aircraft coverage of medical evacuations of severely wounded personnel in September 1970. Lastly, there was a scruffy Seawolf gunner and lowest-ranking airman, Norm Stayton, who dove from his helicopter into a canal, with its surface covered by kerosene that was completely afire. Although wounded by enemy guns, after repeated attempts he was able to rescue a severely burned soldier.

Since the squadron lacked a home base in the United States, its leaders did not have the kind of political influence they would have had if there was a recognized squadron head available there. It is unfortunate that none of the squadron's Navy Cross recipients would receive the nation's highest award since each had deserved to be considered for it. Not surprising, all of these actions of valor were rescue missions. And not unlike Weseleskey's successful mission, these rescues also exposed the Seawolf crews to great danger. On a positive note, it seems that their reporting seniors had the fortitude and vision to refrain from instigating any court-martial proceedings against these men for placing the lives of their fellow aircrews in great peril.

The Department of the Navy had to make the critical choices regarding which sailor or Navy airman deserved the Medal of Honor. In a war with so many heroic accomplishments on the part of America's servicemen, it appeared that the combat heroics of the four other Seawolves would fall short of meeting the Navy's requirement that "there must be no margin of doubt or possibility of error in awarding this honor."[4]

Weseleskey would never receive the Medal of Honor that so many of his shipmates thought he deserved though it was not for lack of effort made in submitting upgrade proposals, both on the part of his former HA(L)3 copilot Tom Crull in 1998, who, years after his Vietnam tour, decided to try to set the record straight, and by the author of this work, in early 2003.

Crull mustered an assemblage of Weseleskey's former crews and shipmates familiar with the rescue incident and the June 1967 incident on the *Garrett County* LST, when Weseleskey was relieved of his OINC job for registering a complaint not in compliance with "chain of command" procedures. For an officer to be taken off such an assignment and placed at a desk in purgatory, would have indicated the termination of a career.

Crull's witnesses attested to Weseleskey's character, his loyalty, and his dedication to accomplishing the mission to which he was assigned.[5] Retired U.S. Navy Captain (then Lieutenant) Jimmy Glover was the detachment maintenance officer who testified that "The gun-ships were not safe to fly in combat...they were not receiving proper support for the quad M-60 machine guns." Glover also has stated his opinion that the animosity toward Weseleskey displayed "by the CO and his staff was so strong that it persisted throughout our tour in HA(L)3 and still exists today after 30 years...."[6]

After returning from R&R in Japan, Weseleskey, in a cheerful mood, got back to his flying routine on February 27. He flew every day through March 6, when a Detachment Five helicopter ditched at sea with no serious casualties. There had not been a fatal accident since Johnson's helicopter flew into the Bassac River on September 1, concluding a string of five fatal flying incidents beginning July 21.

This meant that there were six months of steadiness and stability at the squadron after such a difficult and painful start. In addition, the squadron received accolades from all over the Delta for its countless rescues and general contributions to the Navy's Game Warden mission. The detachment at Vinh Long even earned a Presidential Unit Citation, the highest unit award given during the war.

So after Weseleskey's March 9 heroic rescue mission, during which two crewmen were seriously wounded, it would appear that OINC Rosenthal's efforts at "maintaining an even keel" were thwarted, and by the man who had become Rosenthal's polarizing nemesis. And, of course, the same undercurrent of hostility existed at the headquarters level, both of which seemed to finally converge on Weseleskey. Head of maintenance LCDR Bouchard could never have been more clear-minded in his recommendation to Weseleskey to get letters of support and witness statements in order to defend his actions.

Rosenthal and Spencer accepted neither the heroic nature of Weseleskey's rescue mission nor its legitimacy. They seemed more comfortable with charging Weseleskey with unnecessary risk-taking of the lives of his crew, destruction of government property, and failure to follow standard operating procedures. They were furious. Furthermore, they held Weseleskey responsible for the wounded crewmen. As he had on many previous occasions, Weseleskey maintained his composure and with the help of junior pilot Crull, LCDR Bouchard, the witnesses arriving to drop off statements, the wounded Army advisor (of course) who unhesitatingly had the investigator escorted from his hospital room, and Sam Aydelotte, the administrative officer at the headquarters who had recommended against the court-martial action, the Article 32 investigation was quietly withdrawn.

Weseleskey's earlier Assistant OINC at Detachment One, and supporter of his effort at approaching the leadership in announcing the unsatisfactory aircraft status, LCDR Matte Gache, pointedly felt that Weseleskey had been unfairly treated by his superiors at HA(L)3, as "there is no doubt in my mind that the downgrading of this award was a result of this vendetta against Weseleskey because he rocked the boat..."[7]

Years later, looking at the mission from a more sober perspective and taking into account precedent-setting history as well as applying an understanding of decisions made during the stress of combat, retired Admiral Jerry Miller expressed his opinion with a thoughtful statement to the Secretary of the Navy in the author's letter to upgrade Weseleskey's Navy Cross to a Medal of Honor. In it he stated, "I strongly support the upgrade," considering that Weseleskey "is a man whose natural instincts place the rescue of others above his own safety, regardless of the odds against success."[8]

Miller further asserted that before jeopardizing the lives of his crew, "he (Weseleskey) polled them and got a 'roger' from all, announcing that he had an 'all-volunteer crew.'"[9] Not only did this demonstrate his leadership, it allowed the crew to feel that they were to be active participants in the mission.

Miller also recognized Weseleskey's ability as a pilot and, in consideration of the fact that the squadron was "not equipped with the best" helicopters, the Admiral felt that he deserved a Distinguished Flying Cross as well as a Medal of Honor.

In reviewing and considering the witness statements and other materials laid out before him, Admiral Miller seemed surprised that a court-martial had been considered. In his opinion, there should "absolutely not" have been a charge against Weseleskey for not accompanying his wingman back to base after his helicopter was hit by enemy fire. After all, "in combat, rules, regulations, and squadron doctrine are very suspect" and "in no way can a doctrine be devised that will cover all situations." He felt that "the risk to his wingman and crew appeared minimal compared to the situation being faced by the wounded in the firefight on the ground" and "they needed *immediate* help, which Weseleskey and his crew provided."[10]

Admiral Miller, having served during the Korean War, recalled the December 1950 incident in which Navy pilot Lieutenant (junior grade) Tom Hudner not only jeopardized his own life but destroyed his F4U Corsair fighter by crashing his plane in a futile attempt to save the life of his downed wingman, Jesse Brown.

Having been shot down by antiaircraft fire during a firing run in North Korea, Brown was forced to crash land his plane at the base of a snow-covered mountain. After Brown's hard wheels-up landing, Hudner observed him to be incapacitated but alive, trapped in the cockpit of his airplane, which was buckled by the impact of the crash, waving weakly for help. In an act reminiscent of Weseleskey's determination to save the Army advisors, Hudner, who avoided asking permission of his flight leader, radioed, "I'm going in" before crash landing his plane on a snowy hillside in an attempt to extricate Brown, which he was unable to do.[11]

Miller heard of the lively discussion by senior staff officers on the bridge of the Task Force 77 flagship following the news of Hudner's action. One senior officer wanted to court-martial Hudner, while the admiral on the bridge decided that Hudner deserved the Medal of Honor. And so it was, with Tom Hudner being revered ever since. In his statement to the Secretary of the Navy, Miller asserted that "Weseleskey's case is equal to or superior to that of Hudner in warranting CMOH recognition."[12]

Thus the decision was a subjective one, which Miller ascribes as "one of the weak aspects of the awards and medals program."[13] It appears that the HA(L)3 leadership at Vung Tau decided to exploit the wounds suffered by the two crewmen and the severe damage to the helicopters and try (at least initially) to put Weseleskey in the dock. But that would not happen.

Regardless of what CO Spencer and OINC Rosenthal felt about Weseleskey's aggressive flying, self-confidence, and proud demeanor or his focus on receiving the medals he deserved, the March 9 rescue mission in Cao Lanh warranted a fresh look, an objective eye, and an even hand. After all, Weseleskey's extraordinary act of bravery on this particular day was much more than had been expected of him but not less than he was willing to sacrifice.

Endnotes

Introduction

1. Zaffiri, *Westmoreland*, p. 245.
2. Ibid.
3. Ibid.
4. Ibid.
5. Kutler, *Encyclopedia of the Vietnam War*, p. 220.
6. Fall, *Street Without Joy*, p. 397.
7. Ibid.
8. Zaffiri, *Westmoreland*, p. 308.
9. Ibid, p. 375.
10. *Pacific Stars and Stripes*, February 12, 1968.
11. Ibid, February 13, 1968.
12. Ibid, February 14, 1968.
13. Ibid, February 18, 1968.
14. Ibid, February 19, 1968.
15. Ibid, March 6, 1968.
16. Pham Phi Hung, interview.
17. Collier, *Medal of Honor*.
18. Ibid, p. 235.

Chapter 1

1. Cutler, *Brown Water, Black Berets*, p. 159.
2. Game Warden Problems, p. 1.
3. Ibid, p. 2.
4. Game Warden Expansion.
5. Game Warden History, p. 4.
6. Spencer, Oral History.

Chapter 2

1. Weseleskey, interview (early life).
2. Ibid.
3. Ibid.
4. Weseleskey, email, June 6, 2017.
5. Ibid.
6. Aydelotte, interview.
7. Weseleskey, interview.
8. Ibid.
9. Naval message, February 21, 1967.
10. Ibid.
11. Weseleskey, Sally, interview, August 21, 2004.
12. Ibid.
13. Spencer, Oral History, November 1998.
14. Ibid.

Chapter 3

1. Weseleskey, OINC designation letter.
2. Spencer, Oral History, 1998.
3. Weseleskey, interview, June 26, 2004.
4. Ibid.
5. Spencer, email to author.
6. Weseleskey, DFC Citation, June 10, 1967.
7. Weseleskey, DFC Citation, June 20, 1967.

8. HA(L)3 Newsletter, Vol. 1, No. 1.
9. Spencer, email to author.
10. Ibid.
11. Weseleskey, interview.
12. Ibid.
13. Gache, interview.
14. Ibid.
15. Ibid.
16. Weseleskey, interview.
17. Naval message, June 28, 1967.
18. Weseleskey, interview.
19. Naval message, June 30, 1967.
20. Gache, interview.
21. Spencer, Oral History, 1998.
22. Spector, *After Tet*, p. 65.
23. Ibid.

Chapter 4

1. Gache, interview, July 27, 2004.
2. Weseleskey, interview, April 14, 2004.
3. *Wolfpack*. Vol. 1, No. 1, June 27, 1967.
4. Leaf, interview, July 17, 2004.
5. Gache, interview, October 23, 2006.
6. Leaf, interview, July 17, 2004.
7. Ibid.
8. Gache, email, June 23, 2004.
9. Gache, interview, July 11, 2004.
10. Leaf, interview, July 17, 2004.
11. Gache, email, June 23, 2004.
12. Leaf, interview, July 17, 2004.
13. Waluda/Meussner, interview, July 25, 2004.
14. Leaf, interview, July 17, 2004.
15. Martin, monograph, January 1968.
16. Gache, June 23, 2004.
17. Calamia, message, June 28, 2017.
18. Calamia, interview.
19. Leaf, interview, July 17, 2004.

20. Ibid.
21. Spencer, Oral History, 2000, p. 20.
22. Ibid.

Chapter 5

1. Weseleskey, interview.
2. *Naval Aviation News*, January 1967.
3. Aydelotte.
4. Ibid.
5. Weseleskey, interview.
6. HA(L)3 Message.
7. Weseleskey, interview.
8. Ibid.
9. Ibid.
10. Ibid.

Chapter 6

1. Aydelotte, interview, December 23, 2004.
2. Ibid.
3. HA(L)3 Roster, August 5, 1967.
4. Meussner/Waluda, interview, July 25, 2004.
5. Wright, interview, January 14, 2008.
6. Weseleskey, interview.
7. Aydelotte, interview, December 23, 2004.
8. Duncan, statement, January 12, 1968. Treanor, SS. 1st Lieutenant "Report of Proceedings, Collateral Investigation," January 5, 1968, 199th Aviation Co. San Francisco.
9. Stratton, statement, January 13, 1968.
10. Ibid.
11. Bradfield, statement, January 13, 1968.
12. Stratton, statement, January 13, 1968.

13. Weseleskey, statement, January 12, 1968.
14. Ibid.
15. Citation: Navy and Marine Corps Medal.

Chapter 7

1. Westmoreland, *Soldier Reports*, p. 318.
2. Ibid.
3. Ibid.
4. Ibid.
5. 716th MP Battalion website.
6. The future of this man from New York would be a life of PTSD suffering from guilt for abandoning his MP compatriots.
7. Prados, *Tet*, p. 161.
8. *The Twenty-Five Year Century*, p. 194.

Chapter 8

1. Weseleskey, interview.
2. Ibid.
3. Wilson, interview.
4. Rosenthal, interview.
5. Ibid.
6. Sheider, interview.
7. Miller, R., interview.
8. Morris, interview.
9. Williams, J., interview.
10. Maestas, interview.
11. Cahill, interview.
12. Schwaneback, interview.
13. Keller, interview.
14. Jones, interview.
15. Ibid.
16. Koenig, interview.
17. Ibid.
18. Ibid.
19. Ibid.
20. Farrell, interview.
21. Pickett, interview.
22. Williamson, interview.
23. Bouchard, interview.
24. Fields, interview.
25. Smith, interview.
26. Catling, interview.
27. Crull, interview.
28. Miller, E., interview.
29. Roberson, interview.
30. Ibid.
31. Ibid.
32. Williams, K., interview.
33. Ibid.
34. Wilson, interview.
35. Ibid.
36. Pham Phi Hung, interview.
37. Ibid.
38. Ibid.
39. Duong Van Ca, interview.
40. Pham Thanh Tu, interview.
41. Ibid.
42. Jim Williams, interview.
43. Ibid.
44. Ibid.
45. Cahill, interview.
46. Miller, R., interview.
47. Ibid.
48. Ibid.
49. Jones, interview.
50. Ibid.
51. Ibid.
52. Ibid.
53. Keller, J., interview.
54. Miller, E., interview.
55. Weseleskey, interview.
56. Rosenthal, interview.
57. Wilson, G., interview.
58. Ibid.
59. Ibid.
60. Weseleskey, interview.
61. Ibid.
62. Ibid.
63. Bouchard, interview.

64. Ibid.
65. Ibid.
66. Crull, interview.
67. Ibid.
68. Williamson, interview.
69. Farrell, interview.
70. Ibid.
71. Ibid.
72. Ken Williams, interview.
73. Ibid.
74. Ibid.
75. Ibid.
76. Ibid.
77. Roberson, interview.
78. Weseleskey, interview.
79. Ibid.
80. Ibid.
81. Ibid.
82. Farrell, interview.
83. Ibid.
84. Jones, interview.
85. Miller, R., interview.
86. Maestas, interview.
87. Oliva, interview.
88. Roberson, interview.
89. Pickett, interview.
90. Schwanebeck, interview.
91. Cahill, interview.
92. Weseleskey, interview.
93. Pickett, interview.
94. Crull, interview.
95. Bouchard, interview.
96. Catling, interview.
97. Weseleskey, interview.
98. Ibid.
99. Spencer, interview.
100. Ibid.
101. Ibid.
102. Pham Phi Hung, interview.
103. Colonel Duong Van Ca, interview.
104. Rosenthal, interview.
105. Dept. of the Army, 13th Combat Aviation Battalion Action Summary, April 19, 1968.
106. Weseleskey, interview.
107. Spencer, interview.
108. Spencer: Bronze Star Medal Citation.
109. Weseleskey, interview.
110. Aviators Flight Log Book (Weseleskey).
111. Weseleskey, letter to Sally from Tokyo, February 1968.

Chapter 9

1. Tom Buckley, *Reporting Vietnam*, p. 242.
2. Sister Joan Gormley, interview.
3. Pham Phi Hung, interview.
4. Sister Mary Hayden, interview.
5. Ibid.
6. Ibid.
7. Sister Joan Gormley, interview.
8. Joe Bouchard, interview.
9. Weseleskey, interview.
10. Robin Miller, interview.
11. Pham Phi Hung, interview.
12. Robin Miller, interview.
13. Sister Joan Gormley, interview.
14. Sister Mary Hayden, interview.
15. Sister Joan Gormley, interview.
16. Sister Mary Hayden, interview.
17. Ibid.
18. Bay Nguyen, Go Vap, June 20, 2002, interview.
19. Mrs Anh, interview.
20. Mrs Bay, interview.
21. USAF, email.
22. Colonel Stuart Hughes, interview.
23. Mrs Bay, interview.

24. Ibid.
25. Air Force Command Center Duty Log.

Chapter 10

1. Huchthausen, statement.
2. Jacobs, interview.
3. Pham Phi Hung, interview.
4. Weseleskey, interview.
5. Lewis, statement.
6. Jacobs, interview.
7. Weseleskey, interview.
8. Jacobs, interview.
9. Ibid.
10. Weseleskey, interview.
11. Ibid.
12. Jacobs, interview.
13. Conklin, interview.
14. Ibid.
15. Weseleskey, interview.
16. Ibid.
17. Huchthausen, interview.
18. Ibid.
19. Wilson, interview.
20. Ibid.
21. Weseleskey, interview.
22. Kenton, interview.
23. Weseleskey, interview.
24. Jacobs, interview.
25. Weseleskey, interview.
26. Pham Phi Hung, interview.
27. Kenton, statement.
28. Weseleskey, interview.
29. Wilson, interview.
30. Jacobs, interview.
31. Wilson, interview.
32. Weseleskey, interview.
33. Wilson, interview.
34. Ibid.
35. Weseleskey, interview.
36. Jacobs, interview.
37. Pham Phi Hung, interview.
38. Jacobs, interview.
39. Wilson, interview.
40. Ibid.
41. Weseleskey, interview.

Chapter 11

1. Catling, interview, April 22, 2006.
2. Miller, E., interview, August 12, 2006.
3. Catling, interview, April 22, 2006.
4. Miller, E., interview, August 12, 2006.
5. Przbyszewski, interview, August 20, 2006.
6. Miller, E., interview, August 12, 2006.
7. Conklin, interview, November 10, 2002.
8. Catling, interview.
9. Bouchard, interview.
10. Miller, E., interview, August 12, 2006.
11. Weseleskey.
12. Ibid.
13. Rosenthal, interview, May 12, 2006.
14. Crull, email, April 30, 2007.
15. Bouchard, interview.
16. Ibid.
17. Ibid.
18. Crull, email, April 30, 2007.
19. Roberson, interview, October 13, 1998 statement.
20. Weseleskey, interview.
21. Bouchard, interview.
22. Weseleskey.
23. Crull, April 30, 2007.
24. Weseleskey, interview.
25. Miller, E., interview.
26. Spencer had no recollection of Mackey visit.

27. Jacobs, interview, September 22, 2002.
28. Ibid.
29. Ibid.

Chapter 12

1. Weseleskey.
2. Spencer, interview.
3. Rosenthal Obituary, Pensacola News Journal, March 15, 2016.
4. Jacobs, Century, *If Not Now, When.*
5. Jacobs, interview, October 13, 2017.
6. NBC Nightly News broadcast, June 5, 2011.
7. Weseleskey, email, August 5, 2007.
8. Puller, *Fortunate Son.*
9. *U.S. Naval Institute Proceedings*, November 2002.
10. Weseleskey, email, May 8, 2007.
11. BUPERS order.
12. *U.S. Naval Institute Proceedings.*
13. SEAL Team One letter.
14. *Outpost*, Key West.
15. Weseleskey, email, May 19, 2007.
16. Ibid.
17. Ibid.

Chapter 13

1. Weseleskey, interview.
2. Ibid.
3. Ibid.
4. Ibid.

Epilogue

1. Seawolf Association website history.
2. Wages, Clarence J., Oral History.
3. Seawolf Association website history.
4. U.S. Navy Medal of Honor instruction.
5. Tom Crull's medal upgrade, October 6, 1998.
6. Glover, letter to Tom Crull.
7. Gache, email to author.
8. Retired Vice Admiral Jerry Miller, statement.
9. Ibid.
10. Ibid.
11. Ibid.
12. Ibid.
13. Ibid.

Acknowledgements

I especially wish to thank the many witnesses who provided statements of their individual actions and also rallied behind the story, for making significant contributions to this body of work. Captain Tom Crull (USNR, Retired) of Texas provided a great number of leads, photographs, and items of personal information and was unwavering in his support. Being closely acquainted with the subject of this story, he was always available to listen to and to comment on many of my ideas.

The subject of this story and his wife Sally sent me a trove of information, including flight logbook copies, medal write-ups, photos, personal letters, poems, and other related materials. Captain Weseleskey was aware that I was not acting as his publicity agent, and he had the fortitude to give me leeway and not press any issues he might have had on his mind.

I also express my deep gratitude to Commander Dave Winkler of the Naval Historical Foundation, who gave me my training wheels by allowing me to write several oral histories, including one of HA(L)3 Commanding Officer Captain Robert Spencer, for his fine organization.

Always keeping in mind during my interviews the cliché, "the fog of war," at first I had reservations about the truthfulness of some statements being thrown at me. But only in rare instances during my 40-plus interviews was I able to prove details incorrect. If I felt that they were not credible, and not able to be confirmed, out of respect for the reader, I omitted them. However, I was truly impressed by how many stories, seemingly fictional, fit in neatly with the stories of others. Yes. Memories do fade with the passage of time. However, in this wartime biography and chronology of events, there appeared to be a higher degree of memory retention than I had ever expected. The many Army and Navy veterans proved this to me during the interviews, and I must apologize if at times I pressed hard for clarification of details.

I thank my good friend John Heine, whose Vietnam experience as a marine helicopter pilot serving during the Tet Offensive and whose grammar expertise gave him the ability to advise me on the proper sequences of events, and at the same time do some preliminary editing.

I also owe a deep debt of gratitude to Mark Flanigan (Captain, USNR, retired) who in retirement is as sharp as I imagined him to be as a teacher of English at Hunter College and while he was assistant dean at Columbia College during his days in New York. Doing some critical editing for me, I realized that he had become a mentor, and he was instrumental at affording me a perceptive reader's eye from which to judge my manuscript.

In preparation for my trip to Thailand to interview two of the life-long dedicated Good Shepherd Sisters, Joan Gormley and Mary Hayden, who had been caring for their young charges in Vinh Long during Tet, I want to thank both retired Lieutenant Colonel Robin Miller and retired Colonel Lee Sheider, of the U.S. Army, who were thoughtful and kind enough to have made introductions for me. And of course the sincere hospitality extended to me in Nong Khai at the Village Vocational Training Center for young women enabled me to hear firsthand the Sisters' compelling stories.

I thank many individuals from the Socialist Republic of Vietnam for their hospitality during my visits and the courtesies extended to me by the staff at the Ho Chi Minh City External Affairs Bureau. The consular official in Washington, DC, Mr. Nguyen Vu Tu, helped me avoid a great deal of red tape by introducing me to Mr. Nguyen Hoang Phuong during my first trip to Vietnam, and to Ms. Le Mai Huong during my second, which included a visit to the former Vinh Long Army Airfield, now a Vietnamese Army base. In addition, the veterans I interviewed at the local veterans' center in Vinh Long, although not accustomed to dealing with American veterans, were courteous and direct in answering my questions.

Also, it is regrettable that Vice Admiral Gerald E. Miller (USN, retired), having believed in the fascinating story of the subject and having assisted me in my medal upgrade petition (which was denied) to the Department of the Navy, and who deserves a special place in my heart for being a prime source of my inspiration, will not be able to see my finished work as he passed away in 2014.

Finally, to Weseleskey's fellow alumnus of Valley Forge Military Academy, Greg Oviatt, who has 40 years of experience in publishing, I give great credit to for guiding me through the publishing process and for introducing me to international Casemate Publishers, the perfect choice for publishing and distributing my book through their vast network of dealers and military enthusiasts.

Retired Vietnamese General Pham Phi Hung. (Author's photo)

Monument at Vinh Long in tribute to Viet Cong lives lost during Tet Offensive. (Author's photo)

Glossary

ACRAC. Aviation Cadet Recreational Activity Club.

AD (A-1) SKYRAIDER. Fixed-wing single-engine, single seat propeller-driven attack aircraft that first saw service in the late 1940s. It carried a large payload of munitions and could also be fitted for electronic surveillance missions.

ADJC. Aviation Machinist's Mate (Jet Engine) Chief Petty Officer.

AH1G. Bell Helicopter's Huey Cobra attack helicopter.

AK47. Russian made high quality automatic rifle.

ARVN. Army of the Republic of Vietnam.

ASW. Antisubmarine warfare that includes operations by ships, submarines and aircraft.

ARC LIGHT. Code name used to designate high altitude B-52 missions using accurate radar signals.

ARTICLE 32. "In military legal practice, a pretrial proceeding often compared to a civilian pretrial hearing, roughly the military analogue of a grand jury proceeding, except open, without the civilian grand jury's secrecy. A general court martial must be preceded by an Article 32. The government must present sufficient evidence to convince an investigating (presiding) officer that an offense has been committed and that the accused committed it. Following the Article 32, the investigating officer submits a report to the convening authority, recommending the further disposition of the case, if any. The recommendation does not bind the convening authority." Solis, Son Thang, p. 315.

BROWNING RIFLE. Also known as the BAR; a reliable heavy duty rifle first used by the U.S. Army in 1918.

BUNO. Aircraft bureau number assigned to an aircraft.

BUPERS. Bureau of Naval Personnel.

B-52D STRATOFORTRESS. Big belly bomb bays held 84–500 lb. bombs or 42–750 lb. bombs.

BIRD DOG. Single engine, high wing Cessna O-1 aircraft used by the Army and Air Force both as observation aircraft and by forward air controllers for artillery spotting.

BRONZE STAR. Medal for bravery usually issued with combat V device.

BUG SHIP TACTICS. Helicopter night time tactics using high intensity lighting to discover enemy movement.

CAG. Carrier air group commander.

CARIBOU C-7. Twin-engine short take-off and landing fixed wing aircraft.

CELLS. Flights of B-52s comprised of 3 aircraft flying in V-shaped formation.

CIC. Combat Information Center.

CINCPAC. Commander in Chief Pacific Fleet.

CO CHIEN RIVER. One of the three downstream branches of the Mekong River.

COBRAS. Platoon name for 114th AHC located at Vinh Long Army Airfield.

CON THIEN. U.S. Marine combat base near the DMZ that was involved in protracted battles during 1967–68.

COMNAVFORV. Commander naval forces Vietnam.

COMNAVSUPPACT. Commander Naval Support Activity.

COMPHIBTRAPAC. Commander Amphibious Training Command Pacific area.

COMRIVRON. Commander Coastal Riverine Force.

CONEX BOX. Continental Exchange corrugated shipping containers reused for storage.

CONUS. Continental United States.

CTF116. Commander Task Force 116; River Patrol Force that included numerous combat entities serving in Vietnam.

CUMSHAW. The "mysterious acquisition" of materials or equipment/gear not usually available through normal supply channels.

CVA. Attack aircraft carrier.

CYCLIC CONTROL. Metal rod protruding from helicopter deck held by the pilot and used for controlling aircraft by tilting the rotor head.

DA FORM 2404. Equipment Inspection & Maintenance Worksheet.

DISTINGUISHE FLYING CROSS. Medal for heroism issued to aircraft crewmen.

DONG. Lowest unit of Vietnamese currency, in 1968, each valued in at 0.8 cents

DONUT DOLLY. Female Red Cross volunteer.

DUNG ISLAND. Small Island with difficult terrain where the Bassac River enters into the South China Sea.

DUSTOFF UH-1D. Rescue helicopter, usually designated with a red cross on side of aircraft.

EM CLUB. Enlisted Men's club for food and drink.

F-4U. Corsair maneuverable gull winged fighter/bomber used in World War II and Korean War.

FAA. Federal Aviation Administration.

FAC. Forward air controller.

FIREFIGHT. Exchange of small arms fire between opposing forces.

FLEET ANGELS. Helicopter rescue helicopters flown off aircraft carriers.

FLYING SQUIRRELS. Nickname used by Seawolves Detachment 4 prior to establishment of HA(L)3.

FREE FIRE ZONE. Geographic area in which requirements for permission to engage suspected enemy targets were waived, but which was often modified by local commands in order to prevent unnecessary civilian casualties.

FUEL LIGHTER. Special purpose support barge providing fuel for navy river units.

GCA. Ground controlled approach to airfield runway.

GAME WARDEN. Naval force employed to interdict movements of enemy personnel and supplies.

GARRETT COUNTY LST 786. Former 300' World War II naval vessel used to house and support riverine units and often located in the center of large rivers.

GEMINI 12. Space mission in the early 1960s.

GRIPE. Aircraft mechanical problem, usually defined as up or down, indicating whether it can be flown before being repaired.

HC-1. Helicopter Combat Support Squadron One.

HU-1. Helicopter Utility Squadron; predecessor or HC-1.

HMX1. Marine presidential helicopter squadron.

HS-1. Helicopter replacement pilot training squadron located in Key West, Florida.

HS-3. Helicopter Anti-Submarine Warfare squadron located in Norfolk, VA.

HS-11. Helicopter Anti-Submarine Warfare squadron located at Quonset Point and providing helicopters aboard USS *Wasp* on space mission recoveries.

HARNETT COUNTY LST 821. Former World War II naval vessel assigned to one of the Mekong Rivers.

HOOCH/HOOTCH. House, living quarters, or hut.

HUNTERDON COUNTY LST 838. Former World War II naval vessel assigned to one of the Mekong Rivers.

JAG MANUAL. Judge Advocate General legal manual.

JEWISH WAR VETERANS. Oldest American veterans' organization.

JP4. Jet engine fuel that is volatile and having a low flashpoint.

KHE SANH. Marine Corps firebase located in northwest sector of South Vietnam surrounded by hills and encamped NVA artillery divisions similar to Dien Bien Phu.

LPH. Landing Platform Helicopter naval ship.

LST. Landing Ship Tank.

LZ. Landing zone.

LANCERS. Gunship platoon of 114th Aviation Company.

LIGHT FIRETEAM. Two UH-1 gunship helicopters flying as a team.

LOAN TOAN SECRET ZONE. Area off Co Chien River that is home to VC guerillas.

M14 RIFLE. Standard issue Army automatic rifle that fired 7–62 mm rounds.

M-60. Machine gun used by helicopter door gunners that fired 7.62 mm ammunition.

M79 GRENADE. A 40mm explosive projectile launched from a short barrel rifle.

MACV. Military Assistance Command Vietnam.

MAE WEST LIFE PRESERVER. Life preserver with two inflatable air bladders.

MASH. Mobile Army Surgical Hospital.

MAVERICKS. Nickname for Army 175th Assault Helicopter Company gunship platoon.

MEDAL OF HONOR (CMOH). Highest individual award for heroism, presented by the President of the United States.

MEDCAP. Medical Civic Action Program.

MEDEVAC. Medical evacuation in Vietnam, usually by UH-1 helicopter.

MK82 BOMB. General purpose high explosive 500 lb bomb.

MUST. Self-contained medical unit, transportable, in Vietnam.

NAVFORV. Naval Forces Vietnam.

NLF. National Liberation Front.

NVA. North Vietnamese Army.

Ni CO (Vietnamese). Buddhist nun.

NOBLESSE OBLIGE. Social responsibilities that result from power or prestige.

NORTH VIETNAM. Democratic Republic of Vietnam.

OINC (OIC). Officer in Charge.

OUTLAWS UH-1D. Slick troop transport platoon, component of 175th AHC.

PBR. Patrol Boat River. 32 foot armed naval speed boat with fiberglass hull.

PSP. Perforated steel plating.

PTSD. Post Traumatic Stress Syndrome.

PINNACLE. Air Force parlance for the highest level of secrecy.

PLANK OWNER. An individual who was a member of a ship or squadron's crew when the unit received its commissioning.

PLATOON. Military ground unit comprising approximately 50 men.

PRESIDENTIAL UNIT CITATION. Highest award issued to military units.

PUFF THE MAGIC DRAGON C 47. Twin engine aircraft fitted with Gatling machine guns and able to direct a constant stream of rounds at enemy positions.

QUONSET HUT. Long semi-circular shaped building with rounded corrugated metal roof, often used as a barracks.

RF. Regional Force South Vietnamese armed troops.

R&R. Rest and Recreation. Five day vacation taken during one-year tour of combat duty, usually at Asian cities such as Tokyo, Bangkok, Taipei, Singapore, Penang, and occasionally at Sydney.

RED KNIGHTS UH-1D. Transport platoon, division of 114th AHC.

ROWELL'S RATS. Nickname for Seawolves' Detachment Three prior to the establishment of HA(L)3.

R5D- (DC-4). Four engine transport aircraft used by the Navy until 1975.

RUNG SAT SPECIAL ZONE. An area south east of Saigon, also known as Forest of Assassins, that was comprised of mangroves, swamps, and marshes from which the Viet Cong guerillas staged attacks on the main shipping channel that provided transportation of supplies from the South China Sea to MACV.

SAINT CORNELIUS THE CENTURION. Pagan Roman army officer who was the first known Gentile to convert to Christianity.

SCUTTLEBUTT. Rumors spread while sailors gathered around the drinking fountain.

SEAL. Sea Air Land navy commando.

SECDEF. Secretary of Defense.

SERE SCHOOL. Survival, Evasion, Resistance, Escape training school.

SOP. Standard Operating Procedure.

SHORT TIMER. American combatant usually with fewer than 30 days of tour of duty remaining.

SLICK UH-1D. Transport helicopter.

SPC4, SPC5. Specialist rank for junior Army personnel.

SPOOKY. Douglas AC-47 twin engine aircraft armed with 24,000 rounds of 7.62 mm ammo dispensed by machine guns providing devastating firepower on a localized area.

STRATOFORTRESS. Boeing B-52 eight engine long range, high altitude bomber, capable of delivering up to 70,000 lbs. of ordnance with precise accuracy.

STRIKER. Enlisted serviceman in training for a specific technical rating.

STOL. Aircraft considered to be able to take off and land on short airfields or improvised landing areas.

TAD. For Navy/Marine personnel, temporary additional duty, while For Air Force, TDY.

TOC. Tactical operations center.

TARMAC. Short for tarmacadam, a material usually comprised of sand, gravel, and an oil sealer; used as a ground cover.

TET MAU THAN. Year of the Monkey; Lunar New Year 1968.

TOMB OF THE UNKNOWNS. Arlington National Cemetery tomb for remains of unknown soldiers.

UH-1. Iroquois ("Huey") single engine helicopter developed by Bell for the U.S. Army in the early 1960s. Several models were manufactured, enabling it to carry troops or be used in a combat configuration. Standard armament for the early version was the XM-16 system comprised of twin machine guns on each side of the helicopter and pods bearing 7 rockets each, also on each side of the helicopter. When fully loaded with its armament and crew of four, including two door gunners each manning a M-16 machine gun, it became airborne at its maximum gross weight if not exceeding it.

UH-1B BRAVO IROQUOIS. Second model in the series of Huey aircraft.

UH-1C CHARLIE. Successor to UH-1B.

UH-1D MODEL. Huey designed with large cabin to accommodate troops and medical litters.

VIET MINH. Vietnamese Independence League; nationalist organization founded by Ho Chi Minh.

WHITE KNIGHTS. Transport platoon of 114th AHC.

XM-16 UH-1. Armament system.

YELLOW SHEET. Navy aircraft maintenance record keeping system.

12.7 MM. Ammo cartridge for heavy machine gun of similar size to .50 caliber.

83rd MEDICAL DETACHMENT UNIT. Component of 114th AHC.

114th AHC. Assault Helicopter Company assigned to Vinh Long Airfield.

175th AHC. Assigned to Vinh Long Airfield.

611th TRANSPORTATION COMPANY. Maintenance unit, component of 114th AHC.

716th MP BATTALION. Military police unit assigned to Saigon.

816th VC BATTALION. Viet Cong unit assigned to Vinh Long/Sadec area of operations.

Bibliography

Braestrup, Peter. *Big Story* (California: Presidio Press, 1994)

Buckley, Tom. *Profile of General Loan: 1971* (New York: *Harper's Magazine*, April 1972**)**

Collier, Peter. *Medal of Honor* (New York: Artisan, 2003)

Cutler, Thomas J. *Brownwater, Black Berets* (Annapolis: USNI, 1988)

Fall, Bernard B. *Street Without Joy* (Pennsylvania: Stackpole Books, 1961)

Good Shepherd Sisters. *Annals* (2000)

Jacobs, Colonel Jack and Douglas Century. *If Not Now, When?* (New York: Berkeley Caliber, 2008)

Jordan, Kenneth N. *Men of Honor* (Atglen, Pennsylvania: Schiffer Military History, 1997)

Kutler, Stanley I. *Encyclopedia of the Vietnam War* (New York: Charles Scribner's Sons. Simon & Schuster Macmillan, 1996)

Lam Quang Thi. *The Twenty Five Year Century* (Texas: University of North Texas Press, 2001)

Mao Tse-Tung. *Mao Tse-Tung. Selected Works, Volume Two, 1937–1938* (New York: International Publishers, 1954)

McNamara, Robert S. *In Retrospect* (New York: Random House, 1995)

Moore, Captain John E. *Janes Fighting Ships* (New York: Franklin Watts, 1975)

Myerson, Harvey. *Vinh Long* (Boston: Houghton Mifflin Company, 1970)

Nguyen Khac Can and Pham Viet Thuc. *Vietnam Cuoc Chien 1858–1975* (Hanoi, 2000)

Prados, John. *The Warning That Left Something to Chance: Intelligence at Tet. The Tet Offensive* (Connecticut: Praeger Publishers, 1996)

Puller, Lewis B Jr. *Fortunate Son* (New York: Grove Weidenfeld, 1991)

Reporting Vietnam. (New York: Literary Classics of the United States, 1998)

Spector, Ronald H. *Tet, The Bloodiest Year in Vietnam* (New York: The Free Press, Div. of Macmillan, 1993)

Stibbens, Steve and the 114th Aviation Company Association. *Knights over the Delta* (United States: 114th Avn. Co. Assoc. 2002)

Westmoreland, William C. *A Soldier Reports* (New York: Da Capo Press, 1976, 1980)

Zaffiri, Samuel. *Westmoreland* (New York: William Morrow & Co., Inc., 1994)

Other Publications

Key Outpost, Naval Station, Key West, Florida. July 19, 1968.
Naval Aviation News, January 1967.
Pacific Stars and Stripes, February 12, 1968.
NBC Nightly News, You Tube "Journey to Vietnam; A War Veteran's Return" June
    15, 2011.

Articles and Other Write-Ups

Bell, Garnet "Bill." Lt Colonel Charles A. Beckwith, "An Unforgettable Character."
Crull, Tom. Medal Upgrade. October 6, 1998.
SEAL Team Two, CO to HS-1, Weseleskey. November 21, 1968.
Sprinkle, James D. "HELATKLTRON THREE, The Seawolves" *Journal American
    Aviation Historical Society,* Winter, 1988.
Weseleskey, A. E., Weseleskey to CNO. February 12, 1969.
Weseleskey, A. E. "The Seawolf" Helo Pilots of Vietnam. Maryland, *United States
    Naval Institute Proceedings,* May 1968.
Wolfpack. Vung Tau, RVN. Volume No. 1, June 27, 1967.

Author Interviews

U.S. Navy

Aydelotte, Sam. January 21, 2005.
Bacanscas, Al. August 2004.
Bouchard, Joseph, Cdr. USN. October 16, 2002.
Calamia, Joseph. July 13, 2004.
Capozzi, Dave. October 19, 2003.
Catling, Jim. April 22, 2006.
Conklin, Tom. 2006.
Crull, Tom. September 9, 2003.
Farrell, Jimmy. June 12, 2005.
Fields, Chuck. September 9, 15 2003.
Gache, Matte. June 21, 2004, July 23, 2004, October 6, 1998 (statement Crull), June
    2, 7, 2007.
Hughes, Stuart, Lt. Col. USAF. April 7, 2001.
Leaf, Doug. July 17, 2004.
Miller, Everett. 2006.
Miller, Jerry. Statement. February 19, 2003.
Olezeski, Tom. July 13, 2007.
Pickett. March 28, 2005.
Przbyszewski, Vince. August 22, 2006.
Roberson, C. J. May 4, 2004. (Courtesy of Weseleskey, A. E.)

Rosenthal, Eugene. May 12, 2006; April 21, 2007. DOB 1/29/23. (Two days before Tet 1968)

Smith, Fred. October 22, 2003.

Spencer, Robert. August 12, October 6, 15, 2002; June 28, 2003; December 13, 2004; August 14, September 6, 2006.

Wages, Jerry. October 20, 2002.

Weseleskey, A. E. February 29 2004; March 9, 2004; February 9, 2004; June 29, 2004; January 2, 2005; August 21, 2005; May 8, 2007.

Weseleskey, Sally. August 21, 2004.

Williams, Ken. 2003.

Williamson, Jack. June 1, 2003.

Wilson, Glen. September 18, 2003.

U.S. Army

Cahill, James. August 19, 2003.

Coonley, Paul. In Person.

Edert, Norbert., August 18, 2003.

Jacobs, Jack. September 12, 2002; Oct. 13, 2017.

Jones, Buck. September 2, 2003.

Keller, John. 2003.

Koenig, Richard. January 6, 2004.

Maestas, James. September 9, 2003.

Miller, Robin. August 17, 2003.

Morris, John. August 21, 2003.

Oliva, Richard. August 26, 2003.

Reed, Jimmy. August 27, 2003.

Rose, Thomas J. November 9, 2003.

Schwanebeck, Eugene. August 23, 2003.

Sheider, Lee. September 18, 2003.

Williams, James. October 9, 2003.

Other

Nguyen, Bay. June 20, 2002, New York.

VFMA. Jan. July 12, 2007. Valor Monument: Honoring alumni of the Valley Forge Military Academy or college who have earned the Distinguished Service Cross or Navy Cross for valor.

Sculptor: Mr. Nguyen Xuan Tien: Vice chief of art department at Art University in Ho Chi Minh City. 2002.

Former Vietnamese Enemy Combatants Interviewed in Vinh Long, Vietnam

Duong, Van Ca. (Commando leader). July 10, 2003.

Pham Phi Hung. (Battalion commander). July 10, 2003.
Pham Thanh Tu. (Artillery officer). July 10, 2003.

Buddhist Nuns (Nico) Interviewed in Nhi Binh, Hoc Mon Vietnam
Le Thi Anh (head of Buddhist temple). February 2002.
Ms Bay, Buddhist nun (Tran Thi Vang). February 2002.

Good Shepherd Sisters Interviewed in Nongkhai, Thailand
Gormley, Joan. January 26, 2004.
Haydn, Mary. January 26, 2004.

Monographs

Aydelotte, Sam. Routine Patrol Chronicle of War; 1990.
Glickman, Captain Tom. Monograph 1968.
Martin, Cdr. Bill. Report #4, January 1968.
Weseleskey, A. E. Biographical Sketch, January 2, 2003.

Naval Historical Foundation, Oral History Program (Conducted by Author)

Spencer, Robert A. November 11, 1998.
Wages, Jerry. December 16, 30, 2001.
Witham, Burton. September 2007.

Emails

Spencer, Robert. October 2, 2002.
Gache, Matte. July 23, 2004.
Myers, Harold. June 20, 2002. Pinnacle is part of reporting system referring to the level of reporting, "probably indicating the highest Air Force and DOD officials."

Navy Directives, Messages, Instructions, Reports

DA Form 19–24, (1 Sept. 1962), Investigation Report, January 12, 1968.
Game Warden Expansion, SECNAV Memorandum, December 2, 1966.
Game Warden History, OP506E4, December 23, 1968.
Game Warden Problems, Department of the Navy: 1968.
HA(L)3 OINC Designation Letter.
HA(L)3 Safety Instruction.
SECNAVINST 1650. 1G.
Medal of Honor Instruction.

Index